WHERE ARE THE LESSON FILES?

Purchasing this Classroom in a Book gives you access to the lesson files you'll need to complete the exercises in the book.

You'll find the files you need on your **Account** page at peachpit.com on the **Lesson & Update Files** tab.

For complete instructions, see "Accessing the Classroom in a Book files" in the Getting Started section of this book.

The example below shows how the files appear on your **Account** page (the exact list for your book may look a little different). The files are packaged as ZIP archives, which you will need to expand after downloading. You can download the lessons individually or as a single large ZIP file if your network connection is fast enough.

CONTENTS

GETTING STARTED

Adobe® Dreamweaver® CC is the industry-leading web authoring program. Whether you create websites for others for a living or plan to create one for your own business, Dreamweaver offers all the tools you need to get professional-quality results.

About Classroom in a Book

Adobe Dreamweaver CC Classroom in a Book® (2014 release) is part of the official training series for graphics and publishing software developed with the support of Adobe product experts.

The lessons are designed so you can learn at your own pace. If you're new to Dreamweaver, you'll learn the fundamentals of putting the program to work. If you are an experienced user, you'll find that Classroom in a Book teaches many advanced features, including tips and techniques for using the latest version of Dreamweaver.

Although each lesson includes step-by-step instructions for creating a specific project, you'll have room for exploration and experimentation. You can follow the book from start to finish, or complete only those lessons that correspond to your interests and needs. Each lesson concludes with a review section containing questions and answers on the subjects you've covered.

TinyURLs

At several points in the book, we reference external information available on the Internet. The uniform resource locators (URLs) for this information are often long and unwieldy, so we have provided custom TinyURLs in many places for your convenience. Unfortunately, the TinyURLs sometimes expire over time and no longer function. If you find that a TinyURL doesn't work, look up the actual URL provided in the Appendix.

Prerequisites

Before using *Adobe Dreamweaver CC Classroom in a Book (2014 release)*, you should have a working knowledge of your computer and its operating system. Be sure you know how to use the mouse, standard menus, and commands, and also how to open, save, and close files. If you need to review these techniques, see the printed or online documentation included with your Windows or Mac operating system.

Conventions used in this book

Working in Dreamweaver means you'll be working with code. We have used several conventions in the following lessons and exercises to make working with the code in this book easier to follow and understand.

Code font

In many instructions, you will be required to enter HTML code, CSS rules, and properties and other code-based markup. To distinguish the markup from the body of the text instructions, the entries will be styled with a code font, like this:

Examine the following code `<h1>Heading goes here</h1>`

In instances where you must enter the markup yourself, the entry will be formatted in color, like this:

Insert the following code `<h1>Heading goes here</h1>`

Strikethrough

In several exercises, you will be instructed to delete markup that already exists within the webpage or style sheet. In those instances, the targeted references will be identified with strikethrough formatting, like this:

Delete the following values:

```
margin: 10px 20px 10px 20px;
background-image: url(images/fern.png), url(images/stripe.png);
```

Be careful to delete only the identified markup so that you achieve the following result:

```
margin: 10px 10px;
background-image: url(images/fern.png);
```

Missing punctuation

HTML code, CSS markup, and JavaScript often requires the use of various punctuation, like periods (.), commas (,), and semicolons (;) among others, and can be damaged by their incorrect usage or placement. Consequently, periods and other punctuation expected in a sentence or paragraph may be omitted from an instruction or hyperlink whenever it may cause confusion or a possible error, like this:

> Enter the following code `<h1>Heading goes here</h1>`

> Type the following link: `http://adobe.com`

Element references

Within the body of descriptions and exercise instructions, elements may be referenced by name or by class or id attributes. When an element is identified by its tag name, it will appear as `<h1>` or `h1`. When referenced by its class attribute, the name will appear with a leading period (`.`) in a code-like font, like this `.content` or `.sidebar1`. References to elements by their id attribute will appear with a leading hash (#) and in a code font, like this `#top`. This practice matches the way these elements appear in Dreamweaver's tag selector interface.

Windows vs. OS X instructions

In most cases, Dreamweaver performs identically in both Windows and OS X. Minor differences exist between the two versions, mostly due to platform-specific issues out of the control of the program. Most of these are simply differences in keyboard shortcuts, how dialogs are displayed, and how buttons are named. In most cases, screen shots were made in the OS X version of Dreamweaver and may appear differently from your own screen.

Where specific commands differ, they are noted within the text. Windows commands are listed first, followed by the OS X equivalent, such as Ctrl+C/Cmd+C. Common abbreviations are used for all commands whenever possible, as follows:

WINDOWS	OS X
Control = Ctrl	Command = Cmd
Alternate = Alt	Option = Opt

As lessons proceed, instructions may be truncated or shortened to save space, with the assumption that you picked up the essential concepts earlier in the lesson. If you find you have difficulties in any particular task, review earlier steps or exercises in that lesson.

Installing the program

Before you perform any exercises in this book, verify that your computer system meets the hardware requirements for Dreamweaver, that it's correctly configured, and that all required software is installed.

Adobe Dreamweaver must be purchased separately; it is not included with the lesson files that accompany this book. Go to **www.adobe.com/products/dream-weaver/tech-specs.html** to obtain the system requirements.

Go to **https://creative.adobe.com/plans** to sign up for Adobe Creative Cloud. Dreamweaver may be purchased with the entire Creative Cloud family or as a standalone app. Adobe also allows you to try the Creative Cloud and the individual applications for 30 days for free.

Check **www.adobe.com/products/dreamweaver.html** to learn more about the different options for obtaining Dreamweaver.

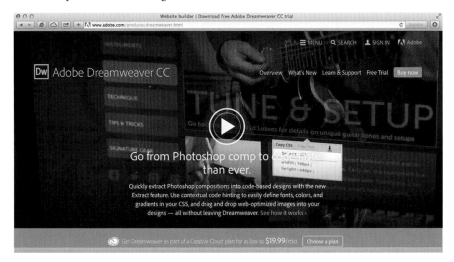

Updating Dreamweaver to the latest version

Although Dreamweaver is downloaded fully and installed on your computer hard drive, periodic updates are provided via the Creative Cloud. Some updates provide bug fixes and security patches, while others supply amazing new features and capabilities. The lessons in this book are based on Dreamweaver CC (2014.1 release) and may not work properly in any earlier version of the program. To check what version is installed on your computer, choose Help > About Dreamweaver in Windows or Dreamweaver > About Dreamweaver on the Macintosh. A window will display the version number of the application and other pertinent information.

If you do not have Dreamweaver, you will first have to install it from scratch from the Creative Cloud or, if you have an earlier version of the program installed, you will have to update Dreamweaver to the latest version. You can check the status of your installation by opening the Creative Cloud manager and logging in to your account.

Check out **https://helpx.adobe.com/creative-cloud/help/download-install-trials.html** to learn how to download and install Creative Cloud to your computer or laptop.

Accessing the Classroom in a Book files

Note: Do not copy one lesson folder into any other lesson folder. The files and folders for each lesson cannot be used interchangeably.

In order to work through the projects in this book, you will first need to download the lesson files from peachpit.com.

To access the Classroom in a Book lesson files:

1   On a Mac or PC, go to www.peachpit.com/redeem, and enter the code found at the back of your book.

2   If you do not have a peachpit.com account, you will be prompted to create one.

3   The downloadable files will be listed under the Lesson & Update Files tab on your Account page.

4   Click the lesson file links to download them to your computer. You can download the files for individual lessons, or download them all at once in one large file.

The files are compressed into Zip archives to speed up download time and to protect the contents from damage during transfer. You must uncompress (or "unzip") the files to restore them to their original size and format before you use them with the book. Modern Mac and Windows systems are set up to open Zip archives by simply double-clicking.

5   Do one of the following:

- If you downloaded DWCC2014_lesson_files.zip, unzipping the archive will produce a folder named **DWCC2014_Lesson_Files** containing all of the lesson files used by the book.

- If you downloaded the lessons individually, create a new folder and name it **DWCC2014.** Download and unzip the individual lesson files to this folder. That way, all the lesson files will be stored in one location.

Recommended lesson order

The training in this book is designed to take you from A to Z in basic to inter-mediate website design, development, and production. Each new lesson builds on previous exercises, using supplied files and assets, to create an entire website. We recommend that you download all lesson files at once and then perform each lesson in sequential order to achieve a successful result and the most complete understanding of all aspects of web design.

The ideal training scenario will start in Lesson 1 and proceed through the entire book to Lesson 13. Each lesson builds the skills and understanding necessary to complete subsequent tasks. We recommend that you do not skip any lessons, or even individual exercises. While ideal, this method may not be a practicable sce-nario for every user. So, each lesson folder contains all the files needed to complete every exercise using partially completed or staged assets, allowing you to complete individual lessons out of order, if desired.

However, don't assume that the staged files and customized templates in each les-son represent a complete set of assets. You may think these folders contain seem-ingly duplicative materials. But these duplicate files and assets, in most cases, can-not be used interchangeably in other lessons and exercises. Doing so will probably cause you to fail to achieve the goal of the exercise.

For that reason, you should treat each folder as a standalone website. Copy the lesson folder to your hard drive, and create a new site for that lesson using the Site Setup dialog. Do not define sites using subfolders of existing sites. Keep your sites and assets in their original folders to avoid conflicts. One suggestion is to organize the lesson folders in a single *web* or *sites* master folder near the root of your hard drive. But avoid using the Dreamweaver application folder or any folders that con-tain a web server, like Apache, ColdFusion, or Internet Information Services (IIS).

Defining a Dreamweaver site

In the course of completing the following lessons, you will create webpages from scratch and use existing files and resources that are stored on your hard drive. The resulting webpages and assets make up what's called your *local* site. When you are ready to upload your site to the Internet (see Lesson 13, "Publishing to the Web"), you publish your completed files to a web host server, which then becomes your *remote* site. The folder structures and files of the local and remote sites are usually mirror images of one another.

The first step is to define your local site:

1 Launch Adobe Dreamweaver CC (2014.1 release) or later.

2 Open the Site menu.

The Site menu provides options for creating and managing standard Dreamweaver sites.

3 Choose New Site.

To create a standard website in Dreamweaver, you need only name it and select the local site folder. Site names typically relate to a specific project or client and appear in the Files panel. This name is intended for your own purposes, so there are no limitations to the name you can create. Use a name that clearly describes the purpose of the website. For the purposes of this book, use the name of the lesson you intend to complete, such as lesson01, lesson02, lesson03, and so on.

4 Type **lesson01** or another name as appropriate, in the Site Name field.

5 Next to the Local Site Folder field, click the Browse for folder icon .

The Choose Root Folder dialog appears.

6 Navigate to the appropriate folder containing the lesson files you downloaded from Peachpit.com (as described earlier), and click Select/Choose.

Note: The main folder that contains the site will be referred to throughout the book as the site root folder.

You could click Save at this time and begin working on your new website, but we'll add one more piece of handy information.

7 Click the arrow ▶ next to the Advanced Settings category to reveal the categories listed there. Select Local Info.

Although it's not required, a good policy for site management is to store different file types in separate folders. For example, many websites provide individual folders for images, PDFs, videos, and so on. Dreamweaver assists in this endeavor by including an option for a Default Images folder. Later, as you insert images from other places on your computer, Dreamweaver will use this setting to automatically move the images into the site structure.

8 Next to the Default Images Folder field, click the Browse for folder icon 🗁. When the dialog opens, navigate to the appropriate images folder for that lesson or site, and click Select/Choose.

Note: Resource folders for images and other assets should always be contained within the main site root folder.

Note: The folder that contains the image assets will be referred to throughout the book as the site default images folder or the default images folder.

If you have already purchased and set up your website domain, you should enter it in this dialog.

9 Enter **http://green-start.org** for the lessons in this book or your own website URL in the Web URL field.

You've entered all the information required to begin your new site. In subsequent lessons, you'll add more information to enable you to upload files to your remote site and test dynamic web pages.

10 In the Site Setup dialog, click Save.

The site name now appears in the site list drop-down menu in the Files panel. As you add more site definitions, you can switch between the sites by selecting the appropriate name from this menu. When a site is selected or modified, Dreamweaver will build, or rebuild, a cache that examines every file in the folder. The cache identifies relationships between the web pages and the assets within sites, and will assist you whenever a file is moved, renamed, or deleted to update links or other referenced information.

Setting up a site is a crucial first step in beginning any project in Dreamweaver. Knowing where the site root folder is located helps Dreamweaver determine link pathways and enables many site-wide options, such as orphaned-file checking and Find and Replace.

Setting up the workspace

Dreamweaver CC (2014.1 release) includes three main workspaces to accommodate various computer configurations and individual workflows. For this book, the Design workspace is recommended.

1   If the Design workspace is not displayed by default, you can select it from the Workspace drop-down menu on the top-right side of the screen.

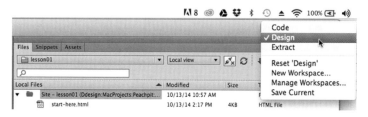

2   If the default Design workspace has been modified—where certain toolbars and panels are not visible (as they appear in the figures in the book)—you can restore the factory setting by choosing Reset 'Design' from the Workspace drop-down menu.

Workspace Layout options can also be accessed from the Window menu.

Most of the figures in this book show the Design workspace. When you finish the lessons in this book, experiment with each workspace to find the one that you prefer, or build your own configuration and save the layout under a custom name.

For a more complete description of the Dreamweaver workspaces, see Lesson 1, "Customizing Your Workspace."

Checking for updates

Adobe periodically provides software updates. To check for updates in the program, choose Help > Updates. For book updates and bonus material, visit your Account page on Peachpit.com and select the Lesson & Update Files tab.

Additional resources

Adobe Dreamweaver CC Classroom in a Book (2014 release) is not meant to replace documentation that comes with the program or to be a comprehensive reference for every feature. Only the commands and options used in the lessons are explained in this book. For comprehensive information about program features and tutorials, refer to these resources:

Adobe Dreamweaver Learn and Support: helpx.adobe.com/dreamweaver.html (accessible in Dreamweaver by choosing Help > Help And Support > Dreamweaver Support Center) has comprehensive content you can search or browse, provided by Adobe. This includes hands-on tutorials, answers to common questions, troubleshooting information, and more.

Dreamweaver Help: helpx.adobe.com/dreamweaver/topics.html is a reference for application features, commands, and tools (press F1 or choose Help > Help And Support > Dreamweaver Online Help). You can also download Help as a PDF document optimized for printing at helpx.adobe.com/pdf/dreamweaver_reference.pdf.

Dreamweaver Forums: forums.adobe.com/community/dreamweaver lets you tap into peer-to-peer discussions and questions and answers on Adobe products.

Adobe Creative Cloud Learn & Support: helpx.adobe.com/support.html provides inspiration, key techniques, cross-product workflows, and updates on new features.

Resources for educators: www.adobe.com/education and edex.adobe.com offer a treasure trove of information for instructors who teach classes on Adobe software. You'll find solutions for education at all levels, including free curricula that use an integrated approach to teaching Adobe software and can be used to prepare for the Adobe Certified Associate exams.

Also check out these useful links:

Adobe Add-ons: creative.adobe.com/addons is a central resource for finding tools, services, extensions, code samples, and more to supplement and extend your Adobe products.

Adobe Dreamweaver CC product home page: www.adobe.com/products/dreamweaver has more information about the product.

Adobe Authorized Training Centers: Adobe Authorized Training Centers offer instructor-led courses and training on Adobe products. See http://training.adobe.com/training/partner-finder.html for a directory of AATC.

1 CUSTOMIZING YOUR WORKSPACE

Lesson overview

In this lesson, you'll familiarize yourself with the Dreamweaver CC (2014.1 release) program interface and learn how to do the following:

- Switch document views

- Work with panels

- Select a workspace layout

- Adjust toolbars

- Personalize preferences

- Create custom keyboard shortcuts

- Use the Property inspector

- Use the Extract workflow

 This lesson will take about 40 minutes to complete. Download the project files for this lesson from the Lesson & Update Files tab on your Account page at www.peachpit.com, store them on your computer in a convenient location, and define a site based on the lesson01 folder, as described in the "Getting Started" section of this book. Your Account page is also where you'll find any updates to the lessons or to the lesson files. Look on the Lesson & Update Files tab to access the most current content.

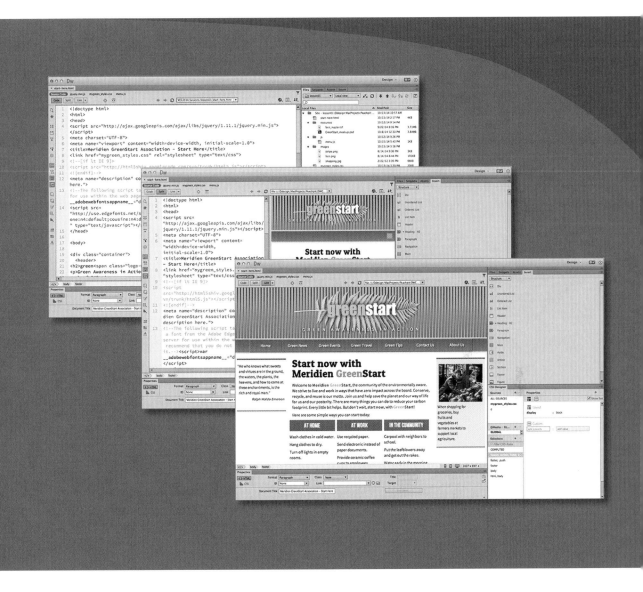

Dreamweaver offers a customizable and easy-to-use WYSIWYG HTML editor that doesn't compromise on power and flexibility. You'd probably need a dozen programs to perform all the tasks that Dreamweaver can do—and none of them would be as fun to use.

Touring the workspace

Dreamweaver is the industry-leading Hypertext Markup Language (HTML) editor, with good reasons for its popularity. The program offers an incredible array of design and code-editing tools. Dreamweaver offers something for everyone.

Coders love the range of enhancements built into the Code view environment, and developers enjoy the program's support for a variety of programming languages and code hinting. Designers marvel at seeing their text and graphics appear in an accurate What You See Is What You Get (WYSIWYG) depiction as they work, saving hours of time previewing pages in browsers. Novices certainly appreciate the program's simple-to-use and power-packed interface. No matter what type of user you are, if you use Dreamweaver you don't have to compromise.

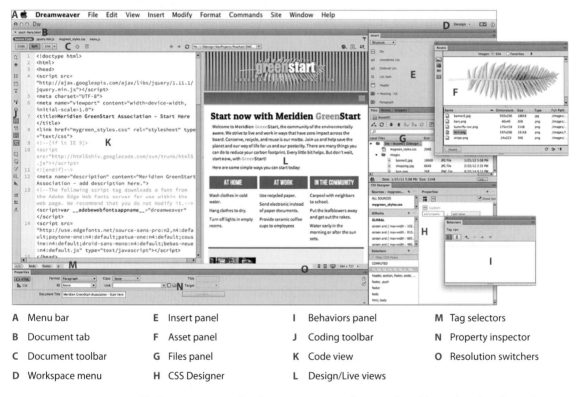

A	Menu bar	E	Insert panel	I	Behaviors panel	M	Tag selectors
B	Document tab	F	Asset panel	J	Coding toolbar	N	Property inspector
C	Document toolbar	G	Files panel	K	Code view	O	Resolution switchers
D	Workspace menu	H	CSS Designer	L	Design/Live views		

The Dreamweaver interface features a vast array of user-configurable panels and toolbars. Take a moment to familiarize yourself with the names of these components.

You'd think a program with this much to offer would be dense, slow, and unwieldy, but you'd be wrong. Dreamweaver provides much of its power via dockable panels and toolbars that you can display or hide and arrange in innumerable combinations to create your ideal workspace. In most cases, if you don't see a desired tool or panel, you'll find it in the Window menu.

This lesson introduces you to the Dreamweaver interface and gets you in touch with some of the power hiding under the hood. If you want to follow along on the tour, choose File > Open. In the lesson01 folder, choose **start-here.html**, and click Open.

Switching and splitting views

Dreamweaver offers dedicated environments for coders and designers as well as a new option that allows you to work with Photoshop mockups.

Design view

Design view shares the workspace with Live view and focuses the Dreamweaver workspace on its WYSIWYG editor, which provides a reasonable depiction of the webpage as it would appear in a browser. To activate Design view, choose it from the Design/Live views drop-down menu in the Document toolbar. Most HTML elements and basic cascading style sheet (CSS) formatting will be rendered properly within Design view, with a major exception for CSS3 properties, dynamic content, and interactivity, such as link behaviors, video, audio, jQuery widgets, some form elements and others.

Design view

Code view

Code view focuses the Dreamweaver workspace exclusively on the HTML code and a variety of code-editing productivity tools. To access Code view, click the Code view button in the Document toolbar.

Code view

Split view

Split view provides a composite workspace that gives you access to both the design and the code simultaneously. Changes made in either window update in the other instantly. To access Split view, click the Split view button in the Document toolbar. Dreamweaver splits the workspace horizontally by default.

Split view (horizontal)

● **Note:** Split view can pair Code view with either Design or Live view.

You can split the screen vertically by enabling the Split Vertically option on the View menu. When the window is split, Dreamweaver also gives you the option for how the two windows display. You can put the code window on top or bottom or left or right. You can find all these options on the View menu.

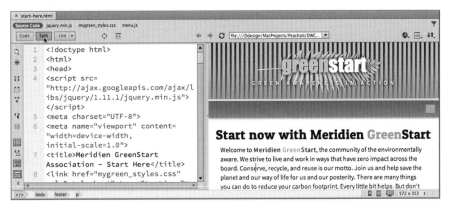

Split view (vertical)

Live view

To speed up the process of developing modern websites, Dreamweaver also includes a fourth display mode called Live view, which provides a browser-like preview of most dynamic effects and interactivity. To use Live view, choose it from the Design/Live views drop-down menu in the Document toolbar. When Live view is activated, most HTML content will function as it would in an actual browser, allowing you to preview and test most applications. In previous versions of Dreamweaver, the workspace in Live view was not editable. This has all changed. You can edit text, add and delete elements, create classes and ids, and even style elements, all in the same window. It's like working on a live webpage right inside Dreamweaver. Live view is integrally connected to the CSS Designer, allowing you to create and edit advanced CSS styling and build fully responsive webpages without having to switch views or preview the page in a browser.

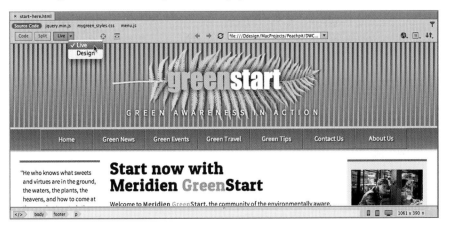

Live view

Live Code

Live Code is an HTML code-troubleshooting display mode available whenever Live view is activated. To access Live Code, activate Live view, and then click the Live Code button at the top of the document window. While active, Live Code displays the HTML code as it would appear in a live browser on the Internet. The code window will interactively render changes to the elements, attributes, and styling.

Live Code mode

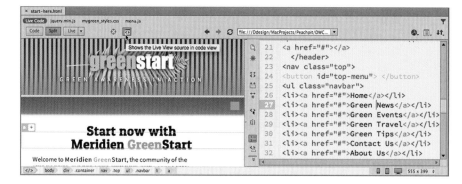

Inspect mode

Inspect mode is a CSS troubleshooting display mode available whenever Live view is activated. It is integrated with the CSS Designer and allows you to identify CSS styles applied to content within the page by moving the mouse cursor over elements within the webpage. The Live view window highlights the targeted element and displays the pertinent CSS rules applied or inherited by that element. You can access Inspect mode at any time by clicking the Live view button whenever an HTML file is open and then clicking the Inspect button at the top of the document window.

Inspect mode

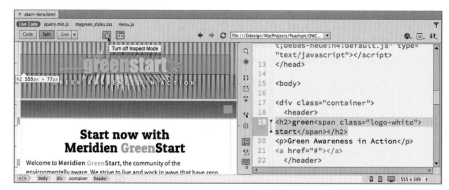

Working with panels

Although you can access most commands from the menus, Dreamweaver scatters much of its power in user-selectable panels and toolbars. You can display, hide, arrange, and dock panels at will around the screen. You can even move them to a second or third video display if you desire.

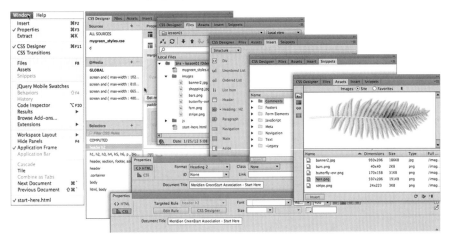

Standard panel grouping

The Window menu lists all the available panels. If you do not see a specific panel on the screen, choose it from the Window menu. A checkmark appears next to its name in the menu to indicate that the panel is open. Occasionally, one panel may lie behind another on the screen and be difficult to locate. In such situations, simply choose the desired panel from the Window menu and the panel will rise to the top of the stack.

Minimizing

To create room for other panels or to access obscured areas of the workspace, you can minimize or expand individual panels in place. To minimize a panel, double-click the tab containing the panel name. To expand the panel, click the tab again.

Minimizing a panel by double-clicking the tab

You can also minimize one panel within a stack of panels individually by double-clicking its tab. To open the panel, click once on the tab.

Minimizing one panel in a stack using its tab

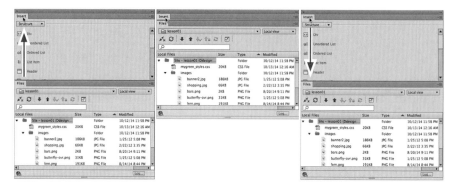

To recover more screen real estate, you can minimize panel groups or stacks down to icons by double-clicking the title bar. You can also minimize the panels to icons by clicking the double arrow icon ▶▶ in the panel title bar. When panels are minimized to icons, you access any of the individual panels by clicking its icon or button. The selected panel will appear on the left or right of your layout, wherever room permits.

Collapsing panel to icons

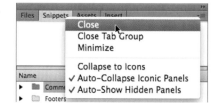

Closing panels and panel groups

Each panel or panel group may be closed at any time. There are several ways to close a panel or panel group; the method often depends on whether the panel is floating, docked or grouped with another panel.

To close an individual panel that is docked, right-click in the panel tab, and choose Close from the context menu. To close an entire group of panels, right-click any tab in the group and choose Close Tab Group.

To close a floating panel or panel group, click the Close icon ✖ that appears in the left corner of the title bar of the panel or panel group. To reopen a panel, choose the panel name from the Window menu. There is no way to reopen a panel group unless it was saved within a specific workspace.

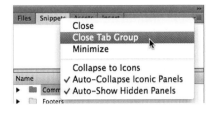

Floating

A panel that is grouped with other panels can be floated separately. To float a panel, drag it from the group by its tab.

Pulling a panel out by its tab

Dragging

You can reorder a panel tab by dragging it to the desired position within the group.

Dragging a tab to change its position

To reposition panels, groups, and stacks in the workspace, simply drag them by the title bar.

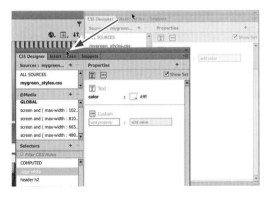

Dragging a whole panel group or stack to a new position

Grouping, stacking, and docking

You can create custom groups by dragging one panel into another. When you've moved the panel to the correct position, Dreamweaver highlights the area, called the *drop zone*, in blue. Release the mouse button to create the new group.

Creating new groups

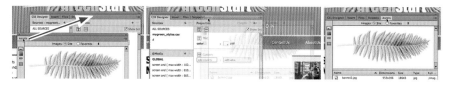

In some cases, you may want to keep both panels visible simultaneously. To stack panels, drag the desired tab to the top or bottom of another panel. When you see the blue drop zone appear, release the mouse button.

Creating panel stacks

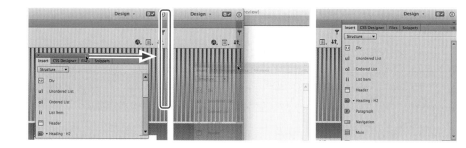

Floating panels can be docked to the right, left, or bottom of the Dreamweaver workspace. To dock a panel, group, or stack, drag its title bar to the edge of the window on which you wish to dock. When you see the blue drop zone appear, release the mouse button.

Docking panels

Selecting a workspace layout

A quick way to customize the program environment is to use one of the prebuilt workspaces in Dreamweaver. These workspaces have been optimized by experts to put the tools you need at your fingertips.

Dreamweaver CC (2014.1 release) includes three prebuilt workspaces: Code, Design and Extract. To access these workspaces, choose them from the Workspace menu located at the top of the document window.

Users who work mostly with code will want to use the Code workspace, because it optimizes the panels and windows to provide an effective workspace for coding.

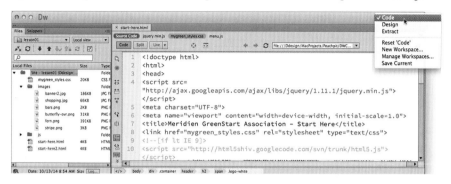

Code workspace

The Design workspace focuses the available screen real estate on the Design and Live view window.

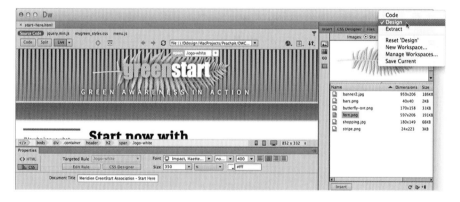

Design workspace

The Extract workspace provides a direct connection to the online interface for extracting CSS styles and image assets from Photoshop mockups uploaded to Creative Cloud. You can upload PSD files directly from Dreamweaver or post them in the Creative Cloud app or website once you are logged in to your account.

Extract workspace

Working with Extract

Extract is a new workflow that has been added to Dreamweaver CC (2014.1 release) that allows you to create CSS styles and image assets from a Photoshop-based mockup. Create your webpage design using text and linked or embedded image layers, and post the file to Creative Cloud where Dreamweaver can access the styles, colors and images to help you build your basic site design.

Build your design in Photoshop using text, images and effects stored in layers.

Post your file to your Creative Cloud online folder right inside Dreamweaver.

Access the various layers from the Extract panel inside Dreamweaver, and copy styles and text, and even download image assets.

Try these features yourself by uploading **GreenStart_mockup.psd** in the lesson01 resources folder to your Creative Cloud account online folder.

Adjusting toolbars

Some program features are so handy you may want them available all the time in toolbar form. Two of the toolbars—Document and Standard—appear horizontally at the top of the document window. The Coding toolbar, however, appears vertically, but only in the Code view window. (You'll explore the capabilities of these toolbars in later exercises.) Display the desired toolbar by choosing it from the View menu. You can also display the toolbar by simply right-clicking at the top of the document window and choosing the desired toolbar from the context menu.

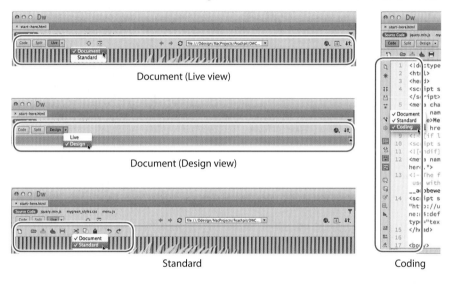

Document (Live view)

Document (Design view)

Standard

Coding

Personalizing preferences

As you continue to work with Dreamweaver, you'll devise your own optimal workspace of panels and toolbars for each activity. You can store these configurations in a custom workspace of your own naming.

To save a custom workspace, create your desired configuration, choose New Workspace from the Workspace menu, and then give it a custom name.

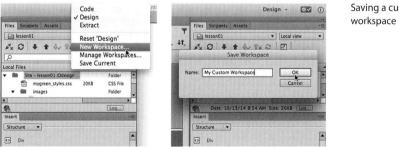

Saving a custom workspace

Creating custom keyboard shortcuts

Another powerful feature of Dreamweaver is the capability to create your own keyboard shortcuts as well as edit existing ones. Keyboard shortcuts are loaded and preserved independently of custom workspaces.

Is there a command you can't live without that doesn't have a keyboard shortcut? Create it yourself. Try this:

1   Choose Edit > Keyboard Shortcuts (Windows) or Dreamweaver > Keyboard Shortcuts (Mac OS).

Note: The default keyboard shortcuts are locked and cannot be edited. But you can duplicate the set, save it under a new name, and modify any shortcut within that custom set.

2   Click the Duplicate Set icon ![icon] to create a new set of shortcuts.

3   Enter a name in the Name Of Duplicate Set field. Click OK.

4   Choose Menu Commands from the Commands pop-up menu.

5   In the Commands window, choose File > Save All.

Note that the Save All command does not have an existing shortcut, although you'll use this command frequently in Dreamweaver.

6 Insert the cursor in the Press Key field. Press Ctrl+Alt+S/Cmd+Opt-S.

Note the error message indicating that the keyboard combination you chose is already assigned to a command. Although we could reassign the combination, let's choose a different one.

7 Press Ctrl+Alt+Shift+S/Cmd+Ctrl+S.

This combination is not currently being used, so let's assign it to the Save All command.

8 Click the Change button.

The new shortcut is now assigned to the Save All command.

9 Click OK to save the change.

You have created your own keyboard shortcut—one you can use in upcoming lessons.

Using the Property inspector

One tool vital to your workflow is the Property inspector. This panel typically appears at the bottom of the workspace. The Property inspector is context-driven and adapts to the type of element you select.

Using the HTML tab

Insert the cursor into any text content on your page and the Property inspector provides a means to quickly assign some basic HTML codes and formatting. When the HTML button is selected, you can apply heading or paragraph tags as well as bold, italics, bullets, numbers and indenting, among other formatting and attributes. In the latest update to Dreamweaver, the Document Title metadata field was moved into the Property inspector. Enter your desired Document Title in this field, and the program adds it automatically to the document <head> section.

HTML Property inspector

Using the CSS tab

Click the CSS button to quickly access commands to assign or edit CSS formatting.

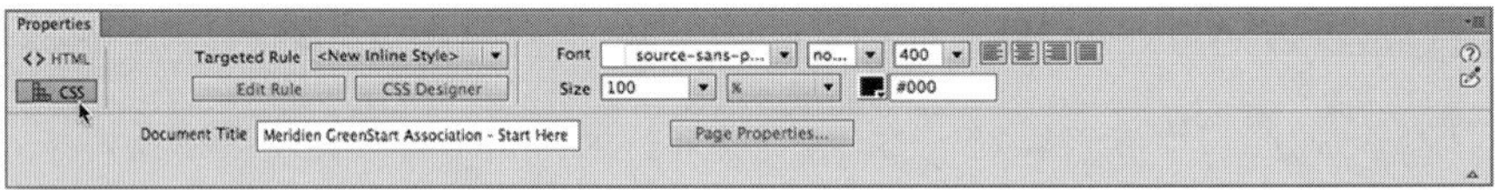

CSS Property inspector

Image properties

Select an image in a webpage to access the image-based attributes and formatting controls of the Property inspector.

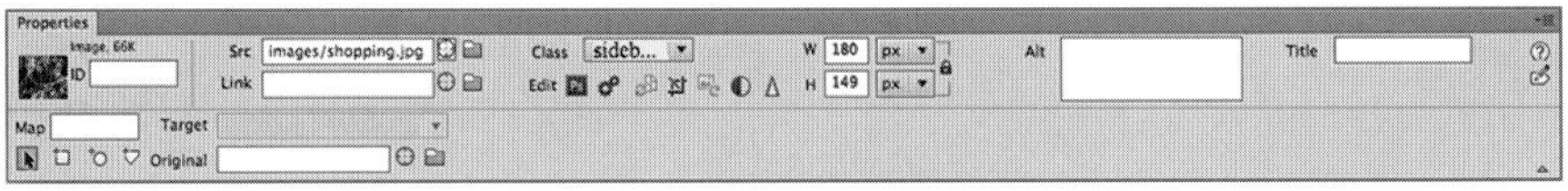

Image Property inspector

Table properties

To access table properties, insert your cursor in a table and then click the table tag selector at the bottom of the document window.

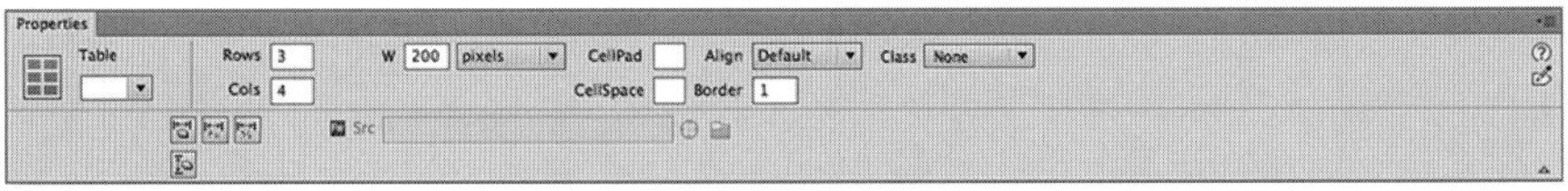

Table Property inspector

Related files interface

Webpages are often built with multiple external files providing styling and pro-gramming assistance. Dreamweaver enables you to see all the files linked to, or *referenced* by, the current document by displaying the filenames in the Related Files Interface at the top of the document window. This interface displays the name of any external file and can actually display the contents of each file; simply select the filename in the display.

The Related File Interface lists all external files linked to a document.

To view the contents of the referenced file, click the name. If you are in Live or Design view, Dreamweaver splits the document window and shows the contents of the selected file in the Code view window. If the file is stored locally, you'll even be able to edit the contents of the file when it's selected.

Use the Related File Interface to edit locally stored files.

To view the HTML code contained within the main document, click the Source Code option in the interface.

Choose the Source Code option to see the contents of the main document.

Using tag selectors

One of the most important features of Dreamweaver is the tag selector interface that appears at the bottom of the document window. This interface displays the tags and element structure in any HTML file pertinent to the insertion point of, or selection by, the cursor. The display of tags is hierarchical, starting at the document root at the left of the display and listing each tag or element in order based on the structure of the page.

The display in the tag selector interface mimics the structure of the HTML code.

The tag selectors also enable you to select any of the elements displayed by simply clicking a tag. When a tag is selected, all of the content and child elements contained within that tag are also selected.

Use the tag selectors to select elements.

The tag selector interface is closely integrated with the CSS Designer panel. By selecting a tag displayed in the interface, the CSS Designer will interactively display the styling applied to the specific element or structure. You may use the tag selectors to style content or to cut, copy, paste, and/or delete elements.

The tag selector is closely integrated with the styling and editing of elements.

Using the CSS Designer

The CSS Designer has been greatly improved in Dreamweaver CC (2014.1 release). Along with its traditional visual method of creating, editing and troubleshooting CSS styling, CSS Designer has gained new productivity enhancements for copying and pasting CSS styles from one rule to another. You can also decrease or increase the specificity of new selector names by pressing the up or down arrow keys, respectively.

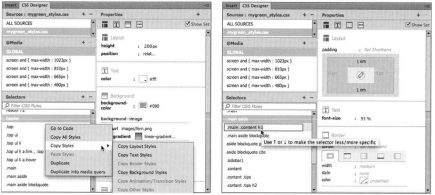

Copy and paste styles from one rule to another.

Make selectors more or less specific using the arrow keys.

The CSS Designer panel consists of four panes: Sources, @Media, Selectors and Properties. The Sources pane allows you to create, attach, define and remove internal and external style sheets. The @Media pane is used to define media queries to support various types of media and devices. The Selectors pane is used to create and edit the CSS rules that format the components and content of your page. Once a selector, or rule, is created, you define the formatting you wish to apply in the Properties pane.

In addition to allowing you to create and edit CSS styling, the CSS Designer can also be used to identify styles already defined and applied, and to troubleshoot issues or conflicts with these styles. To do this, simply insert the cursor into any element. The panes within the CSS Designer will then display all the pertinent style sheets, media queries, rules and properties applied to or inherited by the selected element. This interaction works the same way in all document views.

The display in the CSS Designer responds to the selection or insertion point of the cursor.

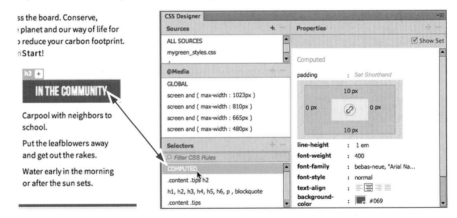

The CSS Designer features two basic modes. By default, the Properties pane will display all available CSS properties in a list, organized in five categories: Layout ▤, Text Ⓣ, Borders ▢, Background ▨, and Other ▥. You can scroll down the list and apply styling as desired. You can also select the option Show Set at the upper-right edge of the window, and the Properties pane will then filter the list down to only the properties actually applied. In either mode, you can add, edit, or remove style sheets, media queries, rules, and properties.

The COMPUTED option collects all styles applied to the selection in one place.

The Properties pane also features a COMPUTED option that displays the aggregated list of styles applied to the selected element. The COMPUTED option will appear any time you select an element or component on the page. When creating any type of styling, the code created by Dreamweaver complies with industry standards and best practices. Dreamweaver will even apply vendor prefixes automatically to certain types of advanced styling as needed.

In addition to using the CSS Designer, you may also create and edit CSS styling manually within Code view while taking advantage of many productivity enhancements like code hinting and auto completion.

Element Quick View

The Element Quick View is another new tool introduced recently that has already been improved in Dreamweaver CC (2014.1 release). It allows you to view the Document Object Model (DOM) to quickly examine the structure of your layout as well as interact with it to select existing elements; now it can also be used to insert new ones by drag and drop.

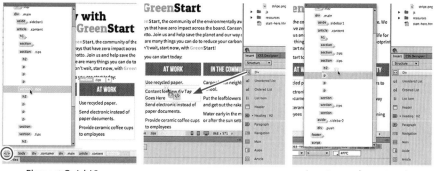

Element Quick View

Insert new elements using Element Quick View.

Element View

Element View is a sort of heads-up display (HUD) that allows you to quickly add ids and classes to elements and even insert references to them in your CSS style sheets and media queries. The Element View HUD appears whenever you select an element in Live view. When an element is selected in Live view, you can change the selection focus by pressing the up and down arrow keys; Element View highlights each element in the page in turn, based on its position in the HTML structure.

Create ids using Element View, and add them to existing media queries.

Create classes using Element View, and add them to existing style sheets.

Explore, experiment, learn

The Dreamweaver interface has been carefully crafted over many years to make the job of webpage design and development fast and easy. Feel free to explore and experiment with various menus, panels and options to create the ideal workspace and keyboard shortcuts to produce the most productive environment for your own purposes. You'll find the program endlessly adaptable, with power to spare for any task. Enjoy.

Review questions

1 Where can you access the command to display or hide any panel?

2 Where can you find the Code, Split, Design and Live view buttons?

3 What can be saved in a workspace?

4 Do workspaces also load keyboard shortcuts?

5 What happens in the Property inspector when you insert the cursor into various elements on the webpage?

6 What new features have been added to the CSS Designer?

7 What can you do with Element Quick View?

8 Does Element View HUD appear in Design view?

Review answers

1 All panels are listed in the Window menu.

2 The Code, Split, Design and Live view buttons are components of the Document toolbar.

3 Workspaces can save the configuration of the document window, the open panels, and the panels' size and position on the screen.

4 No. Keyboard shortcuts are loaded and preserved independently of a workspace.

5 The Property inspector adapts to the selected element, displaying pertinent information and formatting commands.

6 CSS Designer now allows you to copy and paste styles from one rule to another and change the specificity of a new selector name by pressing the up and down arrow keys.

7 Element Quick View allows you to visually examine the DOM and select and insert new elements.

8 No. The Element View is only visible in Live view.

2 HTML BASICS

Lesson Overview

In this lesson, you'll familiarize yourself with HTML and learn how to:

- Write HTML code by hand
- Understand HTML syntax
- Insert code elements
- Format text
- Add HTML structure
- Create HTML with Dreamweaver

 This lesson will take about 40 minutes to complete. There are no support files for this lesson.

HTML is the backbone of the web, the skeleton of your webpage. Like the bones in your body, it is the structure and substance of the Internet, although it is usually unseen except by the web designer. Without it, the web would not exist. Dreamweaver has many features that help you access, create, and edit HTML code quickly and effectively.

What is HTML?

"What other programs can open a Dreamweaver file?"

This question was asked by an actual student in a Dreamweaver class; although it might seem obvious to an experienced developer, it illustrates a basic problem in teaching and learning web design. Most people confuse the program with the technology. They assume that the extension .htm or .html belongs to Dreamweaver or Adobe. Designers are used to working with files ending with extensions, such as .ai, .psd, .indd, and so on—it's just a part of their jobs. These extensions are proprietary file formats created by programs that have specific capabilities and limitations. The goal in most cases when using any of these formats is to create a final printed piece. The program in which the file was created provides the power to interpret the code that produces the printed page. Designers have learned over time that opening these file formats in a different program may produce unacceptable results, or even damage the file.

On the other hand, the goal of the web designer is to create a webpage for display in a browser. The power and/or functionality of the originating program has little bearing on the resulting browser display, because the display is all contingent on the HTML code and how the browser interprets it. Although a program may write good or bad code, it's the browser that does all the hard work.

The web is based on the Hypertext Markup Language (HTML). The language and the file format don't belong to any individual program or company. In fact, it is a *non*-proprietary, plain-text language that can be edited in any text editor, in any operating system, on any computer. Dreamweaver is, in part, an HTML editor, although it is also much more than this. But to maximize the potential of Dreamweaver, you first need to have a good understanding of what HTML is and what it can (and can't) do. This lesson is intended as a concise primer on HTML and its capabilities and as a foundation for understanding Dreamweaver.

Where did HTML begin?

HTML and the first browser were invented in 1989 by Tim Berners-Lee, a computer scientist working at the CERN (Conseil Européen pour la Recherche Nucléaire, which is French for European Council for Nuclear Research) particle physics laboratory in Geneva, Switzerland. He intended the technology as a means for sharing technical papers and information via the fledgling Internet that existed at the time. He shared his HTML and browser inventions openly as an attempt to get the scientific community at large and others to adopt them and engage in the development themselves. The fact that he did not copyright or try to sell his work started a trend for openness and camaraderie on the web that continues to this day.

The language that Berners-Lee created over 25 years ago was a much simpler construct of what we use now, but HTML is still surprisingly easy to learn and master. At the time of this writing, HTML was at version 4.01, officially adopted in 1999. It consists of around 90 *tags*, such as html, head, body, h1, p, and so on. The tag is inserted between less-than (<) and greater-than (>) angle brackets, as in <p>, <h1>, and <table>. These tags are used to identify, or *mark up*, text and graphics to enable a browser to display them in a particular way. HTML code is considered properly *balanced* when the markup features both an opening (<...>) and a closing (</...>) tag, such as <h1>...</h1>. When two matching tags appear this way, they are referred to as an *element*; an element entails any contents contained within the two tags, as well. Empty tags, like a horizontal rule, can be written in an abbreviated fashion, using only one tag, such as <hr/>, essentially opening and closing the tag at the same time.

Some elements are used to create page structures, others to structure and format text, and yet others to enable interactivity and programmability. Even though Dreamweaver obviates the need for writing most of the code manually, the ability to read and interpret HTML code is still a recommended skill for any burgeoning web designer. Sometimes it's the only way to find an error in your webpage. The ability to understand and read code may also become an essential skill in other fields as more information and content is created and disseminated via mobile devices and Internet-based resources.

Note: If you are dead set against learning how to read and write good HTML, you should check out Adobe Muse. This program allows you to create professional-looking webpages and complete websites using point-and-click techniques in a graphical user interface similar to Adobe InDesign while never exposing you to the code running behind the scenes.

Basic HTML code structure

Here you see the basic structure of a webpage:

Basic HTML Code Structure

You may be surprised to learn that the only text from this code that displays in the web browser is "Welcome to my first webpage." The rest of the code creates the page structure and text formatting. Like an iceberg, most of the content of the actual webpage remains out of sight.

Writing your own HTML code

Note: Feel free to use any text editor for these exercises. But be sure to save your files as plain-text or text-only.

Note: TextEdit may default to saving the file as rich text (.rtf); in this case you need to choose Format > Format As Plain Text before you can save the file as .html.

Note: Some text editors may try to change the .html extension or prompt you to confirm the choice.

The idea of writing code may sound difficult or at least tedious, but creating a webpage is actually much easier than you think. In the next few exercises, you will learn how HTML works by creating a basic webpage and adding and formatting some simple text content.

1   Launch Notepad (Windows) or TextEdit (Mac).

2   Enter the following code in the empty document window:

```
<html>
<body>
Welcome to my first webpage
</body>
</html>
```

3   Save the file to the desktop as **firstpage.html**.

4   Launch Chrome, Firefox, Internet Explorer, Safari, or another installed web browser.

5   Choose File > Open. Navigate to the desktop, select **firstpage.html**, and then click OK/Open.

Congratulations, you just created your first webpage. As you can see, it doesn't take much code to create a serviceable webpage.

Text editor

Browser

Understanding HTML syntax

Next, you'll add content to your new webpage to learn some important aspects of HTML code syntax.

1   Switch back to the text editor, but don't close the browser.

2   Insert your cursor at the end of the text "Welcome to my first page" and press Enter/Return to insert a paragraph return.

3   Type **Making webpages is fun** on the new line.
    Press the spacebar five times to insert five spaces.
    Finish by typing **and easy!** on the same line.

4   Save the file.

5 Switch to the browser.

Although you saved the changes, you'll notice that the new text doesn't appear in the browser. That's because you never see a webpage "live" on the Internet. It must be first downloaded to your computer and saved, or *cached*, on the hard drive. The browser is actually displaying the page that it downloaded originally. To see the latest version of the webpage, you'll have to reload the webpage. This is a fact that's important to remember as a web designer. People frequently miss changes in a website because they are looking at the cached versions of a page instead of the most current versions. If your website will be updated frequently, it's possible to insert a piece of JavaScript code that will reload a page automatically each time a browser window accesses it.

6 Refresh the window to load the updated page.

▷ **Tip:** In most browsers, you can press Ctrl+R/Command+R to refresh the page view. In Internet Explorer, press the F5 key.

As you can see, the browser is displaying the new text, but it's ignoring the paragraph return between the two lines as well as the extra spaces. In fact, you could add hundreds of paragraph returns between the lines and dozens of spaces between each word, and the browser display would be no different. That's because the browser is programmed to ignore extra white space and honor only HTML code elements. By inserting a tag here and there, you can easily create the desired text display.

Inserting HTML code

In this exercise, you will insert HTML tags to produce the correct text display.

1 Switch back to the text editor.

2 Add the highlighted tags to the text as follows:

```
<p>Making webpages is fun and easy!</p>
```

To add extra spacing or other special characters within a line of text, HTML provides code elements called entities. Entities are entered into the code differently than tags. For example, the method for inserting a nonbreaking space is by typing the   entity.

3 Replace the five spaces in the text with five nonbreaking spaces so that the code looks like the following sample:

```
<p>Making webpages is fun     
and easy!</p>
```

▷ **Tip:** Another method for creating a nonbreaking space in Dreamweaver is by pressing Ctrl+Shift-spacebar/Command+Shift-spacebar. This will generate the named entity * *. In most cases, the two entities are identical in use and performance; however, * * is not a valid entity for some applications, such as EPUB 2.0. Before you use a specific entity, make sure it is compatible with your workflow.

▷ **Tip:** Feel free to copy and paste the entity code to save time.

4 Save the file. Switch to the browser and reload or refresh the page display.

The browser is now showing the paragraph return and the desired spacing.

By adding the tags and entities, the browser can display the desired paragraph structure and spacing.

Although line breaks, spacing, and even indentation are ignored by the browser, web designers and coders frequently employ such whitespace to make the code easier to read and edit. But don't go crazy. Although whitespace doesn't affect the display of a page in a browser, it can contribute to the time it takes to download and render a webpage overall. Whitespace and extraneous code contributes to what web developers call the overall *weight* of a page. When a page has too much weight, it downloads, renders, and operates in a suboptimal manner. Later in the book, we'll talk about how you can minimize this weight to make your pages load quicker and operate at more acceptable speeds.

Formatting text with HTML

Tags often serve multiple purposes. Besides creating paragraph structures and creating whitespace as demonstrated earlier, they can impart basic text formatting, as well as identify the relative importance of the page content. For example, HTML provides six heading tags (<h1> to <h6>) you can use to set headings off from normal paragraphs. The tags not only format the heading text differently than paragraph text, they also impart additional meaning. Heading tags are automatically formatted in bold and often at a larger relative size. The number of the heading (1 through 6) also plays a role: Using the <h1> tag identifies the heading as being the highest in importance by default. In this exercise, you will add a heading tag to the first line.

1 Switch back to the text editor.

2 Add the highlighted tags to the text as follows:

```
<h1>Welcome to my first webpage</h1>
```

Web designers use heading tags to identify the importance of specific content to help improve their site rankings on Google, Yahoo, and other search engines. Headings also help individuals who use screen readers and other assistive devices that allow them to access web-based content.

3 Save the file. Switch to the browser and reload or refresh the page display.

Note how the text display changed. It is now larger and formatted in boldface.

Applying inline formatting

So far, all the tags you have used work as paragraph or standalone elements. These are referred to as *block* elements. HTML also provides the ability to apply formatting and structure to content that's contained within the flow of another tag, or *inline*. A typical use of inline code would be to apply bold or italic styling to a word or a portion of a paragraph. In this exercise, you will apply inline formatting.

1 Switch back to the text editor.

2 Add the highlighted tags to the text as follows:

```
<p>Making webpages is fun     
<strong><em>and easy!</em></strong></p>
```

3 Save the file. Switch to the browser and reload or refresh the page display.

Strong and *emphasis* (em) are used in place of the tags for bold <b> and italic <i> because they provide enhanced semantic meaning for visitors with disabilities or visual impairment, but the result is basically identical.

Most formatting, both inline and otherwise, is properly applied using cascading style sheets (CSS). The <strong> and <em> tags are among the few still acceptable ways to apply inline formatting using specific HTML code elements. Technically speaking, these elements are more intended to add semantic meaning to text content, but the effect is still the same. Today, text tagged with <strong> and <em> still appears by default as bold and italics in most applications.

However, this may change in the near future. There has been an industry-supported move to separate the content from its presentation, or formatting, over the last decade. Although most browsers and HTML readers currently apply default formatting based on specific tags, this may not always be the case. See Lesson 3, "CSS Basics," for a full explanation of the strategy and application of CSS in standards-based web design.

Adding structure

Most webpages feature at least three fundamental elements: a root (typically <html>), <head>, and <body>. These elements create the essential underlying structure of the webpage. The root element contains all the code and content, with the exception of any dynamic code that must load before the page content itself. This dynamic code is usually written in web programming languages such as ASP, Cold Fusion, or PHP. The <head> element holds code that performs vital background tasks, including styling, external links, and other information. The <body> element holds all the visible content, such as text, tables, images, movies, and so on.

The sample page you created doesn't have a `<head>` element. A webpage can exist without this section, but adding any advanced functionality to this page without one would be difficult. In this exercise, you will add `<head>` and `<title>` elements to your webpage.

1   Switch back to the text editor.

2   Add the highlighted tags and content to the text as follows:

```
<html>
<head>
<title>HTML Basics for Fun and Profit</title>
</head>
<body>
```

3   Save the file. Switch to the browser and reload or refresh the page display.

Did you notice what changed? It may not be obvious at first. Look at the title bar or window tab of the browser. The words "HTML Basics for Fun and Profit" now magically appear above your webpage. By adding the `<title>` element, you have created this display. But it's not just a cool trick—it's good for your business, too.

The content of the `<title>` tag will appear in the browser title bar when the page is refreshed.

Google, Yahoo, and the other search engines catalog the `<title>` element of each page and use it, among other criteria, to index and rank webpages. The content of the title is one of the items typically displayed within the results of a search. It will also appear automatically when you create a bookmark for that page in your browser. A well-titled page could be ranked higher than one with a bad title or one with none at all. Keep your titles short but meaningful. For example, the title "ABC Home Page" doesn't really convey any useful information. A better title might be "Welcome to the Home Page of ABC Corporation." Check out other websites (especially peers or competitors) to see how they title their own pages.

Writing HTML in Dreamweaver

So, the inevitable question is, "If I can write HTML in any text editor, why do I need to use Dreamweaver?" Although a complete answer awaits you in the following 13 lessons, the question begs for a quick demonstration. In this exercise, you will re-create the same webpage using Dreamweaver.

1 Launch Dreamweaver CC (2014.1 release) or later.

2 Choose File > New.

3 In the New Document window, select Blank Page from the first column.

4 Select HTML from the Page Type section.

5 From the Layout section, choose <none>.

6 If necessary, in the DocType menu, select HTML5.

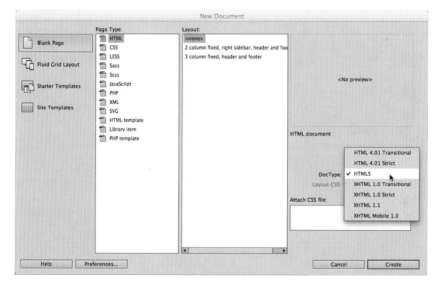

Dreamweaver allows you to create different types of web-compatible files. You will learn more about this dialog box in subsequent lessons.

7 Click Create.

A new document window opens in Dreamweaver. The window may default to one of three displays: Code view, Design view, or Split view.

8 If it's not already selected, click the Code view button in the upper left of the document window.

Split view

Code view   Design view

The advantages of using Dreamweaver to create HTML are evident from the very beginning: As you can see, much of the page structure is created already.

The first thing you should notice in the Code view window is that Dreamweaver has provided a huge head start over using a text editor. The basic structure of the page is already in place, including the root, head, body, and even title tags, among others. The only thing Dreamweaver makes you do is add the content itself.

9 Insert the cursor after the opening <body> tag and type **Welcome to my second page** following the tag.

Both Dreamweaver and text editors allow you to write HTML code. With a text editor, you have to use a separate application to actually see what the webpage looks like. Dreamweaver provides a built-in method for previewing your finished webpage.

● **Note:** Split view may use either Live or Design view to display side-by-side with the Code window. Feel free to choose the one you prefer.

10 Click the Split view button.

In Split view, you can see the HTML code on one side of the document window and a relatively accurate preview of the webpage on the other. Split view will save you hours of time loading and previewing pages in a separate application. Dreamweaver also makes it a simple matter to format the first line with a specific HTML tag.

48   LESSON 2   HTML BASICS

11 Move the cursor to the beginning of the "Welcome to my second page" text. Type < to open the code-hinting feature.

Dreamweaver automatically opens a drop-down list of compatible HTML, CSS, JavaScript, and other supported code elements. This is Dreamweaver's code-hinting feature.

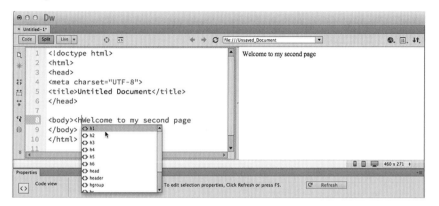

When activated, code hinting provides a drop-down list of applicable HTML, CSS, and JavaScript elements, as well as some in other languages.

12 Double-click h1 from the list to insert it in the code. Type > to close the element.

13 Move the cursor to the end of the text. Type </ at the end of the sentence.

Note how Dreamweaver closes the <h1> element automatically. But many coders add the tags as they write.

14 Press Enter/Return to insert a line break. Type <p and press Enter/Return to insert the element. Type > to close the tag.

15 Type **Making webpages in Dreamweaver is even more fun!** and then type </ to close the <p> element.

Tired of hand-coding yet? Dreamweaver offers multiple ways for formatting your content.

16 Select the word "more." In the HTML tab of the Property inspector, click the **B** and the *I* buttons to apply the <strong>and <em> tags to the text.

These tags produce the appearance of bold and italic formatting on the selected text.

Something missing?

When you reached for the **B** and *I* buttons in step 16, were they missing? When you make changes in Code view, the Property inspector occasionally needs to be refreshed before you can access the formatting commands featured there. Simply click the Refresh button, and the formatting commands will reappear.

Only two more tasks remain before your new page is complete. Note that Dreamweaver created the `<title>` element and inserted the text "Untitled Document" within it. You could select the text within the code window and enter a new title, or you could change it using another built-in feature.

17 Locate the Title field in the Property inspector and select the "Untitled Document" placeholder text.

18 Type **HTML Basics, Page 2** in the Title field.

19 Press Enter/Return to complete the title.

The title field enables you to change the content of the `<title>` element without having to work in the HTML code.

```
4   <meta charset="UTF-8">
5   <title>HTML Basics, Page 2</title>
6   </head>
```

Welcome to my second page

Making webpages in Dreamweaver is even *more* fun!

The new title text appears in the code, replacing the original content. It's time to save the file and preview it in the browser.

20 Choose File > Save. Navigate to the desktop. Name the file **secondpage** and click Save.

Dreamweaver adds the proper extension (html) automatically.

21 Choose File > Preview in Browser and select your favorite browser.

The completed page appears in the browser window.

Using Dreamweaver you completed the task in a fraction of time it took you to do it manually.

You have just completed two webpages—one by hand and the other using Dreamweaver. In both cases, you can see how HTML played a central role in the whole process. To learn more about this technology, go to the website of the W3 Consortium at www.w3schools.com, or check out any of the books in the "Recommended books on HTML 4" sidebar.

Note: Dreamweaver uses the default web browser on your computer. You may install additional alternate browsers and configure their use in the Dreamweaver Preferences dialog box.

Recommended books on HTML 4

HTML and CSS: Eighth Edition, (Peachpit Press, 2014), ISBN: 0321928830

HTML and XHTML Pocket Reference, 4th Edition, Jennifer Niederst Robbins, (O'Reilly, 2009), ISBN: 978-0-596-80586-9

Head First HTML with CSS & XHTML, Elizabeth and Eric Freeman, (O'Reilly, 2005), ISBN: 978-0-596-10197-8

Frequently used HTML 4 codes

HTML code elements serve specific purposes. Tags can create distinct objects, apply formatting, identify logical content, or generate interactivity. Tags that make their own space on the screen and stand alone are called *block* elements; the ones that perform their duties within the flow of another tag are called *inline* elements. Some elements can also be used to create *structural* relationships within a page, like stacking content in vertical columns or collecting several elements together in logical groupings. Structural elements can behave like block or inline elements or do their work entirely invisible to the user.

HTML tags

The following table shows some of the most frequently used HTML tags. To get the most out of Dreamweaver and your webpages, it helps to understand the nature of these elements and how they are used. Remember, some tags can serve multiple purposes.

Table 2.1 Frequently used HTML tags

TAG	DESCRIPTION	STRUCTURAL	BLOCK	INLINE
`<!--...-->`	Designates an HTML comment. Allows you to add notes within the HTML code that are not displayed within the browser.	✓		
`<a>`	Anchor. The basic building block for a hyperlink.			✓
`<blockquote>`	Quotation. Creates a standalone, indented paragraph.		✓	
`<body>`	Designates the document body. Contains the visible portions of the webpage content.	✓		
` `	Break. Inserts a line break without creating a new paragraph.	✓		
`<div>`	Division. Used to divide webpage content into discernible sections.	✓	✓	
`<em>`	Emphasis. Adds semantic emphasis. Displays as italics by default in most browsers and readers.			✓
`<form>`	Designates an HTML form. Used for collecting data from users.	✓		
`<h1>` to `<h6>`	Headings. Creates headings. Implies semantic value. Default formatting is bolded.		✓	
`<head>`	Designates the document head. Contains code that performs background functions, such as meta tags, scripts, styling, links, and other information not overtly visible to site visitors.	✓		
`<hr />`	Horizontal Rule. Empty element that generates a horizontal line.	✓	✓	
`<html>`	Root element of most webpages. Contains the entire webpage, except in certain instances where server-based code must load before the opening `<html>` tag.	✓		
`<iframe>`	Inline Frame. A structural element that can contain another document.	✓		✓
`<img />`	Image.	✓		✓
`<input />`	Input element for a form such as a text field.	✓		✓
`<li>`	List Item.		✓	
`<link />`	Designates the relationship between a document and an external resource.	✓		
`<meta />`	Metadata.	✓		
`<ol>`	Ordered List. Defines a numbered list. List items display in a numbered sequence.	✓	✓	
`<p>`	Paragraph. Creates a standalone paragraph.		✓	
`<script>`	Script. Contains scripting elements or points to an internal or external script.	✓		
`<span>`	Designates a document section. Provides a means to apply special formatting or emphasis to a portion of an element.			✓
`<strong>`	Adds semantic emphasis. Displays as bold by default in most browsers and readers.			✓
`<style>`	Calls CSS style rules.	✓		
`<table>`	Designates an HTML table.	✓	✓	
`<td>`	Table Data. Designates a table cell.	✓		
`<textarea>`	Multi-line text input element for a form.	✓	✓	
`<th>`	Table Header.	✓		
`<title>`	Title.	✓		
`<tr>`	Table Row.	✓		
`<ul>`	Unordered List. Defines a bulleted list. List items display with bullets by default.	✓	✓	

HTML character entities

Entities exist for every letter and character. If a symbol can't be entered directly from the keyboard, it can be inserted by typing the name or numeric value listed in the following table:

Note: Some entities can be created using either a name or a number, as in the copyright symbol, but named entities may not work in all browsers or applications. So, either stick to entities' numbers, or test the specific named entities you wish to use.

Table 2.2 HTML character entities

CHARACTER	DESCRIPTION	NAME	NUMBER
©	Copyright	©	©
®	Registered trademark	®	®
™	Trademark		™
•	Bullet		•
–	En dash		–
—	Em dash		—
	Nonbreaking space		

Go to www.w3schools.com/html/html_entities.asp to see a complete list of entities.

Introducing HTML5

The current version of HTML has been around for over 10 years and, like many technologies, has not kept pace with the advances that have occurred on the web, such as in smartphones and other mobile devices. The World Wide Web Consortium (W3C)—the standards organization responsible for maintaining and updating HTML and other web standards—has been working diligently on updating the language. It released the first working draft of HTML5 (written as one word) in January 2008, with regular updates since then and the latest published as recently as June 2014. Although adoption of the new standard wasn't envisioned until 2020 at the earliest, W3C accelerated the plan and now wants to finalize HTML5 before the end of 2014. So what does all this mean for current or up-and-coming web designers? It means you have to work in two worlds at the same time.

Why? Adoption of the new language is not a mandatory process. The entire community works together cooperatively to develop and implement the new technology. As a result, there's no final deadline and no Internet police that enforce HTML5's adoption or proper use. Today, the current crop of web browsers is working to incorporate the new features outlined in the HTML5 specifications, but the support is not complete, and varies from browser to browser. In some cases, the browser manufacturers even disagree on how certain features should be

Note: HTML 4 was adopted in 1998, and even to this day browsers do not display pages in the same way.

implemented. Until the specifications are finalized, HTML5 sits in a state of *partial* adoption and implementation that may continue for some time to come.

Some designers and developers are taking a "wait and see" approach, maintaining good web design practices and implementing HTML5 features when they are safe and it makes sense to do so. Others have the attitude that "it's all good" and are starting to rely heavily on HTML5 tools and techniques. These designers and developers feel that early adopters will attract users interested in the latest and greatest and that by "jumping the shark," older non-HTML5 compliant browsers will be abandoned more quickly. Still others simply look to their site analytics and design pages that will function properly for the majority of their visitors. In any case, backward compatibility to HTML 4.01 is a primary goal of the W3C and will continue well into the future. So no matter what category you fall into, don't worry; there's no threat that older webpages and sites will suddenly explode or disintegrate in a new browser or mobile device.

What happened to XHTML?

All this talk of HTML5 may make some designers wonder, "What happened to XHTML?" XHTML is a flavor of HTML that seemed destined to take over the Internet. Work was even progressing on the next version when it was suddenly eclipsed by HTML5 a few years ago. While most of the language is identical to HTML, XHTML follows the rules that govern the creation of XML, which can help prevent users from creating badly formed code, among other things.

Although the popularity of XHTML never took off with the majority of designers, the work being done on the next version continues even now. Older sites currently based on XHTML will continue to function fine even as HTML5 is rolled out and adopted. In previous versions of Dreamweaver, XHTML was the default doctype for all new webpages. While HTML5 is the current default doctype, you can select XHTML in the New Document dialog.

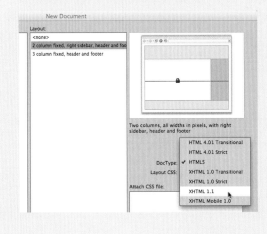

In this book, we will focus more on the first approach. Our lessons and exercises will use the HTML5 features and techniques that have widespread support and utility, but stick to tried-and-true techniques elsewhere. Additionally, we will also explore some of the newer, experimental features of HTML5, but leave their adoption on your own sites up to you.

What's new in HTML5

Every new version of HTML has made changes to both the number and purpose of the tags that make up the language. HTML 4.01 consisted of approximately 90 tags. HTML5 has removed some of those HTML 4 tags from its specification altogether and some new ones have been adopted or proposed.

Changes to the list usually revolve around supporting new technologies or different types of content models, as well as removing features that were bad ideas or ones infrequently used. Some changes simply reflect customs or techniques that have been popularized within the developer community over time. Other changes have been made to simplify the way code is created, to make it easier to write and faster to disseminate.

HTML5 tags

The following table shows some of the important new tags in HTML5. At the moment, HTML5 includes well over 100 tags. Almost 30 old tags have been deprecated, which means that HTML5 features nearly 50 new tags in total. As we move through the exercises of this book, we will use many of these new HTML5 tags as appropriate and explain their intended role on the web. Take a few moments to familiarize yourself with these tags and their descriptions; you'll be using many of them in the following lessons.

Go to www.w3schools.com/html5/html5_reference.asp to see the complete list of HTML5 elements.

Table 2.3 Important new HTML5 tags

TAG	DESCRIPTION	STRUCTURAL	BLOCK	INLINE
`<article>`	Designates independent, self-contained content, which can be distributed independently from the rest of the site.	✓	✓	
`<aside>`	Designates sidebar content that is related to the surrounding content.	✓	✓	
`<audio>`	Designates multimedia content, sounds, music, or other audio streams.	✓		✓
`<canvas>`	Designates graphics content created using a script.	✓		
`<figure>`	Designates a section of standalone content containing an image or video.	✓	✓	
`<figcaption>`	Designates a caption for a `<figure>` element.	✓		✓
`<footer>`	Designates a footer of a document or section.	✓	✓	
`<header>`	Designates the introduction of a document or section.	✓	✓	
`<hgroup>`	Designates a set of <h1> to <h6> elements when a heading has multiple levels.	✓		
`<nav>`	Designates a section of navigation.	✓	✓	
`<section>`	Designates a section in a document.	✓	✓	
`<source>`	Designates media resources for media elements, a child element of video, or audio elements. Multiple sources can be defined for browsers that do not support the default file type.	✓		✓
`<track>`	Designates text tracks used in media players.	✓		
`<video>`	Designates video content, such as a movie clip or other video streams.	✓		

Semantic web design

Many of the changes to HTML have been made to support the concept of *semantic web design*. This movement has important ramifications for the future of HTML, its usability, and the interoperability of websites on the Internet. At the moment, each webpage stands alone on the web. The content may link to other pages and sites, but there's really no way to combine or collect the information available on multiple pages or multiple sites in a coherent manner. Search engines do their best to index the content that appears on every site, but much of it is lost due to the nature and structure of old HTML code.

HTML was initially designed as a presentation language. In other words, it was intended to display technical documents in a browser in a readable and predictable manner. If you look carefully at the original specifications of HTML, it basically looks like a list of items you would put in a college research paper: headings, paragraphs, quoted material, tables, numbered and bulleted lists, and so on.

The Internet before HTML looked more like MS DOS or the OS X Terminal applications. There was no formatting, no graphics, and no user-definable color.

The element list in the first version of HTML basically identified how the content would be displayed. These tags did not convey any intrinsic meaning or significance. For example, using a heading tag displayed a particular line of text in bold, but it didn't tell you what relationship the heading was to the following text or to the story as a whole. Is it a title or merely a subheading?

HTML5 has added a significant number of new tags to help us add semantic meaning to our markup. Tags, such as `<header>`, `<footer>`, `<article>`, and `<section>`, allow you for the first time to identify specific content without having to resort to additional attributes. The end result is simpler code and less of it. But most of all, the addition of semantic meaning to your code allows you and other developers to connect the content from one page to another in new and exciting ways—many of which haven't even been invented yet. It's truly a work in progress.

New techniques and technology

HTML5 has also revisited the basic nature of the language to take back some of the functions that over the years have been increasingly handled by third-party plug-in applications and programming. If you are new to web design, this transition will be painless because you have nothing to relearn, no bad habits to break. If you already have experience building webpages and applications, this book will guide you safely through some of these waters and introduce the new technologies and techniques in a logical and straightforward way. But either way you don't have to trash all your old sites and rebuild everything from scratch. Valid HTML 4 code will remain valid for the foreseeable future. HTML5 was intended to make web design easier by allowing you to do more with less work. So let's get started!

See www.w3.org/TR/2014/WD-html5-20140617 to learn more about HTML5.

See www.w3.org to learn more about W3C.

Review questions

1 What programs can open HTML files?

2 What does a markup language do?

3 HTML is comprised of how many code elements?

4 What are the three main parts of most webpages?

5 What is the difference between block and inline elements?

6 Is HTML5 the current version of the language?

Review answers

1 HTML is a plain-text language that can be opened and edited in any text editor and viewed in any web browser.

2 A markup language places tags contained within brackets < > around plain-text content to pass information concerning structure and formatting from one application to another.

3 Less than 100 tags are defined in the HTML 4 specifications; HTML5 contains over 100.

4 Most webpages are composed of three main sections: a root, head, and body.

5 A block element creates a standalone element. An inline element can exist within another element.

6 No. The current version is HTML 4.01. HTML5 is considered in draft form since the first specifications were published, but it is not slated to be formally adopted until the end of 2014. Full support may take several years after it is finalized.

3

CSS BASICS

Lesson overview

In this lesson, you'll familiarize yourself with CSS and learn

- CSS (cascading style sheets) terms and terminology

- The difference between HTML and CSS formatting

- How the cascade, inheritance, descendant, and specificity theories affect how browsers apply CSS formatting

- How CSS can format objects

- New features and capabilities of CSS3

This lesson will take about two hours to complete. If you have not already done so, download the project files for this lesson from the Lesson & Update Files tab on your Account page at www.peachpit.com, store them on your computer in a convenient location, and define a new site in Dreamweaver based on this folder, as described in the "Getting Started" section of this book. Your Account page is also where you'll find any updates to the chapters or to the lesson files. Look on the Lesson & Update Files tab to access the most current content.

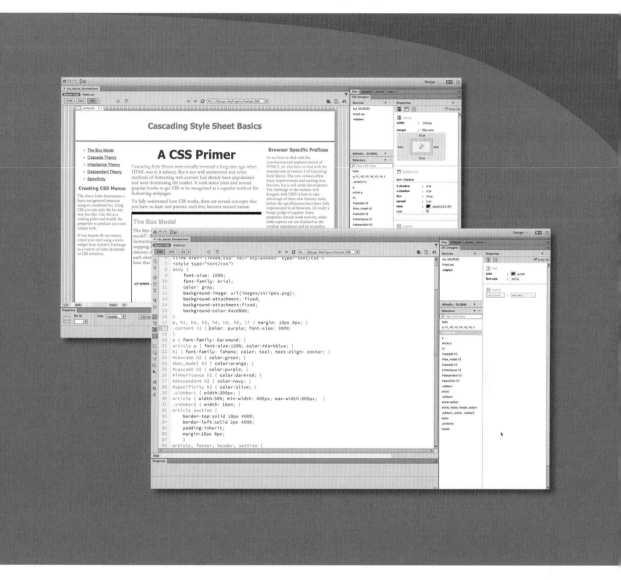

Cascading style sheets control the look and feel of a webpage. The language and syntax of CSS is complex, powerful, and endlessly adaptable. It takes time and dedication to learn and years to master, but a modern web designer can't live without it.

What is CSS?

HTML was never intended to be a design medium. Other than allowing for bold and italic, version 1 lacked a standardized way to load fonts or format text. Formatting commands were added along the way, up to version 3 of HTML, to address these limitations, but these changes still weren't enough. Designers resorted to various tricks to produce the desired results. For example, they used HTML tables to simulate multicolumn and complex layouts for text and graphics, and they used images when they wanted to display typefaces other than Times or Helvetica.

HTML-based formatting was so misguided a concept that it was deprecated from the language less than a year after it was formally adopted in favor of cascading style sheets (CSS). CSS avoids all the problems of HTML formatting, while saving time and money, too. Using CSS lets you strip the HTML code down to its essential content and structure and then apply the formatting separately, so you can more easily tailor the webpage to specific applications.

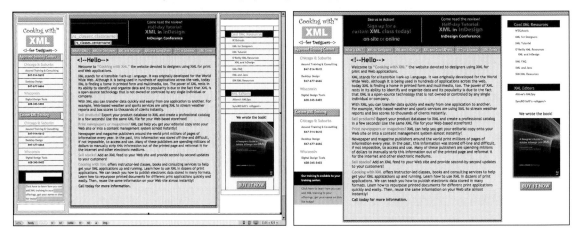

By adding cell padding and margins to the table structure in Dreamweaver (left), you can see how this webpage relies on tables and images to produce the final design (right).

HTML vs. CSS formatting

When comparing HTML-based formatting to CSS-based formatting, it's easy to see how CSS produces vast efficiencies in time and effort. In the following exercise, you'll explore the power and efficacy of CSS by editing two webpages, one formatted by HTML, the other by CSS.

1 Launch Dreamweaver, if it's not currently running.

2 Choose File > Open.

3 Navigate to the lesson03 folder, and open **html_formatting.html**.

4 Click the Split view button. If necessary, choose View > Split Vertically to split Code and Design view windows vertically, top to bottom.

Each element of the content is formatted individually using the deprecated `<font>` tag. Note the attribute `color="blue"` in each `<h1>` and `<p>` element.

Note: "Deprecated" means that the tag has been removed from future support in HTML but may still be honored by current browsers and HTML readers.

5 Replace the word `"blue"` with `"green"` in each line in which it appears. Click in the Design view window to update the display.

The text displays in green now in each line where you changed the color value. As you can see, formatting using the obsolete `<font>` tag is not only slow, but prone to error, too. Make a mistake, like typing greeen or geen, and the browser will ignore the color formatting entirely.

6 Open **css_formatting.html** from the lesson03 folder.

7 If it's not currently selected, click the Split view button.

The content of the file is identical to the previous document, except that it's formatted using CSS. The code that formats the HTML elements appears in the `<head>` section of this file. Note how the code contains only two `color:blue;` attributes.

8 Select the word blue within the code h1 { color: blue; } and type green to replace it. Click in the Design view window to update the display.

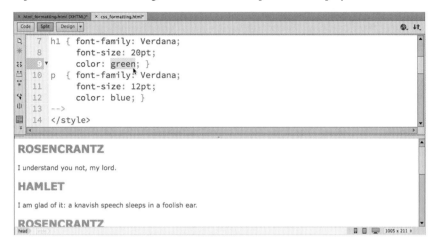

In Design view, all the heading elements display in green. The paragraph elements remain blue.

9 Select the word blue in the code p { color: blue; } and type green to replace it. Click in the Design view window to update the display.

In Design view, all the paragraph elements have changed to green.

In this exercise, CSS accomplished the color change with two simple edits, whereas the HTML <font> tag required you to edit *every* line. Are you beginning to understand why the W3C deprecated the <font> tag and developed cascading style sheets? This exercise highlights just a small sampling of the formatting power and productivity enhancements offered by CSS that can't be matched by HTML alone.

HTML defaults

Many of the nearly 100 HTML 4 tags come right out of the box with one or more default formats, characteristics, or behaviors. So even if you do nothing, much of your text will already be formatted in a certain way. One of the essential tasks in mastering CSS is learning and understanding these defaults. Let's take a look.

1 Open **html_defaults.html** from the lesson03 folder. If necessary, select Design view to preview the contents of the file.

The file contains a range of HTML headings and text elements. Each element exhibits basic styling for traits such as size, font, and spacing, among others.

2 Switch to Split view. If necessary, choose View > Split Vertically to split Code and Design view windows side by side. In the Code view window, locate the `<head>` section and try to identify any code that may be formatting the HTML elements.

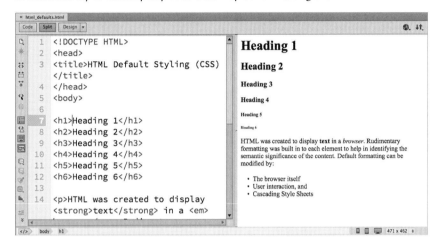

A quick look will tell you that there is no obvious styling information in the file, but the text still displays different kinds of formatting. So where does the formatting come from? And, more importantly, what are the settings?

The answer is: It depends. HTML 4 elements draw characteristics from multiple sources. The first place to look is the W3C, the web standards organization that establishes Internet specifications and protocols. You will find a default style sheet at www.w3.org/TR/CSS21/sample.html that defines the standard formatting and behaviors of all HTML 4 elements. This is the style sheet on which all browser vendors base their default rendering of HTML elements. What this means is that even if you didn't have a single line of CSS code in your webpage, your HTML elements will still display some basic types of styling.

HTML5 defaults?

Over the last decade there has been a consistent movement on the web to separate "content" from its "styling." At the time of this writing, the concept of "default" formatting in HTML seems to be dead. Technically speaking, there are no default styling standards for HTML5 elements. If you look for a default style sheet for HTML5 on w3.org, you won't find one. But for the time being, browser manufacturers are still honoring and applying HTML 4 default styling to HTML5-based webpages. Confused? Join the club.

The ramifications could be dramatic and wide-reaching. Some day, in the not too distant future, HTML elements may not display any formatting at all by default.

Note: If the current trends continue, the lack of an HTML5 default style sheet makes the development of your own site standards even more important.

This doesn't seem to be an imminent danger; HTML5-based webpages continue to display the same default styling we've come to expect. Even if you forget to apply any CSS formatting you can still count on the HTML 4 defaults.

To save time and give you a bit of a head start, we pulled together the following table of some of the most common defaults:

Table 3.1 Common HTML defaults

ITEM	DESCRIPTION
Background	In most browsers, the page background color is white. The background of the elements <div>, <table>, <td>, <th>, and most other tags is transparent.
Headings	Headings <h1> through <h6> are bold and align to the left. The six heading tags apply differing font size attributes, with <h1> the largest and <h6> the smallest. Sizes may vary between browsers.
Body text	Outside of a table cell, paragraphs—<p>, <li>, <dd>, <dt>—align to the left and start at the top of the page.
Table cell text	Text within table cells <td> aligns horizontally to the left and vertically to the center.
Table header	Text within header cells <th> aligns horizontally and vertically to the center.
Fonts	Text color is black. Default typeface and font is specified and supplied by the browser (or by browser defaults specified by the manufacturer, which can be overridden by the user applying preference settings in the browser itself).
Margins	Spacing external to the element border/boundary is handled by margins. Many HTML elements feature some form of margin spacing. Margins are often used to insert additional space between paragraphs and to indent text, as in lists and blockquotes.
Padding	Spacing between the box border and the content is handled by padding. According to the default style sheet, no elements feature default padding.

Browser antics

The next task is to identify the browser (and its version) that is displaying the HTML. That's because browsers frequently differ (sometimes dramatically) in the way they interpret, or *render*, HTML elements and CSS formatting. Unfortunately, even different versions of the same browser can produce wide variations from identical code.

The best practice is to build and test your webpages to make sure they work properly in the browsers employed by the majority of web users—especially the browsers preferred by your own visitors. The breakdown of browser use of your own visitors can differ quite a bit from the norm. They also change over time, especially now, as more and more people abandon desktop computers in favor of tablets and smartphones. In July 2014, the W3C published the following statistics identifying the most popular browsers:

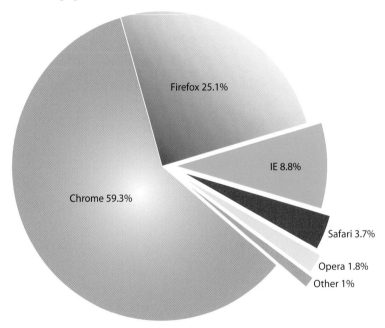

Although it's nice to know which browsers are the most popular among the general public, it's crucial that before you build and test your pages you identify the browsers your target audience uses.

Although this chart shows the basic breakdown in the browser world, it obscures the fact that multiple versions of each browser are still being used. This is important to know because older browser versions are less likely to support the latest HTML and CSS features and effects. To make matters more complicated—although these statistics show trends for the Internet overall—the statistics for your own site may vary wildly.

CSS box model

Browsers normally read the HTML code, interpret its structure and formatting, and then display the appropriate webpage. CSS does its work by stepping between HTML and the browser, redefining how each element should be rendered. It imposes an imaginary box around each element and then enables you to format almost every aspect of how that box and its contents are displayed.

The box model is a programmatic construct imposed by HTML and CSS that enables you to format, or redefine, the default settings of any HTML element.

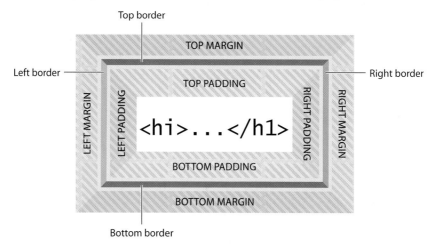

CSS permits you to specify fonts, line spacing, colors, borders, background shading and graphics, margins, and padding, among other things. Most of the time these boxes are invisible, and although CSS gives you the ability to format them it doesn't require you to do so.

1 Launch Dreamweaver, if necessary. Open **boxmodel.html** from the lesson03 folder.

2 If necessary, click the Split view button to divide the workspace between the Code view and Design view windows.

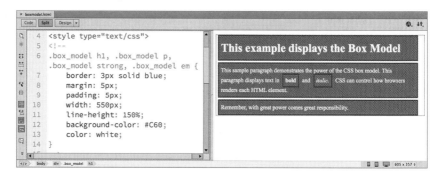

The file's sample HTML code contains a heading and two paragraphs with sample text formatted to illustrate some of the properties of the CSS box model. The text displays visible borders, background colors, margins, and padding. To see the real power of CSS, sometimes it's helpful to see what the page would look like without CSS.

3   Choose View > Style Rendering > Display Styles.

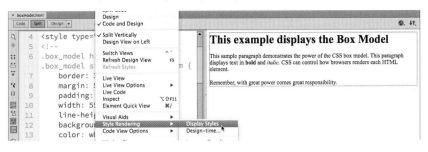

Dreamweaver now displays the page without any applied styling. A basic tenet in web standards today is the separation of the *content* (text, images, lists, and so on) from its *presentation* (formatting). Although the text now is not wholly unformatted, it's easy to see the power of CSS to transform HTML code. Whether formatted or not, this illustrates the importance in the *quality* of your content. Will people still be enthralled by your website if all the wonderful formatting was pulled away?

4   Choose View > Style Rendering > Display Styles to enable the CSS rendering in Dreamweaver again.

The working specifications found at www.w3.org/TR/css3-box describe how the box model is supposed to render documents in various media.

Previewing the completed file

The best way to learn CSS is by creating your own. For the rest of this lesson, you'll learn how CSS works by creating a complete style sheet for a sample HTML file. Let's take a look at the final product of the upcoming exercises.

1   Create a new site based on the lesson03 folder, using instructions in the "Getting Started" section at the beginning of the book.
    Name the site **lesson03**.

2   Open the **css_basics_finished.html** file from the site root.

3 If necessary, switch to Split view and observe the content and code in the two windows.

The file contains a complete HTML page with a variety of elements, including headings, paragraphs, lists, and links all fully formatted by CSS. Note the text styling, as well as the colors and borders assigned to other elements. Some features may not display properly in Design view alone.

4 Switch to Design view only. Activate Live view.

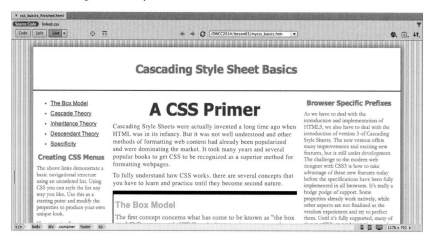

The display changes to show the CSS styling more accurately. A drop shadow now appears around the main content section. As before, the best way to see the true power of CSS is by shutting it off.

5 Choose View > Style Rendering > Display Styles to disable the CSS rendering in Dreamweaver.

The page is no longer formatted by CSS and displays only the default styling you would expect on standard HTML elements. The text now stacks vertically in a single column with no colors, borders, backgrounds, or shadows.

6 Choose View > Style Rendering > Display Styles to enable the CSS rendering in Dreamweaver again.

7 Choose File > Close All.

All sample files close.

As you can see, CSS can style all aspects of a webpage with amazing variety and detail. First, we'll take a look at how you use CSS to format text.

Formatting text

You can apply CSS formatting in three ways: *inline, embedded* (in an internal style sheet), or *linked* (via an external style sheet). A CSS formatting instruction is called a *rule*. A rule consists of two parts—a *selector* and one or more *declarations*. The selector specifies what element, or combination of elements, is to be formatted; declarations contain the styling information. CSS rules can redefine any existing HTML element, as well as define two custom element modifiers called "class" and "id."

A rule can also combine selectors to target multiple elements at once or to target specific instances within a page where elements appear in unique ways, such as when one element is nested within another.

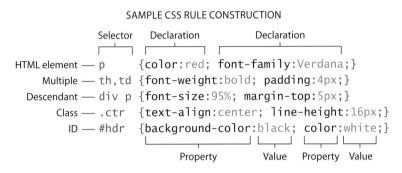

SAMPLE CSS RULE CONSTRUCTION

These sample rules demonstrate some typical constructions used in selectors and declarations. The way the selector is written determines how the styling is applied and how the rules interact with one another.

Applying a CSS rule is not a simple matter of selecting some text and applying a paragraph or character style, as in Adobe InDesign or Adobe Illustrator. CSS rules can affect single words, paragraphs of text, or combinations of text and objects. A single rule can affect an entire webpage, a single paragraph, or just a few words or letters. Basically, anything that has an HTML tag on it can be styled, and there is even an HTML tag specifically intended to style content that has no tag.

There are many factors that come into play in how a CSS rule performs its job. To help you better understand how it all works, the exercises in the following sections illustrate four main CSS concepts, which we'll refer to as theories: cascade, inheritance, descendant, and specificity.

CSS rule syntax: write or wrong

CSS is a powerful adjunct to HTML. It has the power to style and format any HTML element, but the language is sensitive to even the smallest typo or syntax error. Miss a period, comma, or semicolon and you may as well have left the code out of your page entirely.

For example, take the following simple rule:

```
p { padding: 1px;
    margin: 10px; }
```

It applies both padding and margins to the paragraph <p> element.

This rule can also be written properly without spacing as:

```
p{padding:1px;margin:10px;}
```

The spaces and line breaks used in the first example are unnecessary—merely accommodations for the humans who may write and read the code. The browsers and other devices processing the code do not need them. But the same cannot be said of the various punctuation marks sprinkled throughout the CSS.

Use parentheses ( ) or brackets [ ] instead of braces { }, and the rule (and perhaps your entire style sheet) is useless. The same goes for the use of colons ":" and semicolons ";" in the code.

Can you catch the error in each of the following sample rules?

```
p { padding; 1px: margin; 10px: }
p { padding: 1px; margin: 10px; ]
p { padding 1px, margin 10px, }
```

Similar problems can arise in the construction of compound selectors, too. For example, putting a space in the wrong place can change the meaning of a selector entirely.

The `article.content { color: #F00 }` rule formats the `<article>` element and all its children in this code structure:

```
<article class="content"><p>…</p></article>
```

On the other hand, the rule `article .content { color: #F00 }` would ignore the previous HTML structure altogether, and format only the <p> element in the following code:

```
<article class="content"><p class="content">…</p>
</article>
```

A tiny error can have dramatic and far-reaching repercussions. To keep their CSS and HTML functioning properly, good web designers constantly search for any little error, misplaced space, or punctuation mark. As you work through the following exercises, keep a careful eye on all the code for any similar errors.

Cascade theory

The cascade theory describes how the order and placement of rules in the style sheet or on the page affects the application of styling. In other words, if two rules conflict, which one wins out? Let's take a look at how cascade influences CSS formatting.

1 Open **css_basics.html** from the lesson03 folder in Split view.

   The file contains a complete HTML page with various elements, headings, paragraphs, lists, and links that are currently formatted only by default HTML styling.

2 Save the file as **mycss_basics.html** in the site root folder.

   Dreamweaver creates a copy of the file using the new name. The original file is still open. This could cause confusion during the following exercises.

3 Select the document tab for the **css_basics.html** file.
   Choose File > Close.

   The **mycss_basics.html** file should be the only one open.

4 Click the Split view button, if necessary, and observe the `<head>` section in the Code view window for any CSS rules.

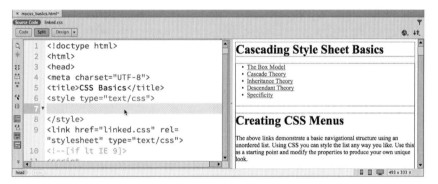

Note that the code contains a `<style>` section but no CSS rules.

5 Insert the cursor between the `<style>` and `</style>` tags.

6 Type `h1 { color:gray; }` and click in the Design view window to refresh the display.

> **Note:** As you type the rule markup, Dreamweaver provides code hints as it did with the HTML code in Lesson 2. Feel free to use these hints to speed up your typing, or simply ignore them and continue typing.

The h1 headings throughout the page now display in gray. The rest of the text still displays the default formatting. Congratulations, you wrote your first CSS rule.

● **Note:** CSS does not require line breaks between rules, but it does make the code easier to read.

7   In Code view, insert the pointer at the end of the rule created in step 6. Press Enter/Return to create a new line.

8   Type h1 { color:red; } and click in the Design view window to refresh the display.

The h1 headings now display in red. The styling of the new rule supersedes the formatting applied by the first. It's important to understand that the two rules are identical except that they apply different colors: red or gray. Both rules want to format the same elements, but only one will be honored.

It's clear the second rule won, but why? In this case, the second rule is the last one declared, making it the *closest* one to the actual content. Whether intentional or not, a style applied by one rule may be overridden by declarations in a subsequent rule.

9   Select the rule h1 { color: gray; }

▶ **Tip:** In Code view, you can also drag and drop code once it's selected.

10 Choose Edit > Cut.

11 Insert the pointer at the end of the rule h1 { color: red; } If necessary, press Enter/Return to insert a new line.

12 Choose Edit > Paste or press Ctrl+V/Cmd+V.

You have switched the order of the rules.

13 Click in the Design view window to refresh the preview display.

The h1 headings display in gray again. Cascade applies to styles whether the rules are embedded in the webpage or located in a separate external, linked style sheet.

14 Select **linked.css** in the Related Files interface.

The contents of the **linked.css** file appears in the Code view window.

15 Insert the pointer in line 2.

Type `h1 { color:orange; }` and press Ctrl+S/Cmd+S to save the file.

Click in the Design view window to refresh the display.

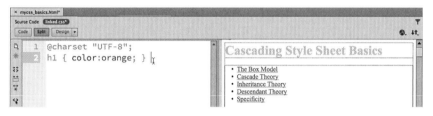

The h1 headings now display in orange.

16 Select Source Code in the Related Files interface.

Locate the `<link>` reference for **linked.css** in the `<head>` section.

The `<link>` element appears after the `<style>` element. Based strictly on cascade this means that any rule that appears in the linked file will supersede duplicate rules in the embedded sheet.

17 Click the line number for the external CSS `<link>` reference.

Drag the entire `<link>` reference above the `<style>` element.

Click in the Design view window to refresh the display.

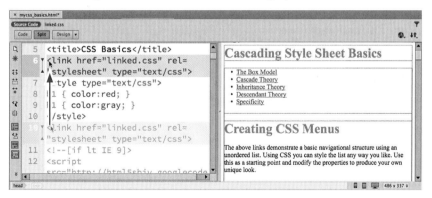

The headings revert to gray.

18 Select File > Save All.

As you can clearly see, the order and *proximity* of the rules within the markup are powerful factors in how CSS is applied. When you try to determine which

Note: !important
is an attribute you
can append to any
CSS value to make it
supersede values set by
other equivalent rules.
It can trump cascade,
inheritance, and
sometimes even more
specific rules.

CSS rule will be honored and which formatting will be applied browsers typically honor the following order of hierarchy, with number 4 being the most powerful:

1. Browser defaults.

2. External or embedded style sheets. If both are present, the one declared last supersedes the earlier entry in conflicts.

3. Inline styles (within the HTML element itself).

4. Styles with the value attribute !important applied.

Inheritance theory

The inheritance theory describes how an element can be affected by one or more rules at the same time. Inheritance can affect rules of the same name as well as rules that format *parent* elements—ones that contain other elements. Let's take a look at how inheritance influences CSS formatting.

1 If necessary, open **mycss_basics.html** from the lesson03 folder. In Split view, observe the HTML code.

The webpage contains headings, paragraphs, lists, and HTML5 semantic elements formatted by HTML defaults, as well as CSS rules created in the previous exercise.

2 Insert the pointer after the rule h1 { color: gray; } in the embedded style sheet. Press Enter/Return to insert a new line.

3 Type h1 { font-family:Arial; } and click in the Design view window to refresh the display.

The h1 elements appear in Arial and gray. The other content remains formatted by default styling.

Now there are four CSS rules that format <h1> elements. Can you tell, by looking at the Design view window, which of the rules is formatting the <h1> text? If you said *two* of them, you're the winner.

At first glance, you may think that the rules formatting <h1> elements are separate from each other. And technically, that's true. But if you look closer, you'll see that the new rule doesn't contradict the others. It's not *resetting* the color attribute as you did in the previous exercise; it's declaring a new, *additional* attribute. In other words, since both rules do something different, both will be honored, or *inherited*, by the h1 element. All <h1> elements will be formatted as gray *and* Arial.

Far from being a mistake or an unintended consequence, the ability to build rich and elaborate formatting using multiple rules is one of the most powerful and complex aspects of cascading style sheets.

4   Insert the pointer after the last h1 rule.
Insert a new line in the code.

5   Type `h2 { font-family:Arial; color:gray; }` and click in the Design view window to refresh the display.

Tip: Rules typically contain multiple property declarations.

The h2 element appears in Arial and gray; it originally displayed in a serif font in black.

6   After the h2 rule, type the following code:

```
h3 { font-family:Arial; color:gray; }
p { font-family:Arial; color:gray; }
li { font-family:Arial; color:gray; }
```

Note: There is no requirement to create rules in any specific order or hierarchy. You may order them any way you please, as long as you keep in mind how the application of styling is governed by cascade and inheritance.

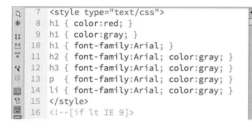

7   Refresh the Design view window display by clicking in it or clicking the Refresh button in the Properties panel.

All the elements now display the same styling, but it took six rules to format the entire page.

Although CSS styling is far more efficient than the obsolete HTML-based method, inheritance can help you optimize your styling chores even more. For example, all the rules include the statement { `font-family:Arial; color:gray;` }. Redundant code like this should be avoided whenever possible. It adds to the amount of code in each webpage as well as to the time it takes to download and process it. By using inheritance, sometimes you can create the same effect with a single rule. One way is to apply styling to a *parent* element instead of to the elements themselves.

8   Create a new line in the <style> section and type the following code:
`article { font-family: Arial; color: gray; }`

If you look through the code, you will see that the <article> tag contains much, but not all, of the webpage content. Let's see what happens if we delete some of our CSS rules.

9 Select and delete the rule ~~h2 { font-family: Arial; color: gray; }~~
Refresh the Design view window display.

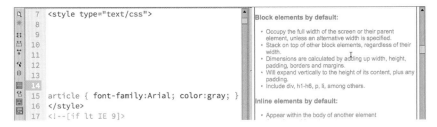

The h2 elements appearing within the <article> element remain formatted as gray Arial. The other h2 element down the page now appears in HTML default styling.

10 Select and delete all h1 rules. Don't forget the one in the **linked.css** file. Refresh the Design view display.

The h1 elements contained within the <article> element continue to be styled. Those outside the <article> element have also reverted to the HTML defaults. Since the rule targets only the <article> element, only the elements contained within it are styled.

11 Select and delete the h3, p, and li rules.
Refresh the Design view display.

```
 7  <style type="text/css">
 8
 9
10
11
12
13
14
15  article { font-family:Arial; color:gray; }
16  </style>
17  <!--[if lt IE 9]>
```

Block elements by default:

• Occupy the full width of the screen or their parent element, unless an alternative width is specified.
• Stack on top of other block elements, regardless of their width.
• Dimensions are calculated by adding up width, height, padding, borders and margins.
• Will expand vertically to the height of its content, plus any padding.
• Include div, h1-h6, p, li, among others.

Inline elements by default:

• Appear within the body of another element

As in step 10, any content contained in the <article> tag remains formatted, while content elsewhere has reverted.

This is the way inheritance works. You could simply recreate the rules to format the other content, but there's a simpler alternative. Instead of adding additional CSS rules, can you figure out a way to use inheritance to format all the content on the page the same way? A hint: Look carefully at the entire structure of the webpage.

Did you think about using the <body> element? If so, you win again. The <body> element contains all the visible content on the webpage and therefore is the parent of all of it.

12 Change the rule selector from `article` to `body` and delete any blank lines.
Choose File > Save All.
Refresh the Design view display.

Once again, all the text displays in gray Arial. By using inheritance, only one rule is needed to format all the content instead of six. You'll find that the <body> element is a popular target for setting various default styles.

Descendant theory

While inheritance provides a means to apply styling to multiple elements at once, CSS also provides the means to target styling to specific elements.

The descendant theory describes how formatting can target particular elements based on their position relative to others. This technique involves the creation of a selector name that identifies a specific element, or elements, by combining multiple tags, as well as id and class attributes. Let's take a look at how descendant selectors influence CSS formatting.

1 If necessary, open **mycss_basics.html** from the lesson03 folder.
In Split view, observe the structure of the HTML content.

The page contains headings and paragraphs in various HTML5 structural elements, such as `article`, `section`, and `aside`. The rule `body { color: gray; font-family:Arial; }` applies a default font and color to the entire page. In this exercise, you will learn how to create descendant CSS rules to target styling to specific elements in context.

2 In Code view, insert the pointer at the end of the `body` rule.
Press Enter/Return to insert a new line.

3 Type `p { font-family:Garamond; }` and refresh the Design view display.

All p elements on the page display in Garamond. The rest of the page continues to be formatted as before.

By creating a selector using the p tag, the font formatting has been overridden for all p elements no matter where they appear. You may be thinking that since the p rule appears *after* the body rule, this type of styling simply relates to the cascade order. Let's try an experiment to see if that's true.

Tip: In this particular page, you could also use the `<div>` element to achieve the same result. But since `<div>` is a frequently used element, it might pose unpredictable conflicts in the future. Since webpages have only one `<body>` element, it is definitely the preferred target.

Note: Dreamweaver frequently edits externally linked files. Use Save All whenever changes on your page may affect multiple files in your site.

Note: Step 3 assumes you have Garamond installed on your computer. If it is not, select another serif style font, like Times.

4 Click the line number for the p rule.

Drag the p rule above the body rule and refresh the Design view display.

The p rule now appears above the body rule, but the styling did not change.

● **Note:** We will examine the role of specificity later in this lesson.

If the styling of p elements was determined simply by cascade, you would expect the headings to revert to gray Arial. Yet here, the styling is unaffected by changing the order of the rules. Instead, by using a more specific tag name in the selector, the new p rule becomes more powerful than the generic body rule. By properly combining two or more tags in the selector, you can craft the CSS styling on the page in even more sophisticated ways.

5 Create a new line after the p rule.

Type `article p { font-size:120%; color:darkblue; }` on the new line.

By adding a p tag immediately after `article` in the selector, you are telling the browser to format only p elements that are children, or *descendants*, of `article` elements. Remember, a *child* element is one contained or nested within another element.

6 Refresh the Design view display.

All paragraphs appearing within the `<article>` element now display in dark blue, 120 percent larger than the other paragraph text on the page.

7 Choose File > Save All.

Although it may be hard to understand at this moment, the other rules—both body and p—are still being inherited by the newly formatted paragraphs. But wherever two or more rules conflict, a descendant selector will win over any less specific styling.

Using classes and ids

So far, you've learned that you can create CSS rules that format specific HTML elements and ones that can target specific HTML element structures or relationships. In some instances, you may want to apply unique formatting to an element that is already formatted by an existing rule. In such cases, you can use CSS classes or id attributes to target that element.

In **mycss_basics.html**, all h1 elements are formatted identically regardless of where they appear in the layout. In the following exercise, you'll use classes and ids to differentiate the styling among the headings.

1 Insert a new line after the rule `article p`

Type `h1 { font-family:Tahoma; color:teal; }` and refresh the display.

All h1 headings now display in teal Tahoma.

Although it's tagged identically to the other h1 headings, "A CSS Primer" is the main heading in the `<article>` element. To make it stand out from the other headings, we can use the class attribute assigned to its parent to target it for special formatting.

2 Create the following new rule `.content h1 { color:red; font-size:300%; }` and refresh the display.

The heading "A CSS Primer" displays in red, 300 percent larger than the body text.

In CSS syntax, the period (.) refers to a *class* attribute, and the hash "#" means *id*. By adding `.content` to the selector, you have targeted the styling only to h1 elements in `<article class="content">`.

In the same way, you can assign custom styling to the subheadings (h2). You can use the id attributes of each `<section>`.

3 Create the following rules:

```
#box_model h2 { color:orange; }
#cascade h2 { color:purple; }
#inheritance h2 { color:darkred; }
#descendant h2 { color:navy; }
#specificity h2 { color:olive; }
```

4 Choose File > Save All. If necessary, refresh the display.

All the h2 headings now display unique colors.

What's important to understand here is that no formatting or additional attributes have been added to any of the headings themselves. They are being formatted based solely on their position within the structure of the code.

Understanding descendant selectors

CSS formatting can be very confusing for designers coming from the print world. Print designers are accustomed to applying styles directly to text and objects, one at a time. In some cases, styles can be *based* on one another, but this relationship is intentional. In print-based styling, it's impossible for one paragraph or character style to affect another unintentionally. On the other hand, in CSS, the formatting of one element overlapping or influencing others all the time.

It may be helpful to think of it as if the elements are formatting themselves. When you use CSS properly, the formatting is not intrinsic to the element but to the entire page and to the way the code is structured. The following exercise will help you understand this concept.

1 In Code view, click the line number for the "The Box Model" heading.

2 Choose Edit > Copy or press Ctrl+C/Cmd+C.

3 Insert the pointer at the end of the h2 element "Cascade Theory" and create a new line.

4 Choose Edit > Paste or press Ctrl+V/Cmd+V and then refresh the display.

The heading "The Box Model" appears following and formatted identically to the heading "Cascade Theory."

5 Insert the pointer at the end of the "Inheritance Theory heading" and create a new line.

6 Press Ctrl+V/Cmd+V to paste the heading again.

The heading matches the styling of the "Inheritance Theory" heading.

As you can see, the formatting of the heading does not travel with the text. That's the point of separating content from presentation—you can insert it anywhere and it will adopt the formatting native to that position. It even works in reverse.

7 In Code view, select and copy the "Inheritance Theory" heading.

8 Insert the pointer after the original "The Box Model" heading and press Ctrl+V/Cmd+V.

```
82  <section id="cascade">        │  Cascade Theory
83  <h2>Cascade Theory</h2>       │
84  <h2>The Box Model</h2>        │  The Box Model
85  <p>The cascade theory describes how the order
    and placement of rules in the style sheet or
```

The heading appears and adopts the same styling as "The Box Model."

Once again, the pasted text matches the formatting applied to the other h2 element within the <article>, ignoring its original styling altogether. Now that you've seen how descendant theory works there's no need for the extra headings.

9 Choose File > Revert. Click Yes to revert the file to the previously saved version.

The ability to separate the content from its presentation is an important concept in modern web design. It allows you great freedom in moving content from page to page and structure to structure without worrying about the effects of residual or latent formatting. Since the formatting doesn't reside with the element itself, it's free to adapt instantly to its new surroundings.

Specificity theory

Conflicts between two or more rules are the bane of most web designers' existence and can waste hours of time in troubleshooting errors in CSS formatting. In the past, designers would have to spend hours manually scanning style sheets and rules one by one trying to track down the source of styling errors.

Specificity describes how browsers determine what formatting to apply when two or more rules conflict. Some refer to this as *weight*—giving certain rules higher priority based on order (cascade), proximity, inheritance, and descendant relationships. One way it does this is by giving numeric values to each part of the selector name. For example, each HTML tag gets 1 point, each class gets 10 points, each id gets 100 points, and inline style attributes get 1000 points. By adding up the component values of the selector, its specificity can be calculated and compared to other rules. The higher specific weight wins.

As you have learned in this lesson, CSS rules often don't work alone. They may style more than one HTML element at a time and may overlap or inherit styling from one another. Each of the theories described so far has a role to play in how CSS styling is applied through your webpage and across your site. When the style sheet is loaded, the browser will use the following hierarchy—with number 4 being the most powerful—to determine how the styles are applied, especially when rules conflict:

1. Cascade

2. Inheritance

3. Descendant structure

4. Specificity

Of course, knowing this hierarchy doesn't help much when you are faced with a CSS conflict on a page with dozens or perhaps hundreds of rules and multiple style sheets. Luckily, Dreamweaver has several tools that can help you in this endeavor. The first one we'll look at is named Code Navigator.

Calculating specificity

Can you do the math? Look at the following list of selectors and see how they add up. Now, look through the list of rules you created in the previous exercises in **mycss_basics.html**. Can you determine the weight of each of those selectors and figure out which rule is more specific on sight?

```
* (wildcard)  { } 0 +   0 +  0 + 0   =     0 points
h1            { } 0 +   0 +  0 + 1   =     1 point
ul li         { } 0 +   0 +  0 + 2   =     2 points
.class        { } 0 +   0 + 10 + 0   =    10 points
.class h1     { } 0 +   0 + 10 + 1   =    11 points
a:hover       { } 0 +   0 +  0 + 1   =    11 points
#id           { } 0 + 100 +  0 + 0   =   100 points
#id.class     { } 0 + 100 + 10 + 0   =   110 points
#id.class h1  { } 0 + 100 + 10 + 1   =   111 points
style=" "     { } 1000 + 0 + 0 + 0   = 1000 points
```

Code Navigator

Code Navigator is an editing tool within Dreamweaver that allows you to instantly inspect an HTML element and assess its CSS-based formatting. When activated, it will display all the embedded and externally linked CSS rules that have some role in formatting a selected element, and it will list them in the order of their cascade application and specificity. Code Navigator works in all Dreamweaver-based document views.

1 If necessary, open **mycss_basics.html** from the lesson03 folder. In Split view, observe the CSS code and the structure of the HTML content. Then, note the appearance of the text in the Design view window.

   The page contains headings, paragraphs, and lists in various HTML5 structural elements, such as `article`, `section`, and `aside`, styled by CSS rules you created in the previous exercises.

2 In Design view, insert the pointer in the "A CSS Primer" heading.

When Code Navigator is enabled, after a moment, an icon that looks like a ship's wheel appears. This icon provides access to Code Navigator.

3 Click the Code Navigator icon. If the Code Navigator does not appear automatically, right-click the heading and choose Code Navigator from the context menu or press Ctrl+Alt+N/Cmd+OptN.

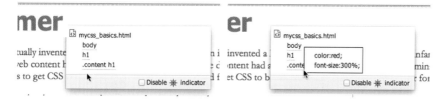

► **Tip:** Code Navigator may be disabled by default. To have it display automatically, deselect the Disable option in the Code Navigator window when it's visible.

A small window appears, displaying a list of three CSS rules that apply to this heading.

If you position the pointer over each rule in turn, Dreamweaver displays any properties formatted by the rule and their values. The rule with the highest specificity (most powerful) is at the bottom of the list.

Unfortunately, Code Navigator doesn't show styling applied via inline styles, so you'll have to check for these types of properties separately and calculate the effect of inline styles in your head. Otherwise, the sequence of rules in the list indicates both their cascade order and their specificity.

When rules conflict, rules farther down in the list override rules that are higher up. Remember, elements may inherit styling from one or more rules, and default styling—that is not overridden—may still play a role in the final presentation. Unfortunately, Code Navigator doesn't display what, if any, default styling characteristics may still be in effect.

● **Note:** Code Navigator doesn't display inline CSS rules. Since most CSS styling is not applied this way, it's not much of a limitation, but you should still be aware of this blind spot as you work with it.

The `.content h1` rule appears at the bottom of the Code Navigator window, indicating that its specifications are the most powerful ones styling this element. But many factors can influence which of the rules may win. Sometimes the specificity of two rules is identical; then, it's simply the order (cascade) in which rules are declared in the style sheet that determines which one is actually applied.

As you saw earlier, changing the order of rules can often affect how the rules work. There's a simple exercise you can perform to determine whether a rule is winning because of cascade or specificity.

4 In the Code view window, click the line number for the `.content h1` rule.

5 Drag the rule to the top of the embedded style sheet.

6 Click in the Design view window to refresh the display.

The styling did not change.

7 In Code view, insert the pointer into the text of the <h1> element "A CSS Primer" and activate Code Navigator.

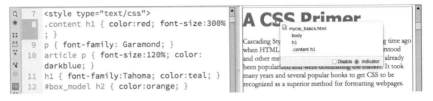

Although the rule was moved to the top of the style sheet, the order of the rules in Code Navigator did not change. The .content h1 selector has a specificity higher than either the body or h1 selectors. In this instance, it would win no matter where it was placed in the code. But specificity can change by simply modifying the selector.

8 Select and delete the ~~.content~~ class notation from the .content h1 selector.

9 Click in the Design view window to refresh the display.

Did you notice how the styling changed? The "A CSS Primer" heading reverted to the color teal and the other h1 headings scaled to 300 percent. Do you know why this happened?

10 Insert the pointer in the "A CSS Primer" heading and activate Code Navigator.

By removing the class notation from its selector it now has equal value to the other h1 rule but, since it is the first one declared, it loses precedence by virtue of its cascade position.

11 Using Code Navigator, examine and compare the rules applied to the headings "A CSS Primer" and "Creating CSS Menus."

The Code Navigator shows the same rules applied to both.

By removing the .content class from the selector, the rule no longer targets only h1 headings in the <article> element; it's now styling all h1 elements on the page.

12 Choose Edit > Undo to restore the .content class to the h1 selector. Refresh the Design view display.

All the headings return to their previous styling.

13 Insert the pointer in the heading "Creating CSS Menus" and activate Code Navigator.

The heading is no longer styled by the `.content h1` rule.

14 Choose File > Save All.

Is it starting to make more sense? Don't worry, it will—over time. Until that time, just remember that the rule appearing last in Code Navigator has the most influence on any particular element.

CSS Designer

Code Navigator was introduced in Dreamweaver CS4 and has been an invaluable aid for troubleshooting CSS formatting. But a new tool may supersede it in the hearts of the Dreamweaver faithful. Like Code Navigator, CSS Designer displays all the rules that pertain to any selected element and allows you to see all the properties affected, but with several key advantages.

When you use Code Navigator, it shows you the relative importance of each rule but you still have to access and assess the effect of all the rules to determine the final effect. Since some elements can be affected by a dozen or more rules this can be a daunting task for even a veteran web coder. CSS Designer eliminates this pressure altogether by providing a separate Properties window that *computes* the final CSS display for you.

If this feature wasn't good enough all by itself, CSS Designer also allows you to access CSS rules individually to edit existing properties or add new ones much more efficiently than before. And best of all, unlike Code Navigator, CSS Designer can even compute the effects of inline styles, too.

1 Open **mycss_basics.html** in Split view.

2 If necessary, choose Window > CSS Designer to display the panel.

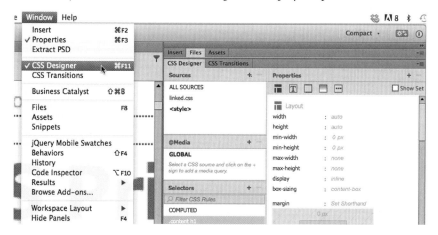

The CSS Designer panel features four windows: Sources, @Media, Selectors, and Properties. Feel free to adjust the heights and widths of the windows as needed. The panel is also responsive: It will take advantage of the extra screen space, if you drag out the edge, by splitting into two columns.

3   Insert the pointer in the heading "A CSS Primer."

The CSS Designer displays a list of the rules and properties applied to the element. In the CSS Designer, the most powerful rules appear at the top of the Selectors window, the opposite of Code Navigator.

4   Click the rule `.content h1` in the Selector panel.

By default, the Properties window of CSS Designer displays a list of properties that you can style for this element. The list is not exhaustive but it contains most of the properties you will need.

Showing a seemingly endless list of properties can be confusing as well as inefficient. For one thing, it makes it difficult to differentiate the properties assigned from those not assigned. CSS Designer allows you to limit the display to only the properties currently applied to the selected element.

5   Click the Show Set option in the CSS Designer panel menu to enable it.

When Show Set is enabled the Properties panel shows only the items that have been set in that rule.

6   Select each rule that appears in the Selectors window and observe the properties of each. To see the expected result of all the rules combined, select the COMPUTED option.

The COMPUTED option analyzes all the CSS rules and generates a list of properties that should be displayed by browsers or HTML readers. By displaying a list of pertinent CSS rules and then computing how the CSS should render, the CSS Designer does the Code Navigator one step better. But it doesn't stop there. While Code Navigator allows you to select a rule to edit it in Code view, the CSS Designer lets you edit the CSS properties right inside the panel itself. And, best of all, it can even compute and edit *inline* styles, too.

7 Select COMPUTED in the Selectors window.
In the Properties window, change the `color` property from `red` to `purple`. Press Enter/Return to complete the change.

▶ **Tip:** Double-click to edit the text-based color name. You can also select colors by using the color picker.

The heading displays in purple. What you may not have noticed is that the change you made was actually entered directly in the rule that contributed the styling.

8 In the Code view window, scroll to the embedded style sheet and examine the `.content h1` rule.

As you can see, the color was changed within the code and added to the proper rule.

9 Save all files.

The CSS Designer is like an amalgam of the Code Navigator and Dreamweaver's old CSS Styles panel. In upcoming exercises you'll get the chance to experience all aspects of the CSS Designer as you learn more about cascading style sheets.

Multiples, classes, and ids, oh my!

By taking advantage of the cascade, inheritance, descendant, and specificity theories, you can target formatting to almost any element anywhere on a webpage. But CSS offers a few more ways to optimize and customize the formatting and increase your productivity even further.

Applying formatting to multiple elements

To speed things up, CSS allows you to apply formatting to multiple elements at once by listing each in the selector, separated by commas. For example, the formatting in these rules:

```
h1 { font-family:Verdana; color:gray; }
h2 { font-family:Verdana; color:gray; }
h3 { font-family:Verdana; color:gray; }
```

can also be expressed like this:

```
h1, h2, h3 { font-family:Verdana; color:gray; }
```

CSS shorthand

Although Dreamweaver will write most of the CSS rules and properties for you, at times you will want, or need, to write your own. All properties can be written out fully, but many can also be written using a shorthand method. Shorthand does more than make the job of the web designer easier; it reduces the total amount of code that has to be downloaded and processed. For example, when all properties of margins or padding are identical, such as:

```
margin-top:10px;
margin-right:10px;
margin-bottom:10px;
margin-left:10px;
```

the rule can be shortened to `margin:10px;`

When the top and bottom and left and right margins or padding are identical, like this:

```
margin-top:0px;
margin-right:10px;
margin-bottom:0px;
margin-left:10px;
```

it can be shortened to `margin:0px 10px;`

But, even when all four properties are different, like this:

```
margin-top:20px;
margin-right:15px;
margin-bottom:10px;
margin-left:5px;
```

they can be shortened to `margin:20px 15px 10px 5px;`

In these three examples, you can see clearly how much code can be saved using shorthand. There are way too many references and shorthand techniques to cover here. To get a full description, check out www.w3.org/community/webed/wiki/CSS_shorthand_reference.

In the following exercises, we'll use common shorthand expressions wherever possible; see if you can identify them as we go.

Creating class attributes

Frequently, you will want to create unique formatting to apply to objects, paragraphs, phrases, words, or even individual characters appearing within a webpage. To accomplish this, CSS allows you make your own custom attributes, called *class* and *id*.

Class attributes may be applied to any number of elements on a page, whereas id attributes should appear only once. If you are a print designer, think of classes as being similar to a combination of Adobe InDesign's paragraph, character, table, and object styles all rolled into one. Class and id names can be a single word, an abbreviation, any combination of letters and numbers, or almost anything, but they may not contain spaces. In HTML 4, ids could not start with a number. There doesn't seem to be any similar restrictions in HTML5 but for backward compatibility you should probably avoid starting class and id names with numbers.

Although there's no strict rule or guide on how to create them, classes should be more general in nature, while ids should be more specific. Everyone seems to have an opinion, but at the moment there is no absolutely right or wrong answer. However, most agree that they should be descriptive, such as `"co-address"` or `"author-bio"` as opposed to `"left-column"` or `"big-text"`. This will especially help to improve your site analytics. The more sense Google and other search engines can make of your site's structure and organization the higher your site will rank in the search results.

To declare a CSS class selector, insert a period before the name within the style sheet, like this:

```
.content
.sidebar1
```

Then, apply the CSS class to an entire HTML element as an attribute, like this:

```
<p class="intro">Type intro text here.</p>
```

Or to individual characters or words using the `<span>` tag, like this:

```
<p>Here is <span class="copyright">some text</span> formatted differently.</p>
```

Creating id attributes

HTML designates `id` as a unique attribute. Therefore, any id should be assigned to no more than one element per page. In the past, many web designers used id attributes to style or identify specific components within the page, such as the header, the footer, or articles. With the advent of HTML5 elements—`header`, `footer`, `aside`, `article`, and so on—the use of id and class attributes for this purpose became less necessary. But ids can still be used to identify specific text elements, images, and tables to assist you in building powerful hypertext navigation within your page and site. You will learn more about using ids this way in Lesson 10, "Working with Navigation."

To declare an id attribute in a CSS style sheet, insert a number sign, or hash mark, before the name, like this:

```
#cascade
#box_model
```

Here's how you apply the CSS `id` to an entire HTML element as an attribute:

```
<div id="cascade">Content goes here.</div>
<div id="box_model">Content goes here.</div>
```

Or to a portion of an element:

```
<p>Here is <span id="copyright">some text</span> formatted
differently.</p>
```

Formatting objects

After the last few exercises, you may be thinking that styling text with CSS is perplexing and difficult to understand. But hold onto your hats. The next concept you'll explore is even more complex and controversial: object formatting. Consider object formatting as specifications directed at modifying an element's size, background, borders, margins, padding, and positioning. Since CSS can redefine any HTML element, object formatting basically can be applied to any tag, although it's most commonly directed at HTML container elements like `<div>`, `<header>`, `<article>`, and `<section>`, among others.

By default, all elements start at the top of the browser screen and appear consecutively one after the other from left to right, top to bottom. *Block* elements generate their own line or paragraph breaks; *inline* elements appear at the point of insertion; *hidden* elements take up no space on the screen at all. CSS can control all of these default constraints and lets you size, style, and position elements almost any way you want them.

Size is the most basic specification, and least problematic, for an HTML element. CSS can control both the width and the height of an element, with varying degrees of success. All specifications can be expressed in *absolute* terms (pixels, inches, points, centimeters, and so on) or in *relative* terms (percentages, ems, or exs).

Width

As you should already be aware, all HTML block elements take up the entire width of the screen by default, but there are a variety of reasons why you'd want to set the width of an element to something less than that. For example, studies have shown that text is easier to read, and more understandable, if the length of a line of type is between 35 and 50 characters. This means that on a normal computer screen a line of type stretching across 1000 or more pixels could include easily 120 characters or more. That's why most websites today break up their layouts and display text in two or more columns at a time.

CSS makes it a simple task to set the width of an element. In this exercise, we'll experiment by applying different types of measurements to the various content elements on the page.

1 Open **mycss_basics.html** from the lesson03 folder.

2 View the page in Split view, and observe the CSS code and HTML structure.

The file contains headings, paragraphs, and lists in several HTML5 semantic elements. The text is partially formatted by several CSS rules, but the structural elements display only default styling.

Fixed widths

The container elements, such as `<div>`, `<header>`, `<article>`, `<section>`, and `<aside>`, each currently occupy 100 percent of the width of the browser window or their parent element, by default. CSS allows you to control the width by applying absolute (fixed) or relative (flexible) measurements.

1 If necessary, open **mycss_basics.html** in Split view.
   In Code view, insert a new line after the last rule in the `<style>` section.

2 Type `.sidebar1 { width:200px; }` to create a new rule to style `sidebar1`. Press Enter/Return to create a new line.

3 Save the file and refresh the Design view display.

The `sidebar1` element now occupies only 200 pixels in width; the other elements in the layout are unchanged.

By using pixels, you have set the width of this element, and its children, by an absolute, or *fixed*, measurement. This means `sidebar1` will maintain its width regardless of changes to the browser window or screen orientation.

4 Select the dividing line between Code and Design view and drag it to the left and right and observe how the different elements react.

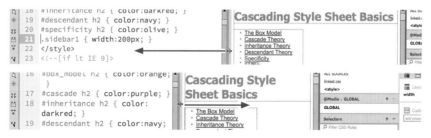

As expected, the element `sidebar1` displays at 200 pixels in width no matter what size the screen assumes. The other containers remain at full screen width. Fixed widths are still very popular all over the Internet, but in some cases you'll want elements to change or adapt to the screen size or user interaction. CSS provides three methods for setting widths using relative, or *flexible*, measurements such as: em, ex, and percentage (%).

Relative widths

Relative measurements set by percentage (%) are the easiest to define and understand. The width is set in relation to the size of the screen: 100% is the entire width of the screen, 50% is half, and so on. If the screen or browser window changes, so does the width of the element. Percentage-based designs are popular because they can adapt instantly to different displays and devices. But they are also problematic because changing the width of a page layout dramatically can also play havoc with your content and its layout.

1 If necessary, open **mycss_basics.html** in Split view.
   Add the `article { width:50%; }` rule.

2 Save the file and refresh the Design view display.

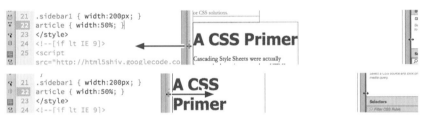

The `<article>` element displays at 50 percent of the screen width. Widths set in percentage adapt automatically to any changes to the screen size.

● **Note:** Hyphenation is not currently supported in HTML. This functionality is under development and may be supported in the near future.

3 Select the dividing line between Code and Design view, drag it to the left and right, and observe how the `<article>` element reacts.

While sidebar 1 remains at a fixed width, the article scales larger and smaller, continuing to occupy 50 percent of the width no matter what size the screen becomes.

Observe how the text wraps within the element as it changes in size. Note how it stops scaling when the frame shrinks to the size of the largest word and how the box model diagram juts out of the element below certain widths. Do you think these issues would affect the page's readability or usability?

Many designers forego the use of percentage-based settings for these reasons. While they like the fact that the containers scale to fit the browser window, they'd prefer that it would stop scaling before it affects the content detrimentally. This is one of the reasons for which the properties `min-width` and `max-width` were created.

4 Add the highlighted notation in `article { width:50%; min-width:400px; }` and save the file.

```
19   #descendant h2 { color:navy; }
20   #specificity h2 { color:olive; }
21   .sidebar1 { width:200px; }
22   article { width:50%; min-width:400px;
        }
```

The `min-width` property prevents the element from scaling smaller than 400 pixels. Note that the `min-width` specification unit is "pixels." This is important, because when combining the `width` setting with `min-width` or `max-width`, you must use differing measurement units, or only one of the specifications will be applied. To see the effect of the `min-width` specification, you need to use the entire screen.

5 Switch to Design view and refresh the display, if necessary. Drag the right edge of the document window left and right. Observe how the `<article>` element reacts.

The `<article>` displays at 50 percent of the screen width as you scale it smaller. When the screen becomes narrower than 800 pixels, the `<article>` stops scaling and remains at a fixed width of 400 pixels. To limit scaling at the upper end, you can also add the `max-width` property.

6 Insert the highlighted notation in the rule `article { width:50%; min-width:400px; max-width:700px; }` and save the file.

```
21   .sidebar1 { width:200px; }
22   article { width:50%; min-width:400px; max-width:700px;   }
23   </style>
24   <!--[if lt IE 9]>
```

7 Refresh the Design view display and drag the right edge of the document window left and right.

The `<article>` displays at 50 percent of the screen only between the widths of 800 pixels to 1400 pixels, where it stops scaling at the dimensions specified.

It's all relative, or not

Ems and exs are kind of a hybrid cross between fixed and relative systems. The em is a measurement that is more familiar to print designers. It's based on the size of the typeface and font being used. In other words, use a large font and the em gets bigger; use a small font and the em gets smaller. It even changes based on whether the font is a condensed or expanded face.

This type of measurement is typically used to build text-based components, like navigation menus, where you want the structure to adapt to user actions that may increase or decrease the font size on a site but where you don't want the text to reflow.

1   If necessary, open **mycss_basics.html** in Split view.
     Add the `.sidebar2 { width:16em; }` rule and save the page.

2   Refresh the Design view display.

     The element `sidebar2` displays at the width of 16 ems.

     Although ems are considered a relative measure, they behave differently than widths set in percentages. Unfortunately, em measurements don't display properly in the Design view; to see the exact relationship, you'll need to use Live view.

3   Switch to Live view. Scroll down to view `sidebar2`.

     The "Browser Specific Prefixes" heading should exactly fit the width of the element without breaking to two lines or leaving any extra space.

4   Refresh the display if necessary and drag the right edge of the document window left and right.

     The element seems to react like an element with a fixed measurement; it doesn't change size as you make the screen bigger and smaller. That's because the "relative" nature of ems isn't based on screen size but on the "font" size.

5   Switch to Split view.
     Add the highlighted code to the body `{ font-size:200%; font-family:Arial; color:gray; }` rule and refresh the display.

     All the text on the page scales 200 percent. The text in `sidebar1` and the `<article>` element has to wrap to fit within the container. On other hand, `sidebar2` actually scales larger to accommodate the bigger text. Note how using ems also preserves the line endings of all the text.

     There's one small caveat when you use ems: The measurement is based on the base font size of the nearest parent element, which means it can change any time the font size changes within the element's HTML structure. And you always need to remember that the relative size of the em is influenced by inheritance.

6 Change the `font-size` property for `body` to `100%` and save the file.

The text in the page returns to its previous size.

By assigning various widths to the containers, we're setting up the basic structure for creating a multicolumn layout. The next step would be to start repositioning these containers on the page. But CSS positioning can be tricky; lots of factors can affect the display and interaction of these elements. Before we move the containers to their final positions, it may help you to understand these techniques better if we first apply some borders and background effects to make them easier to see.

Borders and backgrounds

Each element can feature four individually formatted borders (top, bottom, left, and right). These are handy for creating boxes around paragraphs, headings, or containers, but there's no requirement to use all four borders on every element. For example, you can place them at the top or bottom (or both) of paragraphs in place of `<hr />` (horizontal rule) elements, or to create custom bullet effects.

Borders

It's easy to create different border effects using CSS.

1 If necessary, open **mycss_basics.html** in Split view and observe the CSS and HTML code.

We can assign borders to text or containers.

2 Add the following rule and properties to the `<style>` section:

```
article section {
  border-top:solid 10px #000;
  border-left:solid 2px #ccc; }
```

3 Refresh the display.

A custom border appears at the top and left sides of each `section` in the `<article>` element. The border gives a visible indication of the width and height of the HTML section. At the moment, the borders sit uncomfortably close to the text, but don't worry, we'll address this issue later. Let's apply borders to the other main containers now.

> **Note:** By combining these tags in one selector and using CSS shorthand this new rule saves at least 11 lines of code.

4 Add the following rule and properties:

```
article, footer, header, section { border:solid 1px #999; }
```

5 Refresh the display.

A one-pixel gray border appears on the `article`, `footer`, `header`, and every `section` element on the page, including the ones already formatted in step 2.

As described earlier, it's not unusual for an element to be formatted by two or more rules. Even though the `<section>` elements in the `<article>` were already styled with borders on the top and left, they have inherited the one-pixel border from the second rule, for the right and bottom sides.

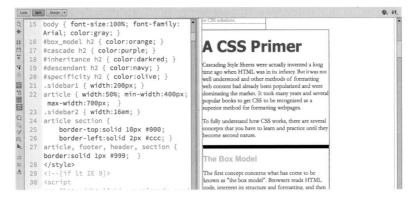

It's also important to point out that there is no extraneous markup within the actual content; all the effects are generated by CSS code alone. That means you can quickly adjust, turn on and off effects, and move the content easily without having to worry about graphical elements or extra code cluttering it up.

Now that you can see the outer boundaries of each container, keep a wary eye on each to see how they react to the CSS styling in the upcoming exercises.

Backgrounds

By default, all element backgrounds are transparent, but CSS lets you format them with colors, images, or both. If both are used, the image will appear above, or in front of, the color. This behavior allows you to use an image with a transparent background to create layered graphical effects. If the image fills the visible space or is set to repeat, it may obscure the color entirely.

1   Open **mycss_basics.html** from the lesson03 folder in Split view.
    Observe the CSS and HTML code.

    Backgrounds can be assigned to any visible, block or inline element. If you want the background to appear behind the entire webpage, assign it to the body element.

2   In Code view, add the `background-color:#ccc;` property to the existing body rule and refresh the display.

```
 8   .content h1 {
 9       color: purple;
10       font-size: 300%;
11   }
12   p { font-family: Garamond; }
13   article p { font-size:120%; color:darkblue
     ; }
14   h1 { font-family:Tahoma; color:teal; }
15   body { font-size:100%; font-family:Arial;
     color:gray; background-color:#ccc; }
16   #box_model h2 { color:orange; }
```

Cascading Style Sheet Basics

- The Box Model
- Cascade Theory
- Inheritance Theory
- Descendant Theory
- Specificity

Creating
CSS Menus

The background of the document window is now filled with light gray.

Background colors may make content hard to read. Studies show that white is still the best color on which to read text. Let's fill the main text containers with a white background.

3 Add the `background-color:#fff;` property to the `article, footer, header, section` rule and refresh the display.

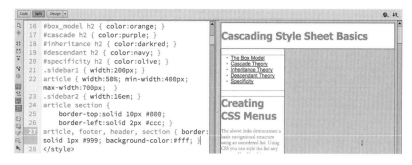

Each of the targeted containers now displays a white background.

Websites have been using graphical backgrounds for many years. In the beginning, images or icons were used to create wallpaper effects. Since the connection speeds of the Internet were much slower in those days, these images typically were very small. Today, large images are becoming a popular way to apply a custom look to websites everywhere. Let's experiment with both types.

4 Add the `background-image:url(images/street.jpg);` property to the body rule and refresh the display.

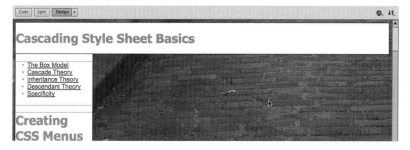

A photograph of a street scene appears in the background of the page, the exact composition of which is determined by the width and height of your document window.

By default, background images display at 100 percent of their original size and attach at the upper-left corner of the screen. If you check the dimensions of the image, you'll see that it's 1900 pixels by 2500 pixels and nearly 4 MB in size. That's big enough to fit almost any type of screen, but some aspects of a background image can't be seen properly in Design view.

5 Switch to full Design view and activate Live view.

Live view renders web content for a browser-like environment.

6 Drag the right edge of the document window left and right and observe how the background image reacts to the changing window size.

The background image does not respond to the changing window. As the window closes, the right side of the image is hidden. It would look better if the image scaled along with the window.

● **Note:** Background-size, like many CSS properties, can be specified in fixed or relative measurements. The specification can be expressed in one or two values. When you use two values, the first applies the width, the second the height.

7 Switch to Code view. Add the `background-size:100% auto;` property to the body rule and refresh the display.

This property makes the background image scale automatically to fit the width of the browser screen. CSS allows you to control many aspects of the background image to make it look and respond better on a variety of devices.

8 Add the background-position: center center; and background-attachment:fixed; properties to the body rule and switch to Live view.

9 Drag the right edge of the document window left and right and scroll the screen down to view the page content.

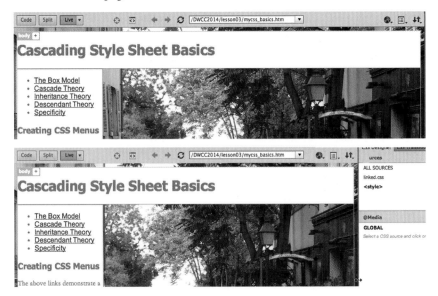

The background image no longer scrolls along with the content and remains centered, regardless of how the window changes.

With more people accessing the Internet with high-speed connections, this type of large background image is becoming more popular. Although the user has to download an image that may be several megabytes, they only have to do it once, and the image will be cached in most cases for those regularly visit the site or visit multiple pages.

Yet the size of such images is a detraction many designers will not accept. They know how large images can cause undesirable delays as webpages and resources download. Another method that is still very popular is to create a simpler background graphic that produces a repeating pattern, or wallpaper. These types of graphics are usually only a few KB yet can produce beautiful, sophisticated effects.

10 Switch to Code view.

Change the body rule in the following manner:

```
background-image:url(images/stripes.png);
background-color:#acd8b6;
```

This new graphic is 15 pixels by 100 pixels and only 2 KB. Even on a slow connection, this graphic will download almost instantly. However, its small size requires a few changes to the styling.

11 Delete the following properties from the body rule:

```
background-size:100% auto;
background-position:center center;
background-attachment:fixed;
```

By default, background images are intended to repeat vertically and horizontally. But before we allow this to happen, make the following changes to get a better idea of what's going to happen.

12 Add the `background-repeat:repeat-x;` property to the body rule and switch to Split view.

You can see the graphic repeating horizontally across the top of the page. If you allow the graphic to repeat vertically as well, the wallpaper effect is seamless.

13 Delete the `background-repeat:repeat-x;` properties from the body rule and refresh the display.

Without the `repeat-x` property, the background will repeat vertically *and* horizontally by default; the graphic is now repeating across the entire page.

14 Save the file.

Combined with the right color or gradient, these types of backgrounds are both attractive and efficient in the use of resources. The choice is yours. No matter what type you choose, be sure to fully test any background treatments. In some applications, CSS background specifications are not fully supported or are supported inconsistently.

Positioning

As you have already learned, block elements generate their own line or paragraph breaks; inline elements appear at the point of insertion. CSS can break all these default constraints and let you place elements almost anywhere you want them to be.

As with other object formatting, positioning can be specified in *relative* terms (such as left, right, center, and so on) or by *absolute* coordinates measured in pixels, inches, centimeters, or other standard measurement systems. Using CSS, you can even layer one element above or below another to create amazing graphical effects. By using positioning commands carefully, you can create a variety of page layouts, including popular multicolumn designs.

1   If necessary, open **mycss_basics.html** in Split view.
    Observe the CSS and HTML code.

    The file contains headings, paragraph text, and various HTML5 container elements partially formatted by CSS. The rules, created in a previous exercises, set specific sizes on the main container's `sidebar1`, `sidebar2`, and `article` elements so they no longer take up the entire width of the screen. In the same way—using only CSS—you can control the positioning of all of these elements on the page. There are several ways to do this, but the *float* method is by far the most popular. The options for the `float` property are `left`, `right`, and `none` and can have a dramatic effect on the positioning of the targeted elements. If no property is actually set by CSS, the default styling is `none`.

● **Note:** The `float` property can also be applied individually to the existing rules for these elements. Using this method makes it easier to update the property by simply editing one value.

2   Create the rule `.sidebar1, article, .sidebar2 { float:right; }` and save the file.

3   Switch to Design view and refresh the display.

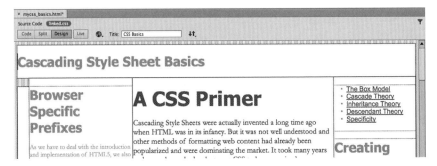

    Depending on the width of your screen, the sidebar and article elements now display horizontally, side by side from right to left in the document window. By using `float:right`, the elements display from right to left on the screen. Notice how `sidebar1` appears on the far right, followed by `article` and then by `sidebar2`. If you change the float value, you can produce the opposite effect.

4 Change the `float:right` property to `float:left` and refresh the display.

All three elements reverse directions, now starting on the left.

As you can see, the `float` property takes an element out of the normal HTML flow. By setting widths smaller than the default 100 percent on the sidebars and the article, `float` allows these block elements to behave in a totally different manner and *share* the space with each other. And `float` is also a dynamic property; it reacts to the width of the document window.

5 Drag the right edge of the document window left and right to change the width of the display.

As the window narrows, there's no longer enough space to accommodate the widths of the individual elements. They are forced to move down into the open space below. When the window gets wider, the elements move up to share the space again. This type of behavior allows websites to display rows of items that adapt automatically to any type of screen, no matter how big or small. As you make the window larger, if there is room for it, the footer element may also slip up into the row with the other three.

You may be saying, "But the footer isn't floated!" and you'd be right. But this is one of the consequences of using `float`: The first subsequent *non*-floated element will share the space with any floated ones if it doesn't have a specific width or other property set that prevents it. The first non-floated block element will honor all the width, margin, and padding settings of any floated element and then occupy 100 percent of the space left over. At times, you may take advantage of this type of behavior to create certain types of multicolumn layouts. However, for this layout, we want the footer to stay at the bottom.

You can force an element to move or position itself differently by simply setting a specific width to the parent container, or to the children themselves, that will preclude them from sharing the available space. At the moment, the combined width of the three floated elements is less than the width of the whole screen, which allows the footer to sneak in if the screen is wide enough. To prevent this from happening, you need to limit the amount of space the floated elements can use.

6 Add a new rule `.container { width:1050px; }` and refresh the display. If necessary, switch to Live view.

The `div` element displays at a width of 1050 pixels.

Now there's not enough room for the elements to float all the way across the screen, but the footer is still trying to sneak into the layout at the bottom of `sidebar2`. There is a CSS property specifically designed to keep this from happening.

7 Create a new rule `footer { clear:both; }` and refresh the display.

The footer moves down to the bottom of the page again.

Although we fixed this situation with a single CSS property, it's not always that easy. Unfortunately, as powerful as CSS positioning seems to be, it is the one aspect of CSS that is most prone to misinterpretation by the browsers in use today. Commands and formatting that work fine in one browser can be translated differently or totally ignored—with tragic results—in another. In fact, specifications that work fine on one page of your website can even fail on another page containing a different mix of code elements.

Note: For this current layout, the footer could suffice with `clear:left`. But the footer is an element that should clear all potential content elements on the page; therefore we chose to use `clear:both`.

Height

Sidebar 1, sidebar 2, and article contain different amounts of content and display at different heights. We could set a fixed height for all three that would work on this page, but what dimension would work on the other pages of the site?

Height is not specified as frequently on the web as width is. That's mainly because the height of an element or component is usually determined by its content, combined with any assigned margins and padding. Setting a fixed height can often result in undesirable effects, such as truncating, or *clipping*, text or pictures. If you must set a height, the safest way is to use the `min-height` property.

1 In the `.sidebar1, article, .sidebar2` rule, add the `min-height:1000px;` property and refresh the display.

    Sidebars 1 and 2 now display at a minimum height of 1000 pixels and will grow as needed to match the length of their content.

    On a different page, setting a common element height might work, but with the amount of content in this article, a common element height isn't really a solution to the problem at hand. The main issue is the graphical background on the page. It makes it pretty obvious that sidebars 1 and 2 are shorter than the article element.

    One answer would be to ditch the page background graphic altogether and apply a background color that matches the one used in the elements. Or, you could simply apply a matching background color to the <div> containing the layout itself.

2 Add the `background-color:#fff;` property to the `.container` rule and save the file.

    The background color for all the elements is now identical.

For all intents and purposes, the heights of sidebar 1, sidebar 2, and article are irrelevant. If not for the gray borders applied to each, you'd have no idea how tall the elements are at all. Problem solved.

Margins and padding

Margins control the space outside the boundaries, or borders, of an element; padding controls the space inside an element, between its content and its border. It doesn't matter whether the borders are visible or not; the effective use of such spacing is vital in the overall design of your webpage.

Margins

Margins are used to separate one block element from another.

1 If necessary, open **mycss_basics.html**.

Margins and padding don't always render properly in Design view.

2 Switch to Design view and activate Live view.
Observe the page layout and styling.

The page displays a header, three columns, and a footer. The column elements are touching each other, and the text within each column is touching the edges of each container.

Note: In most cases, horizontal margins between two adjacent objects combine to increase the total spacing. On the other hand, only the larger of the two settings is honored for vertical margins between two adjacent elements.

3 In the `.sidebar1, article, .sidebar2` rule, add the property `margin:5px;` and refresh the display.

The new property adds five pixels of spacing outside the borders of each targeted element.

4 Deactivate Live view. Click an edge of the `<article>` element.

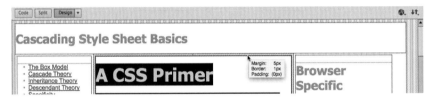

Design view highlights the element and displays a hashed pattern to provide a visual representation of the margin specifications. In HTML 4, the "align" attribute was used to align elements left, right, or center. This attribute was deprecated in the HTML5, and CSS has no specific method for centering block elements. Until something better comes along, you can use margins to center content on the screen.

5 Add the `margin: 20px auto;` property to the `.container` rule and refresh the display.

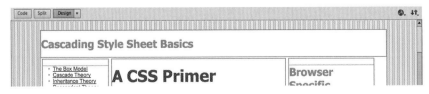

The content centers in the window. In this CSS shorthand notation, the *auto* value applies equal amounts of spacing to the left and right sides of the article.

You've added spacing between the elements. Now, let's add some spacing inside the elements, too.

Padding

The text inside the layout is touching the borders within the containers. Padding puts spacing between the content and an element's border.

1 Add the `padding: 5px;` property to the `.sidebar1, article, .sidebar2` rule.

2 Add the `padding:10px` property to the `footer` rule and refresh the display.

   The text inside the targeted elements is spaced away from all four element borders.

   Did you notice that the subsections in the article element didn't inherit the padding themselves? The text is still touching the border of its element. This may be confusing, because earlier we discussed how styling is inherited from a parent element. While it works for many properties, inheritance isn't a guarantee, for several reasons.

   Inheriting text formatting from a parent element makes a lot of sense if you think about it. You would want the text to have the same font, size, and color. But is the same logic true for *structural* properties, like width, height, padding, and margins? For example, if you set a width of 300 pixels on the container `div` element, would you want all the child elements, such as sidebar 1 and 2 and article, to inherit the same width, too? For this reason and others, padding and margins are a few of the properties that are not inherited via CSS.

3 Add the `padding: 5px;` property to the `article section` rule and refresh the display.

4 Click the edge of the `<article>` element to select it.

You can see five pixels of padding appear within each of the targeted elements. Did you notice how the elements grew slightly larger when you applied padding? Margins, padding, and even borders increase the width and height of an element. Add too much, and you might break your carefully constructed layout.

5 Change the padding value in `.sidebar1, article, .sidebar2` to `15px;` and refresh the display.

Increasing the padding has broken the layout. Sidebar 2 no longer can fit beside the article element, and it has moved down the page until it can find enough space. This type of conflict happens frequently in web design. There is a constant interplay between the elements and the CSS, which can produce undesirable results like this. Luckily, in this case, the solution is as simple as the cause.

6 Change the padding value in the rule `.sidebar1, article, .sidebar2` back to `5px;` and refresh the display.

Reducing the padding value has fixed the layout and sidebar 2 once again displays side by side with the other elements.

Normalization

Now you know that margins and padding, among other things, affect the overall size of an element. You've got to factor these specifications into the design of your page components. But, apart from the properties applied directly by the style sheet, don't forget that some elements feature default margin specifications, too. In fact, you can see these very settings in the extra space appearing above and below the headings and paragraphs on the current page.

Many designers abhor these default specifications, especially because they vary so much among browsers. They start off most projects by purposely removing, or *resetting*, these settings, using a technique called *normalization*. In other words, they declare a list of common elements, and reset their default specifications to more desirable, consistent settings.

1 In the CSS section, move the body rule to the top of the style sheet.

Since the styles in the body rule are inherited by all elements on the page, it should be placed as high as possible in the style sheet, if not in first position. Next should come rules designed to normalize basic elements.

2 Add the `p, h1, h2, h3, h4, h5, h6, li { margin: 0px }` rule directly after the `body` rule and save the file.

As you learned earlier, the comma means "and" in CSS syntax, meaning you want to format all the tags listed. This rule resets the default margin settings for all the listed elements. It's important that this rule be placed as high in the style sheet as possible, typically after the `body` rule, if one exists. That way, you can still add margins to specific instances of any of the targeted elements later in the style sheet without worrying about conflicts with this rule.

3 Refresh the display.

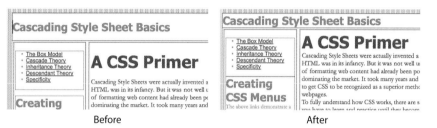

Before   After

The text elements now display without the default spacing.

Using zero margins may be a bit extreme for your tastes, but you get the picture. As you become more comfortable with CSS and webpage design, you can develop your own default specifications and implement them using CSS.

The page has come a long way from the beginning of this lesson. Let's put some final tweaks on the design to match the original finished page.

Final touches

You're nearly finished; the page needs only a few last touches to make it match the design you saw at the beginning of the lesson.

1 Delete the property ~~border:solid 1px #999;~~ from the `article, footer, header, section` rule.

2 Add the highlighted value in the property `margin: 10px 0px;` to the rule `p, h1, h2, h3, h4, h5, h6, li`.

3 Create the following rule:

```
header { padding:30px;
         border-bottom:2px solid #000;
         text-align:center;  }
```

The final style we need to add is a new CSS3 feature.

4 Add the following properties to the `.container` rule:

```
-webkit-box-shadow: 0px 0px 20px 5px rgba(0,0,0,0.40);
box-shadow: 0px 0px 20px 5px rgba(0,0,0,0.40);
```

5 Save the file and refresh the display.

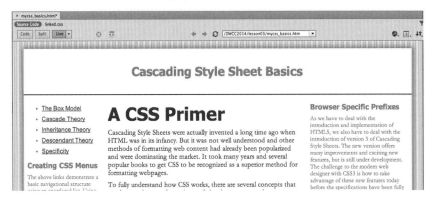

The sample page is complete.

Congratulations! You styled an entire page with CSS.

CSS3 overview and support

In the previous exercise, the last two properties both seemed to apply a drop shadow to the main content container. Did you notice that one used a `-webkit-` prefix? This notation is a temporary accommodation for certain browsers as they implement new CSS3 properties. The specifications provide some amazing, and long-needed, new features for styling the modern web.

The Internet doesn't stand still for long. Technologies and standards are evolving and changing constantly. The members of the W3C have been working diligently to adapt the web to the latest realities, such as powerful mobile devices, large flat-panel displays, and HD images and video—all of which seem to get better and cheaper every day. This is the urgency currently driving the development of HTML5 and CSS3.

Although these standards have not been officially adopted, browser vendors are racing to implement many of the new features and techniques. The current plan by the W3C is to formally adopt HTML5 and CSS3 sometime before the end of 2014, and this may already be the case when you read this. Either way, Dreamweaver won't leave you in the lurch. The latest version provides many new features based on these evolving standards, including ample support for the current mix of HTML5 elements and CSS3 formatting. As new features and capabilities are developed, you can count on Adobe to add them to the program as quickly as possible using Creative Cloud.

As you work through the lessons that follow, you will be introduced to and actually implement many of these new and exciting techniques in your own sample pages.

CSS3 features and effects

There are over two dozen new features in CSS3. Many are ready now and have been implemented in all the modern browsers; others are still experimental and are supported less fully. Among the new features, you will find

- Rounded corners and border effects

- Box and text shadows

- Transparency and translucency

- Gradient fills

- Multicolumn text elements

All these features and more can be implemented via Dreamweaver today. The program will even assist you in building vendor-specific markup when necessary. To give you a quick tour of some of the coolest features and effects brewing, we've provided a sample of CSS3 styling in a separate file.

1   Open **css3_demo.html** from the lesson03 folder. Display the file in Split view and observe the CSS and HTML code.

Some of the new effects can't be previewed directly in Design view. You'll need to use Live view or an actual browser to get the full effect.

2   Activate Live view to preview all the CSS3 effects.

The file contains a hodgepodge of features and effects that may surprise and even delight you—but don't get too excited. Although many of these features are already supported in Dreamweaver and will work fine in modern browsers, there's still a lot of older hardware and software out there that can turn your dream site into a nightmare. And there's at least one additional twist.

Some of the new CSS3 features have not been standardized, and certain browsers may not recognize the default markup generated by Dreamweaver. In these instances, you may have to include specific vendor commands to make them work properly. Like the box shadow in the previous exercise, these commands are preceded by a vendor prefix, such as `-ms-`, `-moz-`, and `-webkit-`. If you look carefully in the code of the demo file, you'll be able to find examples of these within the CSS markup.

```
× mycss_basics.html   × css3_demo.html

Code   Split   Design ▼                                              ⊙. ↓↑.

59  .columns {
60      font-family: "Trebuchet MS", Arial, Helvetica, sans-serif;
61      font-size: 100%;
62      width: 95%;
63      margin-right: auto;
64      margin-left: auto;
65      -moz-column-count: 2;
66      -webkit-column-count: 2;
67      -moz-column-gap: 20px;
68      -webkit-column-gap: 20px;
69      column-count: 2;
70      column-gap: 20px;
71  }
```

Additional CSS support

CSS formatting and application is so complex and powerful that this short lesson can't cover all aspects of the subject. For a full examination of CSS, check out the following books:

- *Bulletproof Web Design: Improving Flexibility and Protecting Against Worst-Case Scenarios with HTML5 and CSS3 (3rd edition)*, Dan Cederholm (New Riders Press, 2012) ISBN: 978-0-321-80835-6

- *CSS3: The Missing Manual*, David Sawyer McFarland (O'Reilly Media, 2013) ISBN: 978-1-449-32594-7

- *HTML5 & CSS3 for the Real World*, Alexis Goldstein, Louis Lazaris, and Estelle Weyl (SitePoint Pty. Ltd, 2011) ISBN: 978-0-9808469-0-4

- *Stylin' with CSS: A Designer's Guide (2nd edition)*, Charles Wyke-Smith (New Riders Press, 2009) ISBN: 978-0-321-52556-7

Review questions

1   Should you use HTML-based formatting?

2   What does CSS impose on each HTML element?

3   True or false? If you do nothing, HTML elements will feature no formatting or structure.

4   What four "theories" affect the application of CSS formatting?

5   What is the difference between block and inline elements?

6   True or false? CSS3 features are all experimental, and you shouldn't use them at all.

Review answers

1   No. HTML-based formatting was deprecated in 1997 when HTML 4 was adopted. Industry best practices recommend using CSS-based formatting instead.

2   CSS imposes an imaginary box on each element and can then apply borders, background colors and images, margins, padding, and other types of formatting.

3   False. Even if you do nothing, many HTML elements feature default formatting.

4   The four theories that affect CSS formatting are cascade, inheritance, descendant, and specificity.

5   Block elements create standalone structures; inline elements appear at the insertion point.

6   False. Many CSS3 features are already supported by modern browsers and can be used right now.

4 WEB DESIGN BASICS

Lesson overview

In this lesson, you'll learn the following:

- The basics of webpage design
- How to create page thumbnails and wireframes
- How to use Photoshop to generate site image assets automatically

This lesson will take about 45 minutes to complete. If you have not already done so, download the project files for this lesson from the Lesson & Update Files tab on your Account page at www.peachpit.com, store them on your computer in a convenient location, and define a new site in Dreamweaver based on this folder, as described in the "Getting Started" section of this book. Your Account page is also where you'll find any updates to the chapters or to the lesson files. Look on the Lesson & Update Files tab to access the most current content.

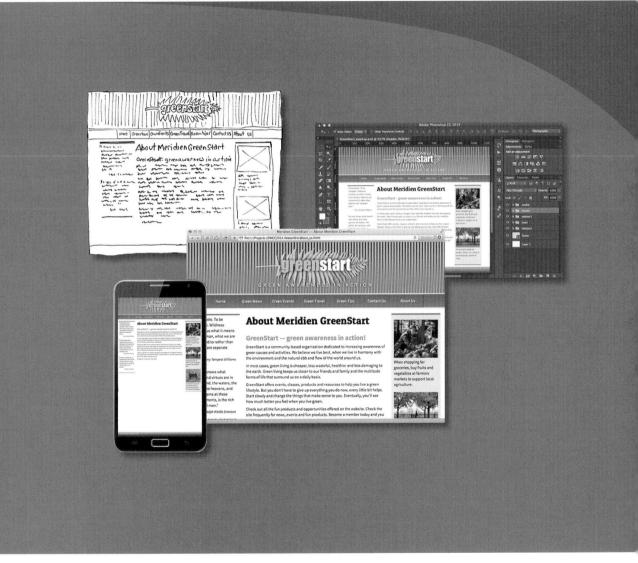

Whether you use thumbnails and wireframes, Photoshop or just a vivid imagination, Dreamweaver can quickly turn your design concepts into complete, standards-based CSS layouts.

Developing a new website

Before you begin any web design project for yourself or for a client, you need to answer three important questions:

- What is the purpose of the website?
- Who is the audience?
- How do they get here?

What is the purpose of the website?

Will the website sell or support a product or service? Is your site for entertainment or games? Will you provide information or news? Will you need a shopping cart or database? Do you need to accept credit card payments or electronic transfers? Knowing the purpose of the website tells you what type of content you'll be developing and working with and what types of technologies you'll need to incorporate.

Who is the audience?

Is the audience adults, children, seniors, professionals, hobbyists, men, women, everyone? Knowing *who* your audience will be is vital to the overall design and functionality of your site. A site intended for children probably needs more animation, interactivity, and bright engaging colors. Adults will want serious content and in-depth analysis. Seniors may need larger type and other accessibility enhancements.

A good first step is to check out the competition. Is there an existing website performing the same service or selling the same product? Are they successful? You don't have to mimic others just because they're doing the same thing. Look at Google and Yahoo—they perform the same basic service, but their site designs couldn't be more different from one another.

How do they get here?

This sounds like an odd question when speaking of the Internet. But just as with a brick-and-mortar business, your online customers can come to you in a variety of ways. For example, are they accessing your site on a desktop computer, laptop, tablet, or cell phone? Are they using high-speed Internet, wireless, or dial-up service? What browser are they most likely to use, and what is the size and resolution of the display? These answers will tell you a lot about what kind of experience your customers will expect. Dial-up and cell phone users may not want to see a lot of graphics or video, whereas users with large flat-panel displays and high-speed connections may demand as much bang and sizzle as you can send at them.

So where do you get this information? Some you'll have to get through painstaking research and demographic analysis. Some you'll get from educated guesses based on your own tastes and understanding of your market. But a lot of it is actually available on the Internet itself. W3Schools, for one, keeps track of tons of statistics regarding access and usage, all updated regularly:

- w3schools.com/browsers/browsers_stats.asp provides information about browser statistics.

- w3schools.com/browsers/browsers_os.asp gives the breakdown on operating systems. In 2011, they started to track the usage of mobile devices on the Internet.

- w3schools.com/browsers/browsers_display.asp lets you find out the latest information on the resolutions, or size, of screens using the Internet.

If you are redesigning an existing site, your web-hosting service itself may provide valuable statistics on historical traffic patterns and even the visitors themselves. If you host your own site, you can incorporate third-party tools, such as Google Analytics and Adobe Omniture, into your code to do the tracking for you for free or for a small fee.

As of the fall of 2014, Windows still dominates the Internet (80 to 85 percent), with most users favoring Google Chrome (60 percent), followed by Firefox (25 percent), with various versions of Internet Explorer (8 percent) a distant third. The vast majority of browsers (99 percent) are set to a resolution higher than 1024 pixels by 768 pixels. If it weren't for the rapid growth in usage of tablets and smartphones for accessing the Internet, these statistics would be great news for most web designers and developers. But designing a website that can look good and work effectively for both flat-panel displays and cell phones is a tall order.

Responsive web design

Each day, more people are using cell phones and other mobile devices to access the Internet. Some people may use them to access the Internet more frequently than they use desktop computers. This presents a few nagging problems to web designers. For one thing, cell phone screens are a fraction of the size of even the smallest flat-panel display. How do you cram a two- or three-column page design into a meager 200 to 300 pixels? Another problem is that most device manufacturers have dropped support for Flash-based content on their mobile devices.

Until recently, web design usually required that you target an optimum size (height and width in pixels) for a webpage and then build the entire site on these specifications. Today, that scenario is becoming a rare occurrence. Now, you are presented with the decision to either build a site that can adapt to displays of multiple different dimensions (responsive) or build two or more separate websites to support desktop *and* mobile users at the same time (adaptive).

Your own decision will be based in part on the content you want to provide and on the capabilities of the devices accessing your pages. Building an attractive website that supports video, audio, and other dynamic content is hard enough without throwing in a panoply of different display sizes and device capabilities. The term *responsive web design* was coined by a Boston-based web developer named Ethan Marcotte, in a book by the same name (2011), which describes the notion of designing pages that can adapt to multiple screen dimensions automatically. As you work through the following lessons, you will learn many techniques for responsive web design and implement them in your site and asset design.

Many of the concepts of print design are not applicable to the web, because you are not in control of the user's experience. A page carefully designed for a typical flat panel is basically useless on a cell phone.

Scenario

For the purposes of this book, you'll be working to develop a website for Meridien GreenStart, a fictitious community-based organization dedicated to green investment and action. This website will offer a variety of products and services and require a broad range of webpage types, including dynamic pages using technologies like jQuery, which is a form of JavaScript.

Your customers come from a wide demographic that includes all ages and education levels. They are people who are concerned about environmental conditions and who are dedicated to conservation, recycling, and the reuse of natural and human resources.

Your marketing research indicates that most of your customers use desktop computers or laptops, connecting via high-speed Internet services. You can expect to get 20 to 30 percent of your visitors exclusively via cell phone and other mobile devices, and much of the rest will be using mobile from time to time.

To simplify the process of learning Dreamweaver, we'll focus on creating a fixed-width site design first. In Lesson 5, "Designing for Mobile Devices," you'll learn how to adapt your fixed-width design to work with smartphones and tablets.

Working with thumbnails and wireframes

After you have nailed down the answers to the three questions about your website purpose, customer demographic, and access model, the next step is to determine how many pages you'll need, what those pages will do, and finally, what they will look like.

Creating thumbnails

Many web designers start by drawing thumbnails with pencil and paper. Think of thumbnails as a graphical shopping list of the pages you'll need to create for the website. Thumbnails can also help you work out the basic navigation structure for the site. Draw lines between the thumbnails showing how your navigation will connect them.

Most sites are divided into levels. Typically, the first level includes all the pages in your main navigation menu—the ones a visitor can reach directly from the home page. The second level includes pages you can reach only through specific actions or from specific locations, say from a shopping cart or product detail page.

Thumbnails list the pages that need to be built and how they are connected to each other.

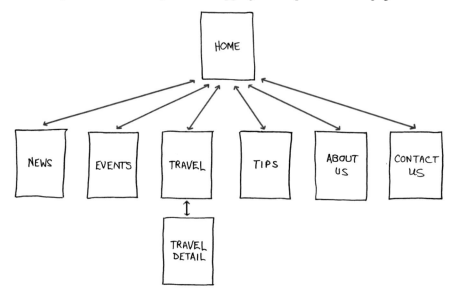

Creating a page design

Once you've figured out what your site needs in terms of pages, products, and services, you can then turn to what those pages will look like. Make a list of components you want or need on each page, such as headers and footers, navigation, and areas for the main content and the sidebars (if any). Put aside any items that won't be needed on every page. What other factors do you need to consider? If mobile devices are going to be an important consideration of your design identity, which of the components will be required or optional for these devices? While many components can be simply resized for mobile screens, some will have to be completely redesigned or reimagined.

Identifying the essential components for each page helps to create an effective page design and structure that will meet your needs.

1. Header (includes banner and logo)
2. Footer (copyright info)
3. Horizontal navigation (for internal reference, i.e., Home, About Us, Contact Us)
4. Main content (one-column with chance of two or more)

Do you have a company logo, business identity, graphic imagery, or color scheme you want to match or complement? Do you have publications, brochures, or current advertising campaigns you want to emulate? It helps to gather them all in one place so you can see everything all at once on a desk or conference table. If you're lucky, a theme will rise organically from this collection.

Desktop or mobile

Once you've created your checklist of the components that you'll need on each page, sketch out several rough layouts that work for these components. Depending on your target visitor demographics, you may decide to focus on a design that's optimized for desktop computers or one that works best on tablets and smartphones.

Most designers settle on one basic page design that is a compromise between flexibility and sizzle. Some site designs may naturally lean toward using more than one basic layout. But resist the urge to design each page separately. Minimizing the number of page designs may sound like a major limitation, but it's key to producing a professional-looking site that's easy to manage. It's the reason why some professionals, like doctors and airline pilots, wear uniforms. Using a consistent page design, or template, conveys a sense of professionalism and confidence to your visitor. While you're figuring out what your pages will look like, you'll have to address the size and placement of the basic components. Where you put a component can drastically affect its impact and usefulness.

In print, designers know that the upper-left corner of a layout is considered one of the "power positions," a place where you want to locate important aspects of a design, such as a logo or title. This is because in western culture we read from left to right, top to bottom. The second power position is the lower-right corner, because this is the last thing your eyes will see when you're finished reading.

Unfortunately, in web design this theory doesn't hold up for one simple reason: You can never be certain how the user is seeing your design. Are they on a 20-inch flat panel or a 2-inch cell phone?

In most instances, the only thing you can be certain of is that the user can see the upper-left corner of any page. Do you want to waste this position by slapping the company logo here? Or make the site more useful by slipping in a navigation menu? This is one of the key predicaments of the web designer. Do you go for design sizzle, workable utility, or something in between?

Creating wireframes

After you pick the winning design, wireframing is a fast way to work out the structure of each page in the site. A wireframe is like a thumbnail, but bigger, that sketches out each page and fills in more details about the components, such as actual link names and main headings. This step helps to catch or anticipate problems before you smack into them when working in the code.

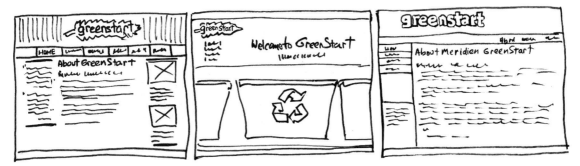

Wireframes allow you to experiment with page designs quickly and easily without wasting time with code.

The wireframe for the final design should identify all components and include specific information about content, color, and dimensions.

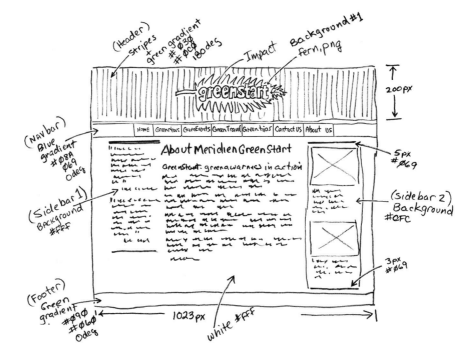

Once the basic concepts are worked out, many designers take an extra step and create a full-size mockup or "proof of concept" using a program like Adobe Fireworks, Photoshop, or even Illustrator. It's a handy thing to do because you'll find that some clients just aren't comfortable giving an approval based only on pencil sketches. The advantage here is that all these programs allow you to export the results to full-size images (JPEG, GIF, or PNG) that can be viewed in a browser. Such mockups are as good as seeing the real thing, but may take only a fraction of the time to produce.

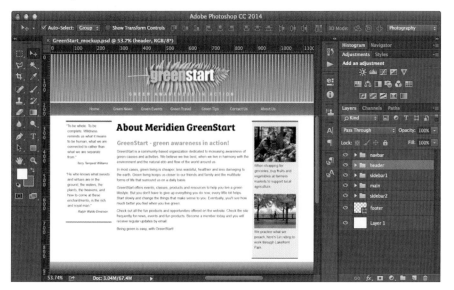

In some cases, creating a mockup in Adobe Photoshop, Adobe Fireworks, or Adobe Illustrator can save hours of tedious coding to receive a needed approval.

In addition to creating graphical mockups, Photoshop has recently added some new tricks geared specifically for web designers, like the new Adobe Generator feature.

Creating web assets using Adobe Generator (optional)

Adobe Generator is one of the new web-oriented tools that allow you to export web assets from a Photoshop file in a variety of sizes, resolutions, and even file types. Best of all, this feature works in real time, exporting image assets from your file based on user-specified attributes added to the layer name. In this exercise, you'll export web image assets from a webpage mockup created in Photoshop.

Working with Adobe Generator

Note: This exercise requires the installation of Photoshop CC or higher and the lesson files for lesson04.

Note: The sample file used in this exercise requires the font Bree Serif, which you can download and install for free from Adobe Typekit. To access this font, and the entire Typekit library, choose Type > Add Fonts from Typekit in Photoshop CC or higher.

In this exercise, you'll work with an Adobe Photoshop document to prepare assets for your web project.

1 Launch Photoshop CC or higher.

2 Open **GreenStart_mockup.psd** from the lesson04 folder.

The Photoshop file contains a complete mockup of the GreenStart site design, comprised of various vector-based design components as well as image assets stored in separate layers. Note the use of colors and gradients in the design.

Tip: It's a good idea to save the file under a different name so you can refer back to the original assets should you make an error.

3 Choose File > Save As. Name the file **myGreenStart_mockup.psd**.

4 If necessary, choose Window > Layers to display the Layers panel.
Observe the names and contents of the layers and layer groups.

The layers and layer groups are named for the webpage components.

5 Open the header layer group, and observe the contents.

The header group contains two text elements and four graphical elements. Often, it's difficult to understand how a graphic component is built or for what purpose it is intended by looking at the layer names alone.

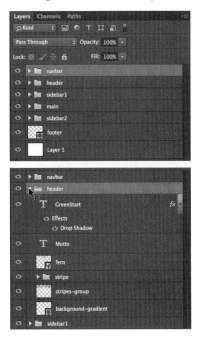

6 In the GreenStart layer, click the eye icon  to toggle the layer visibility off.

The text "greenstart" disappears from the layer.

7 In the fern layer, click the eye icon 👁 to toggle the layer visibility off.

The image of the fern disappears. Using this method, you can identify each element of the header and see what role it plays in the creation of the overall design. The number and type of layers and the level of detail used here aren't necessary for a mockup that you merely want to use for a client approval. This file was set up specifically to create many of the final assets for the page design.

8 Click the eye icon 👁 to toggle the GreenStart and fern layer back on.

Exporting assets from Photoshop

The fern layer will be used to create one component of the header background. Photoshop generates a web asset automatically if you add a file extension to the layer name.

1 Double-click to edit the name of the fern layer to **fern.png**, and press Enter/Return to complete the name.

When activated, Generator works in the background exporting assets in real time.

2 Choose File > Generate > Image Assets.

> **Tip:** To turn off Generator, repeat step 2.

The next time you look at the Generate menu option, a checkmark will appear beside Image Assets, indicating that Generator is active.

3 Choose File > Open.

Navigate to the lesson04 > resources folder.

A new folder has been created and named **myGreenStart_mockup-assets** by Generator. Whenever you add file extensions to the layer names and enable Generator, it creates a folder and fills it with assets automatically, based on the layer names and settings.

4 Navigate to the **myGreenStart_mockup-assets** folder created by Photoshop.

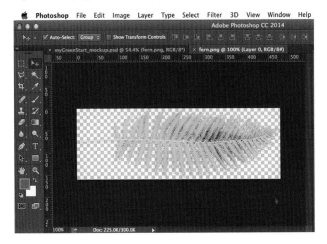

The folder contains a single image: **fern.png**.

5 Open **fern.png**.

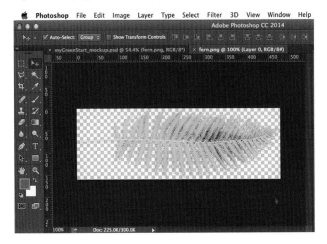

The file contains the fern with a transparent background. Note how the image displays a drop shadow. The shadow is a permanent part of the image, no longer created by a Photoshop effect.

6 Choose Image > Image Size. Note the dimensions and resolution of the image.

The image is 468 pixels by 157 pixels at 72 pixels per inch (ppi).

7 Click OK to close the Image Size dialog.
Close **fern.png**.

Creating multiple assets using Generator

Generator can also modify the default export specifications and even create multiple assets at multiple resolutions.

1 Change the layer name fern.png to **200% fern.png+fern.jpg**, and press Enter/Return to complete the name.

2 Choose File > Open.
If necessary, navigate to the myGreenStart_mockup-assets folder.

> **Note:** If you do not see the images created as described, check to make sure that the command File > Generate > Image Assets is enabled as described in the previous exercise.

The folder contains two images: **fern.png** and **fern.jpg**, both created by Generator.

3 Select **fern.png**, and open the file.

The file contains the fern, but it appears twice as large as the previous image.

4 Open **fern.jpg**.

The file contains the same fern image, but at the original size. JPEGs do not support transparency, so the background is white. There's no need for the JPEG version of the image. Generator can remove assets automatically, too.

5 Change the layer name 200% fern.png+ fern.jpg to **150% fern.png**, and press Enter/Return to complete the name.

The new specification creates a larger, higher-quality image that will display well in regular browsers and on the new crop of higher resolution devices. By your removing "fern.jpg" from the layer name, Generator automatically deletes the JPEG version of the file.

6 Choose File > Open. Navigate to the myGreenStart_mockup-assets folder.

The JPEG version of the file is no longer visible in the folder. As you can see, Photoshop generates assets based on the name of the layer. You can create an entire set of images for your site design from the layers in this file.

7 In the Layers panel, open the header layer group.
Change the name of the stripe layer group to **stripe.png**.

8 Open the sidebar2 layer group.
Change the layer shopping to **shopping.jpg**.
Change the layer biking to **biking.jpg**.

9 Choose File > Open. Navigate to the myGreenStart_mockup-assets folder.

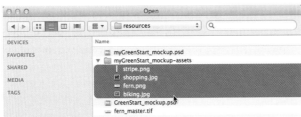

The myGreenStart_mockup-assets folder now contains four image files. These files are identical to the ones you will use to build the site template and populate articles in upcoming lessons. As you can see, Generator offers some handy tools for turning this mockup into real web design assets, but the tricks don't stop there. Photoshop and Dreamweaver have even more collaboration tools to offer, as you will see later.

Check out http://helpx.adobe.com/photoshop/using/generate-assets-layers.html to see a complete explanation of Adobe Generator and how to use it.

Review questions

1   What three questions should you ask before starting any web design project?

2   What is the purpose of using thumbnails and wireframes?

3   Why is it important to create a design that takes into account smartphones and tablets?

4   Why would you use Adobe Photoshop, Illustrator, or Fireworks to design a website?

5   How does Adobe Generator assist in the creation of a website design?

Review answers

1   What is the purpose of the website? Who is the audience? How did they get here? These questions, and their answers, are essential in helping you develop the design, content, and strategy of your site.

2   Thumbnails and wireframes are quick techniques for roughing out the design and structure of your site without having to waste lots of time coding sample pages.

3   Mobile device users are one of the fastest growing demographics on the web. Many visitors will use a mobile device to access your website on a regular basis or exclusively. Webpages designed for desktop computers often display poorly on mobile devices, making the websites difficult or impossible to use for these mobile visitors.

4   Using Photoshop, Illustrator, or Fireworks, you can produce page designs and mockups much faster than when designing in code with Dreamweaver. Designs can even be exported as web-compatible graphics that can be viewed in a browser to get client approvals.

5   Adobe Generator allows you to export site image assets quickly from Photoshop mockups, allowing you to produce multiple sizes and versions of each asset.

5

CREATING A PAGE LAYOUT

Lesson overview

In this lesson, you'll learn how to do the following:

- Insert and format new components into a predefined CSS layout

- Use the CSS Designer to identify applied CSS formatting

- Create advanced CSS background and gradients

- Access and use web-hosted fonts

- Validate HTML code

 This lesson will take about 2 hours 30 minutes to complete. If you have not already done so, download the project files for this lesson from the Lesson & Update Files tab on your Account page at www.peachpit.com, store them on your computer in a convenient location, and define a new site in Dreamweaver based on this folder, as described in the "Getting Started" section of this book. Your Account page is also where you'll find any updates to the chapters or to the lesson files. Look on the Lesson & Update Files tab to access the most current content.

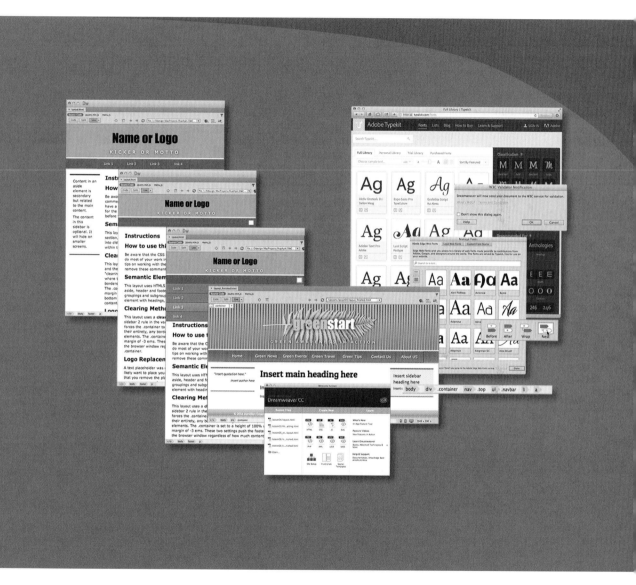

Whether you are designing a single page or an entire
website, Dreamweaver provides all the tools you need
to complete the project on time and under budget.

Using the Welcome Screen

The Dreamweaver Welcome Screen provides quick access to recent pages, easy creation of a range of page types, and a direct connection to several key Help topics. The Welcome Screen appears when you first start the program or when no other documents are open. Let's use the Welcome Screen to explore ways you can create and open documents. The first step is to set up the program interface for a design workflow.

1 Launch Dreamweaver CC (2014.1 release) or later.
   Maximize the program to fill the entire computer display.

   The recommended screen resolution for Dreamweaver is 1280 pixels by 1024 pixels. To get the most out of the program, you really need to run it filling the entire screen.

2 Choose Window > Workspace Layout > Design.

   The Design workspace is optimized for a visual HTML and CSS editing workflow. It will be the default workspace for most of the exercises in the book.

3 In the Create New column of the Welcome Screen, click HTML to create a new, blank HTML page instantly.

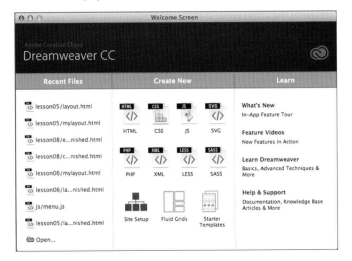

4 Choose File > Close.

   The Welcome Screen reappears.

5 In the Open a Recent Item section of the Welcome Screen, click the Open button.

   This feature allows you to browse for files to open in Dreamweaver.

6 Click Cancel.

The Welcome Screen shows you a list of up to eight of your recently opened files; however, your installation may not display any files at this point if you have not used Dreamweaver until now. Choosing a file from this list is a quick alternative to choosing File > Open when you want to edit an existing page.

You may use the Welcome Screen at any time while working in this book. When you've completed the lessons, you may prefer not to use the Welcome Screen, or even to see it. If so, you can disable it by selecting the Don't Show Again option on the Welcome Screen. To re-enable the Welcome Screen, access the General category of the Dreamweaver Preferences panel.

Previewing your completed file

To understand the layout you will work on in this lesson, preview the completed page in Dreamweaver.

1 In Dreamweaver, press F8 to open the Files panel.
Select **lesson05** from the site list drop-down menu.

2 In the Files panel, expand the lesson05 folder.

3 Double-click **layout_finished.html** to open it.
If necessary, switch to Live view to display the layout in the full document window.

Note: Before beginning this exercise, you must define a new site based on the lesson05 folder, as described in the "Getting Started" section at the beginning of the book.

This page represents the completed layout you will create in this lesson. It is based on the wireframe drawings made in the previous lesson and uses an HTML5 CSS layout built especially for this book. Take a few moments to familiarize yourself with the design and components on the page. Can you determine what makes this layout different from an HTML 4-based design? You will learn more about these differences as you work through this lesson.

4 Position the cursor over each menu item and observe the behavior.

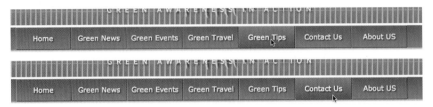

Each menu item changes styling as the cursor passes over it and then returns to its default styling as you move the cursor off. This is called a *rollover* effect, and is based on the default CSS behavior of hyperlinks. You will learn more about this behavior and how to adapt it for your own design requirements later in this lesson.

5 Choose File > Close.

This sample page represents a complex set of HTML, CSS, and JavaScript code that creates a modern, responsive webpage. To build this kind of a layout from scratch would be a daunting task for a beginner. But even many experienced designers don't have the time or budget to build everything from scratch. They prefer, instead, to use partially completed *starter* files, third-party templates, or public frameworks that are available for free or for sale from various websites all over the Internet. In fact, some web-hosting companies actually provide free templates or webpage design when you sign up for their service. Fortunately, you don't have to go out of your way or even pull out your wallet, because Dreamweaver offers you some of its own options built right into the program.

Working with predefined layouts

The goal of using predefined layouts is to find one that closely matches your needs, or to adapt your needs to the available designs. Dreamweaver provides sample CSS layouts and frameworks that you can use to adapt to most types of projects. You can access these samples from the File menu.

1 Choose File > New.

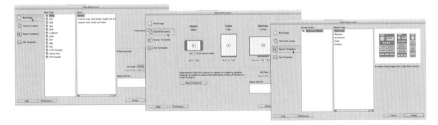

The New Document dialog appears. Dreamweaver allows you to build a wide spectrum of web-compatible documents besides those built using HTML, CSS, and JavaScript. The New Document dialog displays many of these document types, including PHP, XML, and SVG, among others. The predefined layouts, templates, and frameworks, as well as any template you create yourself, can be accessed from this dialog.

At the time of this writing, Dreamweaver CC (2014.1 release) offers two HTML5-based CSS layouts—a Fluid Grid framework and five Responsive Starter layouts. The exact number and features of these layouts may change over time through automatic updates via Creative Cloud. The changes to this list may occur without notice or fanfare, so keep your eyes peeled for new options in this dialog.

All the featured starter layouts use some of the new HTML5 semantic content elements and will help you get some experience with this evolving standard. Unless you need to support older browsers (like IE5 and 6), there's little to worry about when using the newer layouts. Let's take a look at one of the HTML5 layouts.

2 In the New Document dialog, select Blank Page > HTML.

The Layout window of the New Document dialog displays three options: <none>, a 2-column layout, and a 3-column layout.

3 Select **HTML: 3 column fixed, header and footer**.
Click Create.

A new document appears in the workspace, created from the starter layout. Dreamweaver opens files in Live view by default. Although the design appears significantly different than the finished layout you just previewed, at its heart it has all the same components: header, footer, two sidebars, and a main content section. But this design has one limitation that will preclude you from using it.

4 Drag the right edge of the document window to the left to make it narrower.

As the document window narrows, the components don't resize or reformat to adapt to the smaller screen. The predefined Dreamweaver HTML5 layouts are *fixed*-width designs and are not responsive out of the box. But that shouldn't hamper you too much. HTML and CSS are very flexible and allow you to adapt well-designed structures to many purposes. To demonstrate how these layouts can be used as a platform to build almost anything, we took this layout and modified it for you to jump-start the process.

5   Choose File > Close. Do not save the document.

6   Open **layout.html** from the lesson05 folder in Live view.

The sample layout features all the necessary components: header, footer, a navigation menu with four links, two sidebars, and a main content area, all dressed up in a color scheme of neutral gray. As you can see, not only is this layout close to the proposed final design, it's also fully responsive.

● **Note:** The responsive menu relies on resources that require an active Internet connection, and may not function when you are offline.

7   Drag the right edge of the document window to the left.

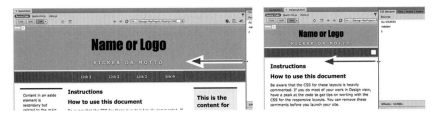

As the window decreases in width, the layout components resize and reformat to adapt to the smaller screen. When the screen reduces to the size of a smart phone, the navigation menu collapses to an icon.

8   Click the square white icon in the upper-right corner.

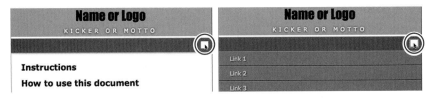

A menu appears with the four navigation links stacked vertically.

9 Position the cursor over each menu item, and observe the behavior.

The styling of each item changes as the cursor passes over it.

10 Click the icon again.

The menu closes.

11 Drag the right edge of the document window to the right.

As the window increases in width, the elements resume their original styling.

12 Position the cursor over each menu item, and observe the behavior.

The rollover behavior in the menus is identical, whether it's vertical or horizontal. This layout will provide a nice starting point for building the main project template that will be used in subsequent lessons. Let's save the file under a new name so you can keep the original in case you need to start over from scratch.

13 Choose File > Save As.

In the Save As dialog, navigate to the site root folder, if necessary. Name the file **mylayout.html**, and click Save.

▶ **Tip:** If Dreamweaver displays the wrong folder, click the Site Root button to display the main folder for the defined site.

Dreamweaver normally saves HTML files to the default folder specified in the site definition, but double-check the destination to make sure your files end up in the right place. All HTML pages created for the final site will be saved in the site root folder. Notice how Dreamweaver made a new file window for **mylayout.html**. There's no need to leave both files open.

14 Select the document tab for **layout.html**.

Choose File > Close.

The original file closes, leaving **mylayout.html** as the only open file. As you work with this page, you will be replacing the placeholder text and modifying the CSS to create the main site template. We'll start by working on the CSS.

Sometimes the best way to understand exactly how much a design depends on CSS is by shutting it off. To shut off the CSS display, you'll first have to switch to Design view.

15 Switch to Design view.

16 Choose View > Style Rendering > Display Styles to disable CSS styling in Design view.

Style display is typically on by default (showing a checkmark in the menu). By clicking this option in the menu, you'll toggle CSS styling off temporarily.

17 Note the identity and order of each page component.

Without CSS, the HTML skeleton is exposed for all to see. It's instructive to know what the page will look like if somehow the cascading style sheet is disabled or not supported by a particular browser. Now it's easier to identify the page components and their structure. Although it's not an absolute requirement, elements that display higher on the page, like <header>, usually are inserted before other elements that appear lower, like <footer>.

Another important aspect you should notice is the navigation menu. Without the CSS styling, the navigation menu reverted back to a simple bulleted, or *unordered*, list with hyperlinks. Not too long ago, this menu would have been built with tables, images, and complex rollover animation. If the images failed to load, the menu usually became a jumbled, unusable mess. The hyperlinks may have continued to work, but without the images there were no words to tell users what they were clicking. On the other hand, navigation built using text-based lists will always be usable, even without styling.

18 Choose View > Style Rendering > Display Styles to turn on CSS styling again.

It's easy to see now how important the CSS is to the final display of the HTML content and structure. Dreamweaver offers several methods for editing CSS. But the main tool is the CSS Designer.

Working with the CSS Designer

In the upcoming exercises in this lesson, you'll modify the existing CSS and add new rules to complete the basic site template design. Before you proceed, it's vital to your role as a designer to understand the existing structure and formatting of a page so that you can effectively complete your tasks. It's always a good idea when using a predefined layout to take a few minutes to examine the underlying HTML and CSS rules and understand what role they perform in the current document. It will also be a good opportunity to familiarize yourself with the CSS Designer and how to use it properly.

1 Open **mylayout.html** from the lesson05 folder in Live view, if necessary.

2 Choose Window > CSS Designer to display it, if necessary.
Choose Window > Workspace Layout > Design.

The CSS Designer has four windows that display different aspects of the CSS structure and styling. If you have a second display, or plenty of screen space, you can take best advantage of the Design workspace, which focuses on visual design, instead of code.

In the Sources window, you'll see the `<style>` tag, indicating that the style sheet is embedded in the `<head>` section of the document. Using an embedded style sheet allows you to work on a single file when building out the initial design, producing faster and more efficient workflows. When the final design is complete, you will learn how to move the CSS styles to an external style sheet, which will allow you to style your entire site using a single file.

In the @Media window, you will see the notation GLOBAL, and three media queries for tablets and phones. In this lesson, we'll concentrate on the GLOBAL styles that target larger screens. In Lesson 6, "Designing for Mobile Devices," you'll learn how to adapt the design for smaller screens.

▶ **Tip:** If you don't see line numbers along the side of your Code view window, choose View > Code View Options > Line Numbers to turn on this feature.

3 Switch to Code view, and locate the opening `<head>` tag (starting at line 3). Locate the `<style type="text/css">` element (line 8). Examine the subsequent code entries.

● **Note:** The CSS markup is contained within an HTML `<!-- -->` comment entry. That's because CSS is not technically valid HTML markup, and may not be supported in some older applications or devices. Using the comment structure allows such applications to ignore the CSS altogether.

All the CSS rules displayed in the list are contained within the `<style>` element.

4 Note the names and order of the selectors within the CSS code.

5 Open the CSS Designer window fully.
In the Sources window, select the `<style>` reference.
In the @Media window, select the GLOBAL reference.
Expand the Selectors panel, and examine the list of rules.

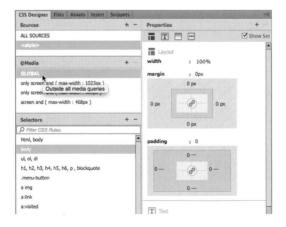

The list displays the same selector names in the same order shown in Code view. When displaying the entire list this way, there is a one-to-one relationship between the CSS code and the CSS Designer. You can see this dynamic relationship by simply clicking a rule in the Selectors window.

6 Select the header rule in the Selectors window.

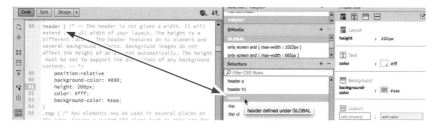

The Code view window focuses on the header rule.

7 Select the .content rule.

The Code view window focuses on the .content rule. This behavior will come in handy from time to time when you need to locate a rule in the code to edit it manually. This shouldn't happen too often, because the CSS Designer can create and edit most of the CSS rules and properties you will ever need. It even enables you to manage the order and placement of the rules in the style sheet.

8 Select the header rule, and drag it above the rule header p. Inspect the CSS markup for the header rule in Code view.

Dreamweaver has moved the rule within the Selectors list, but that's not all. It has also rewritten the code in the embedded style sheet, moving the rule and its specifications to its new position. Arranging related rules together can save time when editing them later, but be careful. The position, or cascade, of rules can affect how they work, and if you move rules around be on the lookout for unintended consequences. Review Lesson 3, "CSS Basics," if you need a refresher on these concepts.

The CSS Designer is one of the most important tools in Dreamweaver, and will save you time and reduce code-entry errors. It is just one of the many productivity enhancements you'll use and master in this book.

▶ **Tip:** If the Code view window does not focus on the selected rule, you may need to insert the cursor in the style sheet manually.

● **Note:** Before you move any other rules, you should first understand what function each one performs and how they relate to one another.

9 Switch to Design view.

In the Selectors window, select the body rule.

Observe the specifications that appear in the Properties window.

Regardless of what view you are in, the CSS Designer remains interactive, responding to the insertion point. Note that the margins and padding are set to zero.

10 Select the ul, ol, dl rule, and observe the values that appear.

The CSS Designer displays changes, showing the specifications of the rule ul, ol, dl. As in the body rule, this rule sets all margin and padding values to zero. Do you know why? An experienced web designer could select each rule in turn and probably figure out the reasons for each of the formats and settings using only the CSS Designer. But in this case, you don't need to resort to hiring a consultant, because the layout provides much of the information you need already.

11 Right-click the rule ul, ol, dl, and choose Go To Code from the context menu.

Dreamweaver displays the document in Split view, and then focuses on the section of code that contains the rule ul, ol, dl in the Code view window. Dreamweaver may display the split horizontally. Many find a vertical split is easier to use for reading and editing code.

12 Choose View > Split Vertically.

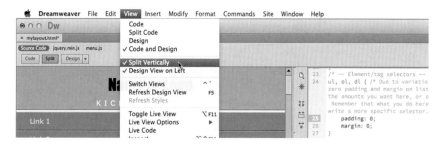

The interface splits Code view and Design view vertically. Observe the text between the opening /* and closing */ notations. This is the way you add comments to cascading style sheets. Like HTML comments, CSS comments can be used to provide behind-the-scenes information that will not be displayed within the browser or affect any elements.

Comments are a good way to leave handy reminders within the body of the webpage or to leave notes to yourself or to others explaining why you wrote the code in a particular fashion. You'll notice that some of the comments are used to introduce a set of rules, and others are embedded in the rules themselves.

13 Scroll down through the style sheet, and study the comments, paying close attention to the embedded ones.

The more you understand what these predefined rules are doing, the better results you can achieve for your final site. Here's what you'll find: the body, `header`, `.container`, `.main`, `.content`, `.sidebar1`, `.sidebar2`, and `footer` rules define the basic structural elements of the page. The `a:img`, `a:link`, `a:visited`, `a:hover`, `a:active`, and `a:focus` rules set up the appearance and performance of the default hyperlink behavior; `.top ul`, `.top ul li`, `.top ul li a:link`, `.top ul li a:visited`, and `.top ul li a:hover` define the look and behavior of the horizontal menu. The remaining rules are intended to reset default formatting or add some desired styling as outlined in the embedded comments.

Managing your CSS effectively and keeping related rules together will pay productivity dividends later, when the style sheet becomes more complicated. It will help you find specific rules more quickly and help to remind you what you have already styled within the page.

14 Save **mylayout.html**.

Now that you are more aware of CSS rules and how you can control them, check out the sidebar "Rules of order" to learn a good technique for creating and ordering your CSS code. Remember, taking special care with how you create rules and where you put them is an essential practice from this point forward.

Rules of order

The CSS Designer is a powerful feature of Dreamweaver. It allows you to create, edit, and manage your CSS rules and media queries all in one place. But things can get out of control very easily if you use it in the wrong way.

To ensure that it produces the correct results each time, always follow these simple steps when creating new CSS rules:

1 In the Sources window, select the style sheet where the new rule will be inserted. Many webpages feature multiple style sheets that may be specialized for certain tasks or devices. Dreamweaver may not allow you to create a new selector if you don't first select the style sheet.

2 In the @Media window, if more than one media query exists, select the specific media query the rule is targeting (or the GLOBAL option, if the rule is targeting all media). If you do not select the proper media query, Dreamweaver will choose for you, with potentially disastrous results. If there are no media queries, GLOBAL is chosen by default.

3 In the Selectors window, select the existing rule you want the new one to follow (optional). If you do not choose, the new rule will probably appear at the end of the style sheet or after the most recent rule created. The position of the rule in the style sheet may be essential to its proper operation. Plus, a well-organized style sheet is much easier to manage.

In an actual exercise, these instructions would probably be written like this:

> In the Sources window, select the style sheet **mygreen_styles.css**.
> In the @Media window, select the **GLOBAL** option.
> In the Selectors window, select the rule `.content h1`
> Click the Add Selector icon ✚ , and create a new rule `.content h2`.

Furthermore, to save space (and some trees), in most cases we'll use a shorthand expression more like this:

> Select **mygreen_styles.css** > GLOBAL > .content h1.
> Create a new rule `.content h2`

This method will also help you select existing rules when editing or adding properties. Don't be surprised, from time to time, if you're pointed back to this sidebar in other exercises in the book as a gentle reminder. You'll appreciate it in the end.

Working with type

Most of the content of your site will be represented in text. Text is displayed in the web browser using digitized typefaces. Based on designs developed and used for centuries on the printing press, these typefaces can evoke all sorts of feelings in your visitors, ranging from security to elegance to sheer fun and humor.

Some designers may use multiple typefaces for different purposes throughout the site. Others select a single base typeface that may match their normal corporate themes or culture. CSS gives you tremendous control over page appearance and the formatting of text. In the last few years, there have been many innovations in the way typefaces are used on the web. The following exercises describe and experiment with these methods.

First, let's see what basic settings are applied to this layout.

1 If necessary, open **mylayout.html** in Live view.

2 In the CSS Designer, select `<style>` > GLOBAL.

By selecting the `<style>` source, the Selectors window displays all the CSS rules as they appear in the embedded style sheet.

3 Select the body rule. In the Properties window, select Show Set, if necessary.

▶ **Tip:** The CSS Designer responds to the size of the document window and the insertion point of the cursor. Always maximize the size of Dreamweaver on your screen and work with Live or Design view filling the entire screen.

● **Note:** When you apply styles to the body element, all elements within the webpage will inherit these specifications by default.

The Properties window of the CSS Designer works in one of two basic modes: displaying all CSS properties or limiting the display to only the properties actually applied. You will experiment with both methods in this lesson.

4 Observe the entry displayed for the `font` property.

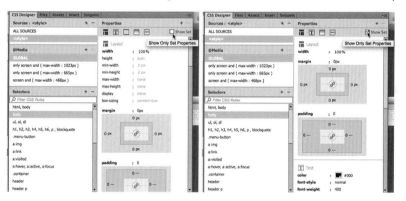

▶ **Tip:** Depending on the size of the window, you may not see the entire attribute for font. Just position the cursor over the font value to see the complete reference.

This setting was written in CSS shorthand that may be hard to understand for beginners. The `font` field displays the following value: 100%/1.4 Verdana, Arial, Helvetica, sans-serif. The attribute is actually composed of three different properties: font-size, line-height, and font-family. Many CSS properties can be written in shorthand like this to economize the code.

The first entry—100%—refers to the font size, and sets it to the default size set in the browser itself. You can use specific measurements if you prefer, such as 18pt, 18px, or .25in. But you can run into trouble with this method when the webpage is displayed on various devices, such as cell phones and tablets. Fixed sizes also don't take into account the resolution of the device or user preferences. Some users like smaller fonts; some need larger sizes.

By using 100%, the rule is setting a threshold for the body rule based on the device or software being used. Then, by using percentages (%) in other rules, you will create a relationship with this base setting that will automatically adjust the type size when the user adjusts the browser default. In other words, if you set the headings to be 200% of the body size, the heading will always be twice the size of the body text, regardless of the device or user interaction.

The second entry—1.4—refers to the line height, called *leading* by print designers, which is the spacing between lines of type in the same paragraph. Written together—100%/1.4—this specification is the same as saying: *font-size/line height*. Written this way, it means 1.4 times the height of the font, or 140%. Most designers prefer a line height between 1.2 and 1.6 for most applications, depending on the font used. These ratios provide good legibility without wasting too much vertical space.

The third entry—Verdana, Arial, Helvetica, sans-serif—refers to the property font-family. But it calls *three* typefaces and a design category, *sans-serif*. Why? Can't Dreamweaver make up its mind?

Face versus font: Know the difference?

People throw the terms *typeface* and *font* around all the time as if they were interchangeable. They are not. Do you know the difference? Typeface refers to the design of an entire family of letterforms. Font refers to one specific design. In other words, a typeface is usually comprised of multiple fonts. Typically, a typeface will feature four basic designs: regular, italic, bold, and bold-italic. When you choose a font in a CSS specification, you usually choose the regular format, or font, by default.

When a CSS specification calls for italic or bold, the browser will normally load the italic or bold versions of the typeface automatically. However, you should be aware that many browsers can actually generate italic or bold effects when these fonts are not present or available. Purists resent this capability, and go out of their way to define rules for italic and bold variations with specific calls to italic and bold versions of the typefaces they want to use.

The answer is a simple but ingenious solution to a problem that has nagged the web from the very beginning. Until recently, the fonts you see in your browser were not actually part of the webpage or the server; they were supplied by the computer browsing the site. Although most computers have many fonts in common, they don't always have the same fonts. So if you choose a specific font, and it isn't installed on the visitor's computer, your carefully designed and formatted webpage could immediately and tragically appear in Courier or some other equally undesirable typeface.

Normal browser display

Same page using the font Giddyup

For most people, the solution has been to specify fonts in groups, or *stacks*; the stack gives the browser a second, third, and perhaps fourth (or more) choice to default to before it picks for itself (egads!). Some call this technique *degrading gracefully*. Dreamweaver CC (2014.1 release) offers nine predefined font groups. If you don't see a combination you like, you can click the Manage Fonts option at the bottom of the Set Font-family pop-up menu and create your own.

Before you start building your own group, remember this: Go ahead and pick *your* favorite font, but then try to figure out what fonts are installed on your visitors' computers, and add them to the list, too. For example, you may prefer the font Hoefelter Allgemeine Bold Condensed, but the majority of web users are unlikely to have it installed on their computers. By all means, select Hoefelter as your first choice; just don't forget to slip in some of the more tried-and-true or *web-safe* fonts, such as Arial, Helvetica, Tahoma, Times New Roman, Trebuchet MS, Verdana and, finally, a design category like serif or sans serif.

In the last few years, a new trend has been gaining momentum to use fonts that are actually hosted on the site or by a third-party service. The reason for the popularity is obvious: Your design choices are no longer limited to the dozen or so fonts from which everyone can choose. You can choose among thousands of designs and develop a unique look and personality that was nearly impossible in the past. But you can't just use *any* font.

Web-hosted fonts offer a vast variety of design options.

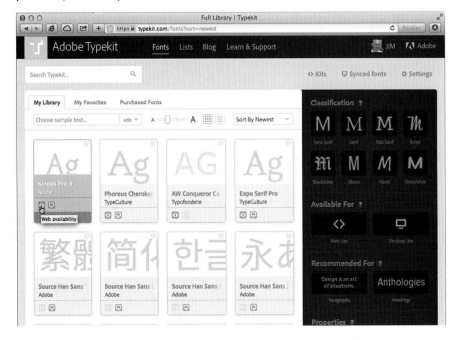

Licensing restrictions prohibit many fonts from web-hosted applications altogether. Other fonts have file formats that are incompatible with phones and tablets. So it's important to look for fonts that are designed and licensed for web applications. Today, multiple sources exist for web-compatible fonts. Google and Font Squirrel are two such sources that even provide some free fonts. Luckily, as a subscriber to Adobe Creative Cloud, you have access to two new services: Adobe Typekit and Adobe Edge Web Fonts.

Typekit is a web-hosted subscription service that offers both print and web fonts. You can subscribe to the service even if you don't have Creative Cloud, but as a subscriber you can access many of the available fonts for free. Adobe Edge Web Fonts is a free service that provides only web fonts, hence its name, and is powered by Typekit. The best thing about Edge Web Fonts is that you can access it directly inside Dreamweaver.

Using Edge Web Fonts

The first choice for most web designers is selecting the base typeface that will display their content. In this exercise, you will see how easy it is to use web fonts to apply a global site typeface by editing a single rule. There's no need to be intimidated about using web fonts—everything you need to implement this technology is built right into Dreamweaver CC.

Note: Edge Web Fonts and other types of hosted fonts are rendered properly in Dreamweaver only in Live view with an active Internet connection.

1 If necessary, open **mylayout.html** in Live view.

2 In the CSS Designer, select `<style>` > GLOBAL > `body`.

3 In the Properties window, deselect the Show Set option.

The Properties window now displays all CSS specifications set for the `body` rule.

4 At the top of the Properties window, click the Text category icon.

The window display focuses on CSS Properties for text. Note how the font setting we reviewed in the previous exercise is now divvied up to its individual properties. You can edit the setting either way, but you may find this method to be easier and more accurate.

5 Locate the `font-family` property, and select the "Verdana, Arial, Helvetica, sans-serif" value.

A window appears showing nine predefined Dreamweaver font stacks. You can select one of these or create your own font specification.

6 At the bottom of the font stack window, click Manage Fonts.

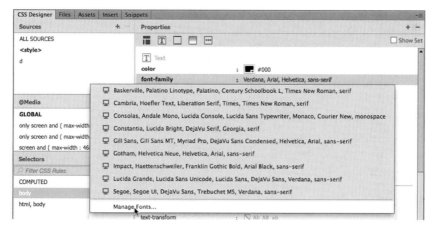

The Manage Fonts dialog gives you three options (tabs) for using web fonts: Adobe Edge Web Fonts, Local Web Fonts, and Custom Font Stacks. The first two tabs provide access to a new technique for using custom fonts on the web. The first, Adobe Edge Fonts, supports the Edge Web Fonts service to access hundreds of fonts in multiple design categories right inside the program. The second, Local Web Fonts, allows you to buy or find free web-compatible fonts that are licensed for this purpose and host them yourself. The third enables you to build font stacks using either the new web-hosted fonts, various web-safe fonts, or a combination of both.

For the site's base font, let's try Edge Web Fonts.

The tab for Adobe Edge Web Fonts displays samples of all the fonts available from the service. You can filter the list to show specific designs or categories of fonts.

7 In the Manage Fonts dialog, select the option "List of fonts recommended for Headings."

The window shows a list of fonts that are typically used for headings and titles. Some designers like to use the same font for both headings and paragraph text.

8 Select the option "List of fonts recommended for Paragraphs," directly below the option for "Headings."

Only one font is displayed: Source Sans Pro. Since this font works well for headings and paragraph text, it's a perfect choice for the site's base font. By applying it to the body rule, it will automatically be applied to headings and paragraphs throughout the site.

9 Click the font sample displayed in the Manage Fonts dialog.
Click Done to close the panel.

A blue checkmark appears on the sample of Source Sans Pro. Once you click Done, Dreamweaver will add the font to the CSS Designer interface and write any code needed in your page to use it in your CSS specifications.

10 In the Properties window, click the font-family property.
Select **source-sans-pro** from the Font list.
If necessary, select 400 from the font-weight property.

Source Sans Pro appears in the font-family property for the body rule. In most cases, the change in the layout will be instantaneous. The entire page, both headings and paragraph text, should now display Source Sans Pro. If you did not see the font style change, Dreamweaver may have not updated the Live view display.

11 If necessary, click the Refresh icon ↻ above the document window.

If this step doesn't display the new font, you may not have a live connection to the Internet at this moment. Because Edge Web Fonts are hosted on the Internet, you won't be able to see them until you establish a live connection or upload this page to a live web server. You will learn how to upload pages to the Internet in Lesson 13, "Publishing to the Web."

12 Save the file.

As you can see, using Edge Web Fonts on your website is really easy. But don't be fooled into thinking they're any less problematic than old-fashioned font stacks. In fact, even if you want to use Edge Web Fonts as your primary font source, the best practice would be to include them in a custom font stack of their own.

Introducing web-hosted fonts

The latest trend around the Internet is the increasing popularity of custom type-faces. For years we've been stuck with the familiar but faded presence of the same web-safe fonts gracing most of our websites: Arial, Tahoma, Times New Roman, Trebuchet MS, Verdana, and so on. To use a less common typeface, your options were to chance fate and flirt with font substitution, or to render the custom typeface as a graphic (and all that entails).

If the concept of web fonts is new to you, you're not alone. At the time of this writing, "web fonts" had only been in existence a little over five years, and only starting to gain widespread popularity for the last two.

The basic concept is relatively simple: The desired font is copied to your website or linked to it from a common web server. Then, the browser loads the font and caches it, as needed.

Here are some handy links to learn more about the new trend in web fonts:

- Adobe Edge Web Fonts: http://html.adobe.com/edge/webfonts
- Adobe Typekit: https://typekit.com

Here are some other font services:

- Extensis WebINK: www.webink.com
- Google Web Fonts: www.google.com/fonts
- Font Squirrel: www.fontsquirrel.com
- MyFonts.com: www.myfonts.com/search/is_webfont:true/fonts

Building font stacks with web fonts

If you're lucky, your web fonts will display every time for every user. But luck can run out, and it's better to be safe than sorry. In the last exercise, you accessed and selected an Edge Web Font and applied it to the base font of the body rule. In this exercise, you'll build a custom stack anchored on your chosen web font.

1 Open **mylayout.html** in Live view, if necessary.

2 In the CSS Designer, select <style> > GLOBAL > body.

3 Select the Text ⊤ category in the Properties window.
Select the font-family value.

The Font list drop-down menu appears.

4 Choose Manage Fonts.

5 In the Manage Fonts dialog, click the Custom Font Stacks tab.

6 In the Available Fonts list, locate the **source-sans-pro** font.
Click the << button to move the font to the Chosen Fonts list.

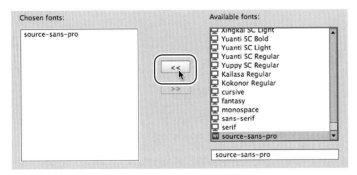

7 Repeat step 6 to add **Trebuchet MS**, **Verdana**, **Arial**, **Helvetica**, and **sans-serif** to the Chosen Fonts list.

Feel free to add more web or web-safe fonts to your list as desired. If any fonts you want to use are not installed on your computer, you can type the names manually into the field at the bottom of the Available fonts window, and then add them to the stack using the << button.

8 Click Done.

9 In the Properties window, open the font-family value.
Select the new custom font stack.

The page display should not change; Source Sans Pro is still the primary font in the list. But the new font stack, based on the new Edge Web Font, will ensure that your text will be formatted in all contingencies.

10 Save the file.

Now you've learned how to specify the look of your text content. Next, you'll learn how to control the size of the text.

Specifying font size

Font size can convey the relative importance of the content on the page. Headings are typically larger than the text they introduce. In our working document, the page content is divided into two areas: the main content and the sidebars. In this exercise, you will learn how to manage the size of the text in both areas to add emphasis as desired.

1 Open **mylayout.html** in Live view, if necessary.

2 Insert the cursor in the main "Instructions" heading.

If you look at the Selectors window, you will see that there is no individual h1 rule formatting this heading. Let's create one now.

3 In the CSS Designer, select `<style>` > GLOBAL > `.content`. Create a new selector `.content h1`

The main heading of the page should stand out from the rest of the text and headings.

4 Add the Edge Web Font **Patua One** as you did in the previous exercise.

5 Create the following properties for the `.content h1` rule:

```
margin-top: 0px
margin-bottom: 15px
font-family: patua-one
font-size: 250%
line-height: 1.4em
```

Note: In this rule you added only a single font. You may think you should have to build a custom font stack, but you don't. That's because the stack created earlier will be inherited by default if this font doesn't display properly.

The main heading increases in size and reformats. Now let's reduce the size of the text in the sidebar section. Before you create any new rules, first try to identify whether any existing rules are already formatting the section.

6 Insert the cursor in one of the `<p>` elements in sidebar 1. Select Show Set in the Properties window.

7 Observe the tag selectors at the bottom of the document window. Examine the list of rules that appears in the Selectors window and the properties assigned to them.

The CSS Designer will identify rules that apply to or are inherited by an element whenever it is selected. The text in this element is contained within three basic elements: <p>, <section>, and <aside>. Eight rules that appear in the Selectors window.

8 Insert the cursor in one of the <p> elements in sidebar 2. Observe the tag selectors at the bottom of the document window. Examine the list of rules that appear in the Selectors window.

The text in this element has a similar structure, and the same eight rules appear in the CSS Designer. But there are no rules specifically targeting or formatting the text in either structure. The basic text styling is inherited from the body rule. Since we want the text in both sidebars to have similar styling, it would be nice to use a single rule to apply it. The best choice would be to use the existing rule .main aside.

> ▶ **Tip:** At times you will use their individual class names to target one or the other sidebar specifically. But, using a generic selector is often better when styling multiple elements at once.

9 In the CSS Designer, select <style> > GLOBAL > .main aside.

10 Create font-size: 95% in the Properties window.

The text in both sidebars now displays at 95 percent of its original size.

11 Save the file.

Now that you have formatted text, let's turn our attention to other aspects of the page design and color scheme.

Creating a CSS background

If you start at the top of the page and work down, the first element to address would be the `<header>`. Using the Photoshop mockup from Lesson 4, "Web Design Basics," as our guide, the `<header>` is comprised of several components, including the company name, motto, logo, and a graphical background. The same effect could be produced using a single image, but that would be the least flexible, not to mention the least accessible, option. Instead, we'll stretch your CSS skills by building a composite design combining text and multiple background effects. This technique will allow the design to be more adaptable to various devices, like cell phones and tablets.

▶ **Tip:** Text is editable in Live view, but not by default. To edit text, double-click it first.

1 If necessary, open **mylayout.html** in Live view.
   Select the text *Name or Logo*.
   Type **greenstart** in all lowercase to replace it.

   Now let's add the company motto.

2 Select the text *KICKER OR MOTTO*.
   Type **GREEN AWARENESS IN ACTION** to replace it.

3 In the CSS Designer, select `<style>` > `GLOBAL` > `header`.
   Examine the CSS properties applied to the element.

The rule sets various properties for the `<header>`, including a background color.

Adding a background image

In this exercise you will first add a background image to the `<header>` element, and then use CSS to adjust its size and position.

1 If necessary, deselect the Show Set option in the Properties window.

   Only when Show Set is deselected does the Properties window display the list of all available CSS specifications. The list is organized into five categories: Layout, Text, Border, Background, and Custom. To focus the display on a particular category, you can use the category icons at the top of the Properties window.

● **Note:**
The Properties window doesn't show every known CSS property. Some advanced or experimental specifications have been left off to save space. If you don't see a property you need, you can always enter it in the Custom section of the panel or within the code itself.

2 Click the Background category icon .

In the **background-image** section, click the in URL field.

Click the Browse icon next to the URL field.

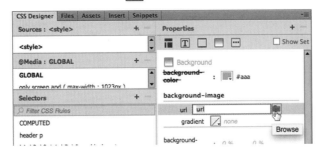

3 In the Select Image Source dialog, navigate to the default images folder. Select **fern.png**, and click Choose/Open.

Background images repeat both vertically and horizontally by default. This image is too tall to repeat vertically, but two ferns appear left to right.

4 In the **background-repeat** property, choose the no-repeat option.

The background image now appears once in the <header> element, aligned to the left side. The background specifications can also control the size and alignment of background images.

5 In the **background-size** property, select % from the **width** value field.

When you set the measurement system, the value defaults to zero (0). If only one value is set, the remaining value is set to auto by default. For the background-size property, a percentage value scales the image based on the size of the parent element. In the Properties window, you can enter the value via the keyboard or by using the mouse.

6 Position the cursor over the **vertical** (right side) value field.
Click and drag to the right to increase the value to **90%**.

The image will scale to 90 percent of the height of the <header> element.

▶ **Tip:** If you find the process of dragging to set the values too difficult you may enter them via the keyboard.

7 In the **background-position** property, select center from the **vertical** (right side) value field.

The image appears centered vertically but still aligns to the left side of the header. The horizontal value defaults to 0%. You can enter a new specification manually as before, or change it interactively using the mouse.

8 Position the cursor over the **horizontal** (left) value field.
Click and drag to the right to increase the value to **47%**.

The fern image is now centered vertically and horizontally in the <header>. In addition to the background image, you can also apply other background effects, like solid colors and even gradients. Since gradients are a new CSS3 specification, it's recommended that you always add a solid color, in case a browser or device doesn't support gradients.

Defining values

Values can be expressed in one or two parts in the Properties window. When the value comes in two parts, numeric values are entered on the left side, while the measurement system (px, em, %) is entered, or selected, on the right. Single-part values (center, left, right, and so on) can be selected from the right side of the field or entered manually.

Predefined values (center, middle, top) or measurement systems can be selected from a hinting menu that pops up when Show Set is deselected. When Show Set is enabled, the hinting menu does not appear at all, and all values must be entered in full, manually.

You may enter the value and measurement system all at once at any time by double-clicking the field.

Adding other background effects

Note: Hexadecimal colors can be written in shorthand, like *#090*, when the numbers are in matched pairs, such as *#009900*. Be aware, however, that any time you enter such shorthand expressions, Dreamweaver may arbitrarily rewrite them in full or swap them with RGB values.

In this exercise, you will add both a background-color and background-gradient to the <header> element.

1 Change the **background-color** in the header rule to #090.

The gray background-color changes to green. In older browsers, this color is a fallback option—it will display if the browser doesn't support CSS gradients. Next, let's create the gradient background for the newer applications and devices.

2 In the **background-image** property of the header rule, click the gradient color picker.

CSS3 gradients are code-intensive effects, but Dreamweaver's gradient color picker makes their specification both fast and easy. The default gradient has two color stops.

3   Set **#060** as the **top** gradient color stop.
Set **#0C0** as the **bottom** gradient color stop.
Set the Linear Gradient Angle to **180** degrees.
Press Enter/Return to complete and apply the gradient.

Note: When you set colors using hexadecimal formats in gradients, Dreamweaver will change them to RGBa notations automatically.

The gradient is applied, but there's a problem. The effect is centered vertically and horizontally behind the fern image but does not fill the entire header. Background gradients are treated as background *images*. Since there's already a background image applied to the element, the gradient uses the same size and positioning specifications that were applied to the fern.

CSS3 allows you to apply multiple background images to an element. It even allows you to apply individual specifications to each effect. Unfortunately, while the CSS Designer can apply both a gradient and an image to the background, it only provides one set of size and positioning specifications. But don't worry. Whenever the CSS Designer lets you down, you can always resort to Code view.

4   Right-click the `header` rule in the Selectors window.
Choose Go to Code from the context menu.

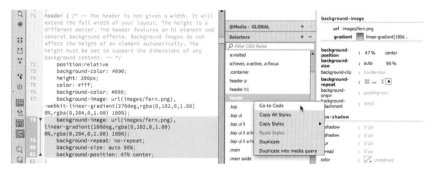

Dreamweaver switches to Split view, inserts the cursor in the Code view window, and focuses on the `header` rule in the style sheet. Note how the `background-image` property shows specifications for both the fern image and the gradient in one declaration. A comma separates the two properties.

If you examine the `background-size` and `background-position` properties, you'll see but a single specification in each. To add a second value for the gradient, you just have to add a comma at the end of each declaration, and then enter the desired values.

▶ **Tip:** Don't forget to add the comma (,) between each specification. They won't work properly without it.

5 Add the following values to these existing properties:

```
background-size: auto 90%, 100% auto;
background-position: 47% center, left top;
```

● **Note:** CSS properties in your code may appear in a different order than that pictured.

```
78      background-image: url(images/fern.png),
        linear-gradient(180deg,rgba(0,102,0,1.00)
        0%,rgba(0,204,0,1.00) 100%);
79      background-repeat: no-repeat;
80      background-size: auto 90%, 100% auto;
81      background-position: 47% center, left top;
```

6 Select Show Set in the Properties window.
   Observe the `header` rule and all the specifications displayed in the CSS Designer.

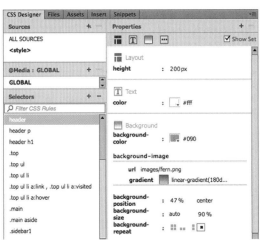

The Properties panel displays the background image and gradient, but only shows one set of specifications for the size and position. You can edit the original set using the CSS Designer, but you'll have to continue to edit any others in Code view, manually.

7 Choose File > Save.

▶ **Tip:** In some cases, you may need to refresh the document window display manually to see the effects of the CSS.

The fern remains formatted as before, but the gradient now fills the entire header.

Now that you've learned how to edit the rule manually, there's nothing stopping you from taking this effect one step further by adding a third background effect to create the vertical stripes as shown in the mockup.

8 Switch to Code view, and locate the first `header` rule in the embedded style sheet.

● **Note:** The stripe.png image is identical to the one created in Lesson 4, "Web Design Basics."

The reference to **fern.png** appears first in the `background-image` property; the gradient in the second. To get the stripes to appear between these two effects, you'll have to insert the new specifications between them, respectively. Be sure to separate each new specification by commas.

9 Modify the following properties:

```
background-image: url(images/fern.png), url(images/stripe.png),
¬ -webkit-linear-gradient(270deg,rgba(0,102,0,1.00)
0%,rgba(0,204,0,1.00) 100%);
background-image: url(images/fern.png), url(images/stripe.png),
¬ linear-gradient(180deg,rgba(0,102,0,1.00) 0%,
¬ rgba(0,204,0,1.00) 100%);
background-repeat: no-repeat, repeat-x;
background-size: auto 90%, auto auto, 100% auto;
background-position: 47% center, left top, left top;
```

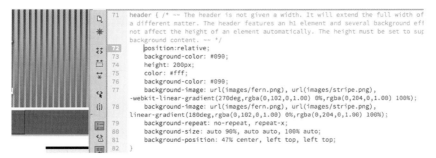

10 Choose File > Save All.

The stripes appear, and repeat horizontally across the header. By using a small graphic that repeats horizontally across the header, you are minimizing the size of the graphics that must be downloaded to create this complete effect. Best of all, if the graphic doesn't download at all, the gradient background is still displayed. In the odd chance that neither the graphic nor the gradient is displayed, the header will display the solid green color applied in step 1.

To complete the header, you need to format the <h1> to match the site color scheme and apply custom styling to the letters "start" in the company name.

Creating custom CSS styling

In this exercise, you'll apply custom styling to a portion of the company name using a span tag and a custom CSS class.

● **Note:** For these steps to work properly, the document window must be wider than 1024 pixels or the GLOBAL media option must be selected.

1   Switch to Live view.
    Insert the cursor in the text "greenstart" in the <header> element.
    Select the h1 tag selector, and observe the CSS Designer.

    The Selectors window displays a list of rules related to the <h1> element and the <header>. The header h1 rule supplies the text color.

2   Select the header rule h1
    Change the color property to #0F0.

The company name displays in bright green, but the color makes the text difficult to see clearly against the fern image. Adding a text shadow would help the text stand out better against the background. You may find it much easier to create the text shadow with Show Set disabled.

3   Deselect Show Set in the Properties window.
    In the header h1 rule, create the following text-shadow properties:

    h-shadow: 0px
    v-shadow: 0px
    blur: 30px
    color: rgba(0,0,0,0.75)

The shadow appears behind the text. The last step is to fill the letters "start" with white. In HTML, you can apply styling to a specific portion of text using the `<span>` tag with a custom class. It's typically easier to create the class first.

4   In the CSS Designer, select `<style>` > GLOBAL.
    Create a new selector `.logo-white`

5   Add the `color: #FFF` property to the new rule.

    You cannot apply a `<span>` in Live view. You'll have to switch to Design or Code view instead.

6   Switch to Design view.
    Select the letters "start" in the company name.

7   In the Property inspector, choose `logo-white` from the Class drop-down menu.

    Note how the tag selector now displays `span .logo-white`.

8   Save all files.

The basic `<header>` design for desktop, or GLOBAL, environments is now complete. The text, logo, and background effects will require some custom specifications for smaller screens, but we'll address that task in Lesson 6, "Designing for Mobile Devices." Instead, let's turn our attention to the next component on the page: the horizontal navigation menu.

Modifying existing content

As you can see, the layout comes equipped with a horizontal navigation menu with four links. The generic hyperlinks are simply placeholders waiting for your final content. Let's change the placeholder text in the menu to match the pages outlined in the thumbnails created earlier, and then modify the styling to match the site color scheme.

1   If necessary, open **mylayout.html** in Live view.

2   Select the text *Link 1*, and change it to **Home**
    Change *Link 2* to **Green News**
    Change *Link 3* to **Green Events**
    Change *Link 4* to **Green Travel**

One of the advantages of using bulleted lists as navigation menus is that Dreamweaver makes it easy to insert new links. You can add links in any document view, although certain views require different techniques.

Adding new items to a navigation menu

In this exercise, you will learn how to insert new items in the navigation menu.

1   In Live view, insert the cursor in the *Green Travel* link.
    Select the li tag selector.

2   Choose Window > Insert to display the Insert panel.
    In the Structure category, click the List Item option.

The position-assist interface appears. This interface enables you to choose where the new element will be inserted: before, after, or nested within the current selection.

3   Click **After**.

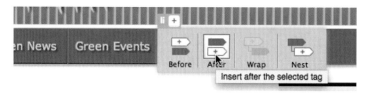

A new list item appears with placeholder text, creating a second row in the menu. The menu is not supposed to break to two lines, but let's finish the entire menu before investigating this issue.

4   Select the placeholder text *Content for li Goes Here*.
    Type **Green Tips** to replace it.

The new item looks like it has a button structure, but it's not formatted like the other links. You could probably figure out what's wrong using Live view, but in this case, the problem may be identified faster in Code view.

5 Click the `<li>` tag selector for the new link item, and switch to Code view. Observe the menu items, and compare the first four with the last one.

```
474   <ul class="navbar">
475   <li><a href="#">Home</a></li>
476   <li><a href="#">Green News</a></li>
477   <li><a href="#">Green Events</a></li>
478   <li><a href="#">Green Travel</a></li>
479 ▾ <li>Green Tips</li>
480   </ul>
```

Can you see the difference? In Code view, the difference is obvious. The last item is tagged with the `<li>` element like the others—as part of the bulleted list—but it doesn't feature the hyperlink placeholder markup `<a href="#">` used in the other items. Since this is the only meaningful difference between the list items, you can rightly assume that the `<a>` markup is conveying at least part of the menu styling. To make *Green Tips* look like the other menu items, you have to add a hyperlink to it, too, or at least a similar placeholder.

6 Select the text *Green Tips* in Code view.
In the Property inspector Link field, type # and press Enter/Return.

```
478   <li><a href="#">Green Travel</a></li>
479 ▾ <li><a href="#">Green Tips</a></li>
480   </ul>
```

`</>` body   div   .container   nav   .top.open   ul   .navbar   li   a

Properties				
`<>` HTML	Format	None	Class	navbar
CSS	ID	None	Link	#
	Document Title	Add Title Here		Page Properties...

The `<a href="#">` notation is added to the text so that it looks like all the others.

7 Switch to Design view.

All the menu items are identically formatted now. New menu items can also be added using Design view.

8 If necessary, insert the cursor at the end of the text *Green Tips*.
Press Enter/Return.

Dreamweaver adds a new `<li>` element but doesn't automatically add placeholder text or a hyperlink.

9 Type **Contact Us**, and select the text.
Enter # in the Link field, and press Enter/Return.

The new *Contact Us* link is complete. You can also add menu items in Code view.

10 Switch to Code view.

In this view, you can choose from several methods for creating a new list item. For example, you can type out the entire element manually, use the Insert panel as in step 4, or use copy and paste.

11 Insert the cursor in the *Contact Us* link.
Select the li tag selector.

By using the <li> element, the selection includes the link markup as well.

12 Choose Edit > Copy or press Ctrl+C/Cmd+C.

13 Press the right arrow key one time.

The cursor moves to the end and outside the <li> element. Although there's no need to insert a new line in the code, it keeps the markup consistent and easier to read.

14 Press Enter/Return to insert a new line.
Choose Edit > Paste or press Ctrl+V/Cmd+V.

```
487    <li><a href="#">Green Tips</a></li>
488    <li><a href="#">Contact Us</a></li>
489    <li><a href="#">Contact Us</a></li>
490    </ul>
```

A duplicate version of the *Contact Us* list item appears.

15 Select the text *Contact Us* in the new <li> element.
Type **About Us** to replace it.

16 Save the file. Switch to Live view.

There are seven items in the menu now in two lines. To match the original mockup, we'll need to somehow fit the menu on one line. Obviously, the current formatting was not designed to accommodate so many items, but that's not a big problem. It's common when using predefined layouts or third-party templates that you will have to modify the original design to conform to your own content or project requirements.

Hyperlink pseudo-classes

The <a> element (hyperlink) provides five *states,* or distinct behaviors, that can be modified by CSS using what are called *pseudo-classes.* A pseudo-class is a CSS feature that can add special effects or functionality to certain selectors, such as the <a> anchor tag:

- The a:link pseudo-class creates the default display and behavior of the hyperlink, and in many cases is interchangeable with the a selector in CSS rules. But the a:link is *more* specific, and will override specifications assigned to a less-specific selector if both are used in the style sheet.

- The a:visited pseudo-class formats the link after it has been visited by the browser. This resets to default styling whenever the browser cache, or history, is deleted.

- The a:hover pseudo-class formats the link when the cursor passes over it.

- The a:active pseudo-class formats the link when the mouse clicks it.

- The a:focus pseudo-class formats the link when accessed via keyboard as opposed to mouse interaction.

When used, the pseudo-classes must be declared in the order listed above to be effective. Remember, whether declared in the style sheet or not, each state has a set of default formats and behaviors.

Styling a navigational menu

Identifying the styling source of a webpage component can be a tedious, time-consuming process. Sometimes it's easy—as with the header element—while others can be more difficult. Often, you'll have to assume the role of CSS detective: combining skillful observation with your experience in both web design and Dreamweaver. Like a good detective, over time you will start to anticipate how layouts and components are structured and styled and be able to quickly identify the prime suspect of any styling problems.

For example, menus like the one used for the GreenStart site's horizontal navigation are typically comprised of a parent <ul> element and one or more children <li> elements. Armed with this knowledge, the first assumption you might make is that the parent <ul> element has a width that's too narrow to permit all seven buttons to sit in one row. By using several Dreamweaver tools together, it should be easy to determine what CSS rule, or rules, you'll need to adjust.

1   Open **mylayout.html** in Live view, if necessary.
    The program window must be maximized to fill the computer display.
    The document window should be wider than 1024 pixels.

The first step in any CSS investigation is to identify the elements involved in a specific component.

2   Insert the cursor in any of the menu items. Examine the tag selector display.

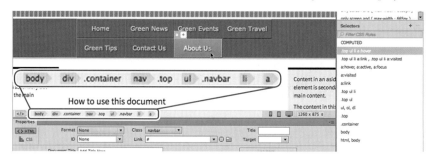

As you click around the layout, the tag selectors change to show you how each component or content element is structured. The tag selector interface reads from right to left, showing the elements nested one inside the other. You should notice that the CSS designer is also changing at the same time, showing the rules applied to, or inherited by, the targeted element. By combining these two behaviors together, you can quickly identify the CSS formatting applied to each element. Don't forget that you can also select the individual tag selectors.

3   Click the a tag selector.

The Selectors window in the CSS Designer lists all the rules that affect this element in some way.

4   Select the Show Set option in the Properties window of the CSS Designer.

The Properties window now displays only active settings.

5   Starting at the top of the list, select each rule in the Selectors window. Inspect each rule, and note all properties assigned by them.

Some rules format the selected element; others pertain to only one of the parent elements, or to the page overall. As you look through each rule, keep an eye out for any *width* properties.

As you inspect the list of rules, you will discover that `.top ul li a:link,` `.top ul li a:visited` applies a width of 7 ems to each menu item, and that `.top ul` sets a width of 33 ems to the parent `<ul>` element. When the menu had only four items these settings provided plenty of space for them, but it's obviously not sufficient for the seven items now in the structure. Since both elements are formatted in ems, assessing the correct width is simply a matter of math: The `<nav>` element will have to be at least 49 ems in width to hold all seven items.

6 Select the rule `.top ul` in the Selectors window.
   Position the cursor over the **width** value.
   Click and drag to the right to increase the value to **49em**.

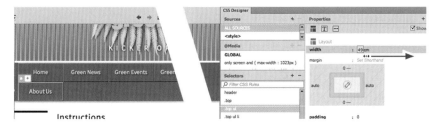

Note: Feel free to enter values using the keyboard.

As you increase the width, two more menu items move up to the first row, but when the width hits 49 ems, the last link stays on the second line. Although 49 ems should be wide enough to support all seven items, other settings can affect the overall width of an element to keep it from fitting, such as any padding and/or borders assigned to them. The solution can be as simple as removing any borders and padding or to continue increasing the width of the parent element until all the elements fit.

7 Increase the width in the rule `.top ul` until the last menu item fits in the same row with the others.

A minimum width of 57 ems enables the entire menu to fit on one line. Now that you have added the new menu items and got them to fit in one row, the next step is to apply the site color scheme to this component. To change the color, let's use the CSS Designer again to find the CSS rules that control this styling.

8 If necessary, insert the cursor in one of the menu items.
   Select the `a` tag selector, and inspect the rules displayed in the CSS Designer.

The CSS Designer displays the same rules affecting the currently targeted element as it did earlier. It's not unusual to discover that more than one rule is responsible for styling a single element and that settings in one rule may conflict with or actually reset those in another.

As you inspect each rule, look for properties that affect the appearance of the individual links and the menu overall, such as color, background color, background gradients, and so on. Keep in mind that rules near the top of the Selectors window have more specificity than ones lower in the list and will override any settings that conflict.

9 Select the `li` tag selector, and inspect the rules displayed in the CSS Designer.

ADOBE DREAMWEAVER CC CLASSROOM IN A BOOK (2014 RELEASE) **169**

10 Select the `.top ul` tag selector, and inspect the rules displayed in the CSS Designer.

After inspecting the styling applied to these elements, you will discover that five rules are responsible for most of the formatting of the menu. The rule `.top` applies the background color for the entire menu.

11 In the CSS Designer, select `<style>` > GLOBAL > `.top`. Deselect Show Set in the Properties window.

12 Change the background color to #069.

The background color changes from gray to a solid blue. Let's add some advanced styling to the background now.

13 In the **background-image** property for `.top`, click the gradient color picker. Set **#069** as the **top** gradient color stop. Set **#08A** as the **bottom** gradient color stop. Set the Linear Gradient Angle to **180** degrees. Press Enter/Return to complete and apply the gradient.

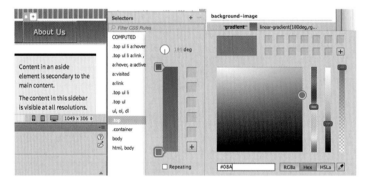

The gradient background supersedes the solid background color. You may have noticed that the menu buttons feature gray borders. The `.top li` rule formats the borders of each menu item.

14 Select `<style>` > GLOBAL > `.top ul li`. Change the values in the following properties:

```
border-top-color: #0AE
border-right-color: #024
border-bottom-color: #024
border-left-color: #0AE
```

By alternating the border color this way, it produces a three-dimensional effect on the menu buttons.

The main feature of the navigation menu is the hyperlink. Hyperlinks are one of the few HTML elements that come with a built-in dynamic behavior, powered strictly by CSS. You experience these behaviors every time you move your cursor over or click the element. It features five distinct states: link, visited, hover, active, and focus. See the sidebar "Hyperlink pseudo-classes" for a full description on hyperlink behaviors and states.

The rule `.top ul li a:link, .top ul li a:visited` supplies the text color for the menu items in the default and visited states. For links in the body of a webpage the two states are usually formatted separately, but in a menu you want these links to be identical.

15 Select `<style> > GLOBAL > .top ul li a:link, .top ul li a:visited`. Change the `color` property to `#FFC`.

The `:hover` pseudo-class is responsible for styling links whenever the cursor is positioned over them. Normally, you'll see this behavior simply as the cursor turning into the pointer icon, but for this dynamic menu the CSS applies completely different background and text colors to create a rollover effect.

16 Select `<style> > GLOBAL > .top ul li a:hover`.
In the **background-image** property, click the gradient color picker.

17 Set **#069** as the **top** gradient color stop.
Set **#08A** as the **bottom** gradient color stop.
Set the Linear Gradient Angle to **0** degrees.
Press Enter/Return to complete and apply the gradient.

This gradient is a mirror image of the one in the `.top` rule. This effect can be tested directly in Live view.

18 Position the cursor over any of the menu items.

The gradient background flips vertically, providing a good contrast from the default menu state. You have styled the components for the interactive part of the navigation menu, but there's one static aspect of the menu that still needs a small tweak: the top border of the menu bar. In the Photoshop mockup, this border is shown in yellow, although it's displayed in white at the moment.

19 Insert the cursor anywhere in the horizontal menu.

Examine the tag selectors for the menu.

Can you identify which of the elements shown in the tag selector interface supports this rule? You can eliminate any element that doesn't stretch across the entire width of the screen, such as the hyperlinks, the list items, and the <ul> element itself. This process of elimination should quickly focus your attention on the <nav> element.

20 Select the `.top` tag selector.

Examine the rules and properties displayed in the CSS Designer.

The Selectors window shows the `.top` rule that contains a property for `border-top`.

21 Select `<style>` > GLOBAL > `.top`

Change the `border-top` color to **#FD5**

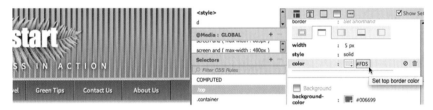

The border changes to a golden yellow.

22 Save the file.

The navigation menu for desktop media is complete. The various media queries will require further modifications, but we'll address those in Lesson 6, "Designing for Mobile Devices." The next task is to build a new semantic structure in sidebar 1.

Building semantic content

Sidebar 1 will be used for environmentally themed quotations. Unlike normal paragraph text, the value of a quotation is usually based on perceived reputation of the author or source. HTML provides several elements designed specifically to identify this type of content.

1 If necessary, open **mylayout.html** in Live view.

2 Insert the cursor in sidebar 1.

Examine the tag selectors showing the structure.

The current structure is based on `<p>`, `<section>`, and `<aside>` elements. Semantically, quotations should be based on the `<blockquote>` element.

3 Select the `section` tag selector. Press Ctrl+T/Cmd+T to edit the tag.

The Quick Tag Editor appears, focused on the `<section>` tag. You'll replace this tag with `<blockquote>`.

4 Select the tag name `section`, and type **blockquote** to replace it.

As you type, the Code Hinting menu focuses on the `<blockquote>` tag. Feel free to press Enter/Return to select and insert the tag using the menu.

5 Press Enter/Return to close the Quick Tag Editor and complete the element.

When it's completed, the default styling of the `<blockquote>` element applies indenting on the left and right. Such indentation is typical of material quoted within a term or research paper, and may be desirable in the main content area, but it's totally unnecessary in the narrow `<aside>` elements. You'll need to create a new CSS rule to format these elements.

6 Select `<style>` > GLOBAL > `.main aside`.

Create a new selector `.main aside blockquote`

The Show Set option should still be active from the previous exercise.

7 Create the following properties in the new rule:

```
margin: 0px 0px 20px 0px
padding: 0px
```

Typically, a blockquote should contain a quotation, either alone or in one or more paragraphs, and an element providing the source or citation. Like `<blockquote>`, the `<cite>` element provides the correct semantic structure in this application.

8 Select the text within the first <p> element.

Replace the text by typing **"Insert quotation here."**

You can see that the opening quotation mark is indenting the first line of text slightly, leaving the text misaligned with the following lines. A technique used by professional typesetters actually *outdents* such items to produce a *hanging* quotation mark.

9 Select <style> > GLOBAL > .main aside blockquote.

Create a new selector aside blockquote p

10 Create the following properties:

```
margin: 0px 0px 5px 0px
padding: 0px .5em
text-indent: -0.5em
```

Although it's hard to see now on the one-line placeholder quotation, the effect is more evident in the following paragraph. The effect on multiline quotations will be quite appealing. Let's convert the second paragraph to create the <cite> element.

11 Insert the cursor in the second <p> element.

Select the p tag selector.

12 Press Ctrl+T/Cmd+T to open the Quick Tag Editor.

Change the p tag to cite, and press Enter/Return to complete the change.

13 Replace the placeholder text within the new <cite> element with the following:

Insert author here

Now we'll create a new rule to style the author name.

14 Select <style> > GLOBAL > .main aside blockquote.

Create a new selector aside blockquote cite

15 Create the following properties in the new rule:

```
display: block
padding-right: .5em
font-size: 90%
text-align: right
font-style: italic
```

The <blockquote> structure is complete and contains a complete semantic structure. To remain semantically correct, each new quotation should be inserted into its own <blockquote> element. The last thing that needs to be done to complete sidebar 1 is to change the color of the top and bottom borders.

16 Select <style> > GLOBAL > .main aside.

This rule formats the borders of both sidebars at once.

17 Change color of the top and bottom borders to #069.

The borders in both sidebars change to dark blue.

18 Save the file.

The basic layout is nearly complete. A simple tweak to Sidebar 2 and the footer, and you will be done with the desktop-based styling.

Positioning elements with Element Quick View

A new workflow that has been added to the Dreamweaver is the ability to manage elements directly in the Element Quick View. The interface allows you to insert and precisely position elements within your layout.

1 Open **mylayout.html** in Live view.

2 Insert the cursor in the first paragraph in sidebar 2.

Semantically, paragraph text should always be introduced by a heading.

3 Choose Window > Insert to display the Insert panel.
In the Structure category, choose **H2** from the Heading drop-down menu.

H1 is displayed by default in the Heading item. Inserting a different heading requires you to first select it from the menu.

4 Click **H2** to insert a new Heading.

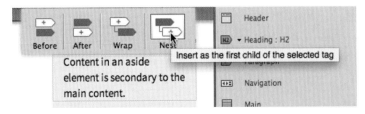

The position-assist interface appears.

5 Click **Nest** to insert the heading within the
<p> element.

A new <h2> element, with some placeholder
text, has been inserted within the <p> element,
creating an invalid HTML structure. You can
tell something is wrong, but it's not obvious
what the problem is in Live view. From time
to time such misplacement errors will occur;
Element Quick View allows you to reposition
elements within your structure.

6 Click the Element Quick View icon **</>** in the tag selector interface.

The Element Quick View pop-up window appears, displaying the document
object model (DOM) outline. The various elements in the page are shown as
icons, indented to show the structure of the code. Some elements are open,
while others may be closed. To see the contents of a closed element, you only
have to click it.

7 If necessary, click `aside .sidebar2` to display its contents.
Click the section icon in `.sidebar2` to display its contents.

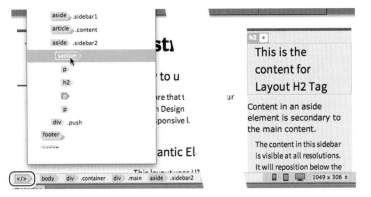

The section contains two p elements and one h2 element. The h2 appears
between the two paragraph tags.

8 Drag the h2 tag to insert it above the first paragraph in Element Quick View.

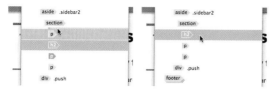

Tip: Watch for the green smart guide indicating where the element will appear.

The h2 should now properly appear above the two paragraphs. Moving and inserting elements correctly in Element Quick View takes some practice. Let's format the new heading and the background of the sidebar.

9 Select the placeholder text *This is the content for Layout H2 Tag*.
Type **Insert sidebar heading here** to replace it.

10 Select the placeholder text in the first paragraph in sidebar 2.
Type **Insert sidebar content here** to replace it.

11 Insert the cursor in the second paragraph.
Select the p tag selector.
Press Delete.

12 Select `<style>` > `GLOBAL` > `.sidebar2`.
Create the new property `background-color: #CFC`

13 Create a new selector `.sidebar2 section h2`

14 Create the following properties in the new rule:

```
margin-bottom: 5px
font-weight: 700
font-size: 130%
line-height: 1.4em
```

15 Save the file.

Sidebar 2 is complete. The last tasks remaining to complete are to insert some new placeholder text and to format the footer.

Inserting placeholder text

Let's simplify the layout by replacing the existing headings and text in the main content area.

1 Double-click to select the heading *Instructions*.
Type **Insert main heading here** to replace the text.

2 Select the heading *How to use this document*.
Type **Insert subheading here** to replace the text.

3 Select the placeholder text in that same `<section>` element.
Type **Insert content here.**

4 Insert the cursor in the next section. Click the `section` tag selector. Press Delete. Select and delete the remaining two `<section>` elements and their contents.

5 Save the file.

Inserting HTML entities

Let's format the footer and insert a generic copyright statement that includes an HTML entity.

1 Insert the cursor in the `<footer>` element. Examine the rules applied to this element and any pertinent styles.

The footer rule applies a background color and other styling to the element.

2 Select `<style>` > GLOBAL > `footer`.

3 Deselect the Show Set option.

4 Click the gradient color picker in the background-image section.

5 Create the following new properties for the `footer` rule:
Set **#060** as the **top** gradient color stop.
Set **#0C0** as the **bottom** gradient color stop.
Set the Linear Gradient Angle to **0** degrees.
Press Enter/Return to complete and apply the gradient.

The background properties from the `header` rule are now applied to the `footer`.

6 Change the `color` property to **#FFC** in the `footer` rule.

7 Select and delete the placeholder text in the footer.

To insert a copyright character you will use an HTML entity.

8 Choose Insert > Character > Copyright.

The copyright symbol © appears in the footer. Dreamweaver inserts the copyright character using the named entity `&copy;` in the code.

9 Press the spacebar to insert a space.
Type **2014 Meridien GreenStart. All rights reserved.**

10 Save the file.

The basic page layout for desktop media is complete.

▶ **Tip:** Modify the copyright date as necessary when you create a new page or update the content.

Validating HTML code

The goal whenever you create a webpage is to create code that will work flawlessly in all modern browsers. As you work making major modifications in the sample layout there's always a possibility that you may accidentally break an element or create invalid markup. These changes could have ramifications in the quality of the code or whether it displays in the browser effectively. Before you use this page as your project template, you should check to make sure the code is correctly structured and meets current web standards.

1 If necessary, open **mylayout.html** in Dreamweaver.

2 Choose File > Validate> Validate Current Document (W3C).

A W3C Validator Notification dialog appears, indicating that your file will be uploaded to an online validator service provided by the W3C. Before clicking OK, make sure you have a live Internet connection.

3 Click OK to upload the file for validation.

After a few moments, you may receive a report listing any errors in your layout. If you are following the instructions in this lesson correctly, the only error displayed suggests that you use <h1> headings only as top-level elements. This error occurred because the <header> and the <article> elements both use h1 headings in their markup.

HTML 4 regarded <h1> elements as the "most important heading" on a page. Best practices for HTML 4 dictated that only one most important heading should appear on each page. In HTML5, no such practice has been established yet, and many designers actually believe that if you're using the new semantic elements you should be able to insert one <h1> in each semantic grouping or section.

In any case, if you want to eliminate the validation error altogether, simply change the logo element in the header into an <h2> or lower-level heading.

4   Switch to Design view.
Insert the cursor into the "greenstart" logo text in the header.
Observe the tag selector.

The tag selector shows an h1 element in the header.

5   In the Property inspector, choose **Heading 2** from the Format drop-down menu.

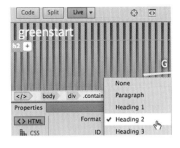

The tag selector now shows an h2 element in the header. The formatting of the logo text has been dropped. The rules formatting it are looking for an h1 element. To restore the styling, you simply have to edit the selector name.

6   In the CSS Designer, select <style> > GLOBAL > header h1.

7   Double-click the selector to edit the name. Change the selector to header h2.

The original formatting has been restored to the logo text. Let's validate the new structure.

8   Choose File > Validate > Validate Current Document (W3C). Click OK to upload the file for validation.

The Validation panel reports that no validation errors were found.

9   Save the file.

Congratulations. You created a workable basic page layout for your project template and learned how to insert additional components, placeholder text and headings; modified existing CSS formatting and created new rules; and validated the HTML code successfully. In the upcoming lessons, you will continue to work on this file to tweak the CSS to make it work on all mobile devices and then set it up as the primary site template.

Review questions

1 Does Dreamweaver provide any design assistance for beginners?

2 What is the advantage of using a graphic as a background image?

3 How can you insert the cursor before or after an element without using Code view?

4 How does the CSS Designer assist in designing your website layout?

5 What advantages does using HTML5-based markup provide?

6 Can you use any font to create a font stack?

7 Why should you validate your webpage?

Review answers

1 Dreamweaver CC (2014.1 release) provides two CSS-based HTML5 starter layouts, a fluid grid framework, and several responsive starter layouts.

2 By inserting graphics as a background image you leave the container free for other content, and gain additional flexibility when designing for mobile devices.

3 Select an element using its tag selector, and then press the left arrow or right arrow key on your keyboard to move the cursor before or after the selected element.

4 The CSS Designer serves as a CSS detective, allowing you to investigate what CSS rules are formatting a selected element and how they are applied.

5 HTML5 offers new elements that provide semantic meaning to HTML structures that allow search engines, like Google and Yahoo, to index your pages more quickly and effectively.

6 Technically, yes, you can declare any font name in your CSS rules. However, normally, the font will only load if the visitor has that font installed on their computer. Today, many designers are hosting custom fonts on their own sites or using third-party font hosting services. But, if you use third-party fonts on your site, be sure to check to make sure it's licensed for web use.

7 Validation checks the code to make sure it is properly created and follows standard web practices.

6 DESIGNING FOR MOBILE DEVICES

Lesson overview

In this lesson, you'll edit and adapt cascading style sheets (CSS) and CSS3 media queries in Dreamweaver for mobile devices and learn how to:

- Edit media queries for mobile and handheld devices, such as tablets and smartphones

- Select and target CSS rules within specific media queries

- Configure page components to work with mobile devices

- Preview these pages in Dreamweaver

- Test responsive designs on multiple mobile devices at once

This lesson will take about 35 minutes to complete. If you have not already done so, download the project files for this lesson from the Lesson & Update Files tab on your Account page at www.peachpit.com. Store them on your computer in a convenient location, and define a new site based on the lesson06 folder, as described in the "Getting Started" section of this book. Your Account page is also where you'll find any updates to the lessons or to the lesson files. Look on the Lesson & Update Files tab to access the most current content.

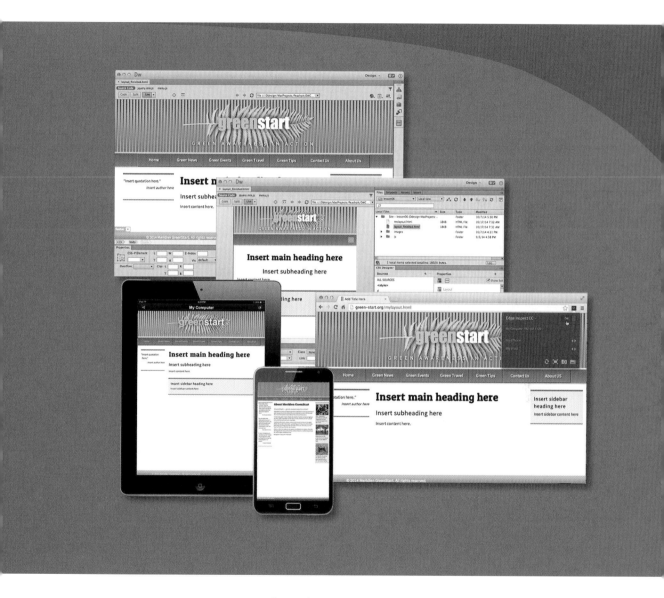

The trend toward designing sites to respond automatically to mobile devices and smartphones continues to grow exponentially. Dreamweaver has powerful tools to get your site mobile-ready.

Responsive design

The Internet was never conceived for smartphones and tablets. For the first decade, the hardest challenge a programmer or developer had to worry about was the difference between a 13- and 15-inch computer monitor. For years, resolutions and screens sizes only got *larger*.

Today, the chances that some or all of your visitors are using a smartphone or tablet to access your site are increasing exponentially day by day. In 2014, statistics show more people were using mobile devices to access the Internet than using desktop computers, and this trend doesn't seem to be slowing down.

To help web designers adapt pages and content to this changing landscape, two basic tools were created: *media type* and *media query*. These functions enable browsers to identify what type of device is accessing the webpage and then load the appropriate style sheet, if one exists.

Media type property

● **Note:** In Lessons 4 and 5, you created the basic design for the website as it should appear on a standard desktop computer display based on the screen media type.

The media type property was added to the CSS2 specifications and adopted in 1998. It was intended to address the proliferation of noncomputer devices that were able to access the web and web-based resources at that time. Customized formatting is useful to reformat or optimize web content for different media or output.

In all, CSS2 included nine individually defined media types.

Table 6.1 Media type properties

PROPERTY	INTENDED USE
all	Speech synthesizers
aural	Speech synthesizers
braille	Braille tactile feedback devices
handheld	Handheld devices (small screen, monochrome, limited bandwidth)
print	Documents viewed onscreen in print preview mode and for printing applications
projection	Projected presentations
screen	Primarily for color computer screens
tty	Media using a fixed-pitch character grid, such as teletypes, terminals, or portable
tv	Television-type devices (low resolution, color, limited-scrollability screens, sound available)

While the media type property works fine for desktop screens, it never really caught on with browsers used on cell phones and other mobile devices. Part of the problem is the sheer variety of devices in all shapes and sizes. Add to this smorgasbord an equally diverse list of hardware and software capabilities, and you've produced a nightmare environment for the modern web designer. But all is not lost.

Media queries

A media query is a newer CSS function that provides code in the webpage to interactively determine not only what kind of device is displaying the page but also what dimensions and orientation it's using. Once the media query knows what type or size of device it has encountered, it instructs the browser to load the specified resources to format the webpage and content. This process is as fluid and continuous as a precision dance routine, allowing the user to switch orientations during a session and have the page and content adapt seamlessly without other intervention. The key to this ballet is the development of style sheets optimized for specific browsers, specific devices, or both.

How your site deals with smartphones and mobile devices depends on whether you're adapting an existing site or developing a new one from scratch. For an existing site, you first have to create a basic method of treating the underlying design of the site's main components. Then, you have to work through each page, one at a time, to assess existing components individually—like images and tables—that do not inherently adapt to the specific environment.

For new websites, the typical approach is to build *in* the adaptability as you create the overall design, and then build each page to achieve maximum flexibility. In either case, to support a truly mobile design, be aware that some site components may need to be replaced, left out of the final design altogether, or swapped out live by JavaScript or by the media query itself. For the time being, there is no single solution to all responsive issues.

Media query syntax

Like the CSS it controls, a media query requires a specific syntax to work properly in the browser. It consists of one or more media types and one or more expressions, or media features, that a browser must test as true before it applies the styles it contains. Currently, Dreamweaver supports 22 media features. Others are being tested or are still under development and may not appear in the interface, but you can add them manually to the code, as necessary.

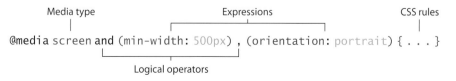

The media query creates a set of criteria to determine whether or not a specific set of rules contained within it is applied in a webpage.

You can create media queries in a variety of ways. For example, they can be designed to work exclusively, by completely resetting the existing styling, or in tandem, by inheriting some styles and modifying specifications only as necessary. The latter method requires less CSS code and is typically more efficient. We will favor it in the upcoming exercises.

To learn more about media queries and how they work, check out www.w3schools.com/cssref/css3_pr_mediaquery.asp.

Previewing your completed file

In this lesson, you will continue to modify the page layout you created in Lesson 5, and adapt it as necessary for use on tablets and smartphones. Let's preview the page in Dreamweaver.

Note: For the following exercise to work properly, the document window must be 1024 pixels or wider.

Note: Since Dreamweaver fully supports all media queries and responsive styling, make sure the program fills the entire width and height of your computer display to perform this lesson properly.

1 Launch Dreamweaver CC (2014.1 release) or later, and maximize the display of the program to fill the entire display, if necessary.

2 Open **layout_finished.html** in Live view.

The document contains the layout completed in Lesson 5, updated for desktop media. The layout is designed to adapt to any screen size. You can check this out by using the responsive media tools built into Dreamweaver. We'll start with the Resolution Switcher controls in the lower-right corner.

3 Click the Desktop Size icon ▢ in the Resolution Switcher interface at the bottom right of the document window.

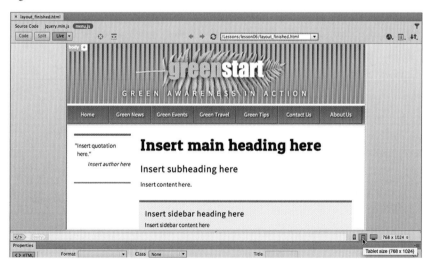

Note how the Desktop Size icon at the bottom of the document window appears selected, or pushed in. The document window resizes to 1000 pixels by 852 pixels. The layout partially changes, adapting to the new dimensions.

4 Click the Tablet Size icon ▢ in the Resolution Switcher interface at the bottom right of the document window.

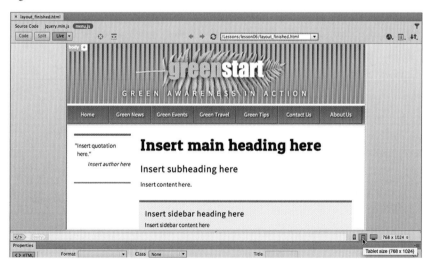

The Live view window resizes to 768 pixels by 1024 pixels. Now the changes are more dramatic. The header and logo have reduced in height; the menu has scaled down in size; sidebar 2 has shifted below the main content and expanded to match its width.

5 Click the Mobile Size icon █ in the Resolution Switcher interface at the bottom right of the document window.

Live view resizes to 480 pixels by 800 pixels. The layout has completely restyled now. Sidebar 1 has vanished; the menu has collapsed to an icon; the main content and sidebar 2 now fill the window from side to side. To return to the normal screen display, you only have to click the icon again in the Resolution Switcher interface

6 Click the Mobile Size icon █ in the Resolution Switcher interface at the bottom right of the document window.

The icon does not appear selected any longer. The document window fills the entire program again, and the layout returns to its original styling. You can also test the responsive styling by adjusting the screen size manually.

7 Select the right edge of the document window, and drag it to the left.

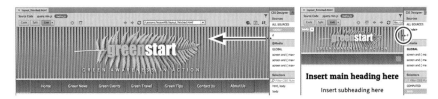

As the window narrows, the styling changes as it did before. You can drag the screen all the way down to the width of the smallest smartphone. Watch the Resolution Switcher interface as you resize the screen to see the exact dimensions of the window.

8 Drag the right edge of the document window to the right to restore its original size and styling.

The Live view display is very accurate and can substitute for an actual browser in most cases.

9 Preview the page in a browser.

The layout will be loaded in the selected browser. Compare the display and responsiveness of the layout.

10 Resize the browser window from full size down to approximately 300 pixels in width. Observe how the browser window mimics the display in Dreamweaver.

The browser display mimics the same behaviors you witnessed in Dreamweaver.

● **Note:** Some browsers will not scale down below a minimum size.

11 Close the browser. Close **layout_finished.html**.

This exercise has demonstrated some of the ways a web design can be adapted to various types of devices and displays, including desktops, tablets, smartphones, and other mobile devices.

Mobile-ready vs. mobile-optimized

Hiding elements, like sidebar 1, is not an ideal solution in all situations. The *hidden* elements and the associated code are still downloaded, even if they're not displayed. If you find yourself hiding an inordinate amount of content, or you see that you have a large number of visitors via phones and tablets, you may want to consider creating a separate mobile-*optimized* site.

A mobile-optimized site is often hosted on a subdomain, like *mobile.yourdomain.com*, and contains pages designed specifically for mobile devices. These sites not only reduce page size; they may also select, or filter, content appropriate for the specific device. For example, some sites remove images, tables, and other large elements that don't scale down very well.

Obviously, producing two or more completely different sites can drastically increase design and maintenance costs, especially if the content changes on a regular basis. It's also not the best plan for optimizing your search engine ranking.

Instead, one good option is to create your website based on an online database or content management system (CMS) like Drupal, Joomla, or WordPress. A CMS can dynamically create pages as needed based on a template and style sheets with no additional effort. You could create pages for your regular site and a mobile-optimized site for multiple screen sizes simply by creating new templates and deciding what content to display on each.

Working with media queries

The GreenStart site design was based on a predefined responsive layout. The original design automatically adapted to changes in the screen size. As you modified the basic design in the previous lesson—such as adding items to the horizontal menu—you could see how the original styling didn't work correctly with the new content. You had to modify various rules to adapt the components to the new content and to apply the site colors and graphical scheme overall.

Identifying media queries

In Lesson 5, the changes to the original CSS styling addressed only desktop media. In this lesson, we'll examine and modify the styling for tablets and smartphones. The first step is to identify the styling that has already been created for mobile devices and what it does.

1 If necessary, launch Dreamweaver CC (2014.1 release) or later.
   Maximize the program to fill the entire screen.

2 Open **mylayout.html** from the lesson06 folder in Live view.

● **Note:** If your screen is too small to display the CSS Designer in two columns, you will still be able complete the lesson.

3 Choose Window > CSS Designer, if necessary, to display the panel.
   While maintaining a document window of 1024 pixels or greater, adjust the width of the panel to display the CSS specifications in two columns.

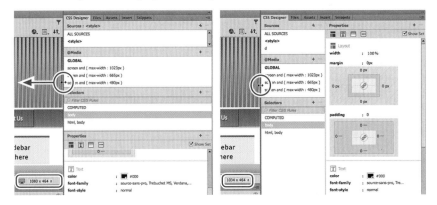

Setting up the CSS Designer in two columns makes working with and editing CSS easier.

4 Select the `<style>` reference in the Sources window of the CSS Designer.
   Examine the items listed in the @Media window (open that window if necessary).

By default, the @Media window lists any media queries defined in the selected document or CSS source file. By selecting the `<style>` reference, you've forced the @Media window to list only media queries defined in that source. This behavior allows you to determine the source of a media query when you need to edit it.

The window displays four items:

```
GLOBAL
screen and (max-width 1023px)
screen and (max-width 665px)
screen and (max-width 480px)
```

The GLOBAL reference includes all CSS rules assigned to the file that are not contained within a media query. The other references represent media queries targeting screen media at various widths. In this case, the media queries specify a max-width to which their styles will apply. When the screen is wider than that specification, the styling within that media query will be ignored. This way, the GLOBAL rule applies the bulk of the styling, while the media queries only need make adjustments to certain components or content as necessary, based on the width of the screen.

Targeting media queries

As you have already learned, the CSS Designer responds to changes in the document window and placement of the cursor by automatically displaying the relevant rules and properties interactively. This behavior also works in reverse. If you select a media query or selector in the panel, Dreamweaver will change the document presentation based on the selection.

> **Tip:** For the full list of selectors to display, you must first select the `<style>` reference in the Sources window.

1 In the @Media window, select the GLOBAL reference.

The Selectors window displays a list of all rules defined in the style sheet but not assigned to a media query.

2 Select the media query `screen and (max-width: 1023px)`.
Observe the rules displayed in the Selectors panel.

> **Note:** When you select a media query, Dreamweaver will automatically adjust the width of the screen based on your own computer display and hardware. Your screen may not match the screen shots exactly, but will fall within the query parameters.

The document window automatically narrows to 1023 pixels or less. The height of the header has decreased, forcing the logo elements to overflow into the horizontal menu. The horizontal menu has broken to two lines again. Sidebar 2 has shifted below the main content and matches its width. This media query styles the page for smaller computer displays and tablets up to 1023 pixels in width.

3   Select the media query screen and (max-width: 665px).

The document window changes to 665 pixels or less. The header has decreased in size again, and the text is overflowing even further down the page. Sidebar 1 has disappeared altogether. The horizontal menu has collapsed into an icon. The main content and sidebar 2 are now stretching nearly the entire width of the document window. This media query takes over the design for devices 655 pixels or smaller.

4   Select the media query screen and (max-width: 480px).

The document window changes to 480 pixels or less. The overall design has further decreased in size. The header content still does not fit the confines of the element. Sidebar 1 now stretches all the way across the window. This media query styles the page for smartphones. To return the document view to normal, you simply have to select the GLOBAL reference again.

5   Select the GLOBAL reference.

The document view returns to full screen and styles the page for desktop media. The Selectors window has some helpful tricks waiting for you, too.

Targeting selectors

Like the media query references, the selectors are tied into the document display.

1   If necessary, open **mylayout.html** from the lesson06 folder in Live view.

2 In the CSS Designer, select `<style>` > GLOBAL > `.content h1`.

The `<h1>` element in the main content area is highlighted in blue. Dreamweaver visually identifies all elements in the layout affected by a specific rule. This behavior is very helpful when you are modifying various components.

3 Select `<style>` > GLOBAL > `.top ul li`.

Dreamweaver highlights all the items in the horizontal menu. These two behaviors combined allow you to troubleshoot and edit the CSS visually.

4 Select `<style>` > `screen and (max-width 1023px)`.

The header and horizontal menu need to be modified to work in this media query. Let's start with the header.

5 Examine the list of rules in the Selectors window.

The list displays a rule to format `header h1`, but in Lesson 5 you changed the `<h1>` element to an `<h2>` to correct the validation error. When changing page elements or structures, it's important to keep an eye out for unintended consequences like this one. Luckily, in this case, it's an easy fix.

6 Change the `header h1` rule to `header h2`.

The text is now formatted by the rule, and resizes to 250 percent. It's too small, but this specification was designed for the placeholder text in the original predefined layout.

▶ **Tip:** If you first select the style sheet and then the media query, you should be able to change the selector name by double-clicking it.

7   Select `<style>` > `screen and (max-width 1023px)` > `header h2`.
    Change the `font-size` property to **350%**.

The logo and motto text fits the background properly again. Now, let's fix the horizontal menu.

8   Insert the cursor in one of the menu items.
    Examine the list of selectors.

    The list contains 10 rules. The goal is to find the rule that sets the width of the menu.

9   Examine the rules to find the one responsible for the menu width.

    The rule `.top ul` sets the width of the parent `ul` element to 28 em.

10 Select `<style>` > `screen and (max-width: 1023px)` > `.top ul`.

11 Increase the width property to **48em**.

The menu fits on a single line. The rest of the page looks fine at the moment. This media query is finished. Let's check the rest of the media references and fix any other problems.

12 Select `<style>` > `screen and (max-width: 665px)`.

    The layout displays at 665 pixels or less. Sidebar 1 is no longer visible, and the header is messed up again. The horizontal menu has collapsed to an icon.

13 Examine the list of rules in the Selectors window.

    There are 15 rules contained in the media query (`max-width: 665px`), five more than in (`max-width: 1023px`). The extra rules are reformatting the horizontal menu. As in the previous instance, the selector name `header h1` needs to be updated.

14 Change the `header h1` rule to `header h2`.

    The text resizes to fit properly over the logo background image.

15 Save the file.

The page looks like it's fully styled now, but there's something hiding in plain sight that may surprise you.

Troubleshooting styles across media queries

When you selected the media query `screen and (max-width: 665px)`, the horizontal menu collapsed to an icon. This is a common theme in responsive designs. Menus are often too large and unwieldy on small screens, so designers frequently reformat menus to display them vertically and to hide until needed. Since the media query is applying completely new styling, it's important to check all aspects of that design before finishing.

1 If necessary, open **mylayout.html** from the lesson06 folder in Live view.

2 Select `<style>` > `screen and (max-width: 665px)`.

The layout displays at 665 pixels or less. The horizontal menu collapses to an icon. It is powered by web-hosted JavaScript and is designed to close automatically if you are connected to the Internet and in Live view.

● **Note:** If you are in Design view or offline, the responsive menu will be open by default. It is not broken.

3 Click the icon displayed in the menu bar.

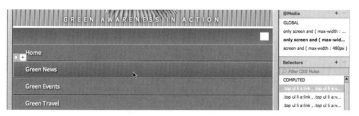

The menu opens to reveal the seven items created in the previous lesson. The menu is still formatted in its original gray color scheme. To apply the new site color theme to these items, you'll need to identify the rules responsible for the current styling.

4 Select one of the menu items.

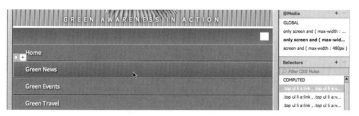

When you select the menu item, it exhibits the *hover* effect you created in Lesson 5. Although you created it for GLOBAL media, this is a good example of how styles can be inherited from other media queries, or even other style sheets.

5 If necessary, select the Show Set option.

Examine the rules and properties displayed in the CSS Designer.

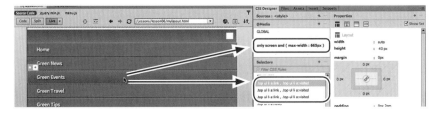

Note: In responsive designs, it's common to see elements styled by rules in several media queries. The CSS Designer will list the rules in order of importance based on the current screen display.

In the @Media window, the media query `screen and (max-width: 665px)` is bolded, indicating that it is actively formatting the layout at this moment. The Selectors window displays rules affecting the chosen element. But, at the top of the list there are *three* copies of the `.top ul li a:link, .top ul li a:visited` rule. This is a common occurrence in responsive designs where components are styled by multiple media queries or style sheets.

6 Select the rule `.top ul li a:link, .top ul li a:visited` at the top of the list. Examine the properties assigned to this rule.

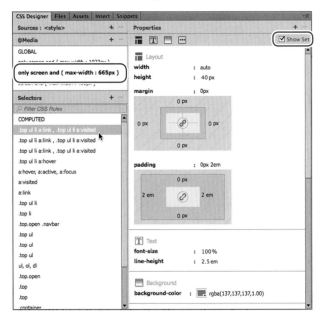

The layout remains at the width of 665 pixels or less, and the media query `screen and (max-width: 665px)` is still highlighted. In the Properties window, you can see values set for width, height, margins, padding, font-size, line-height, and background-color. It's always good to familiarize yourself with styles set by other similar rules.

7 Select the second copy of `.top ul li a:link, .top ul li a:visited` in the list. Examine the properties assigned to this rule.

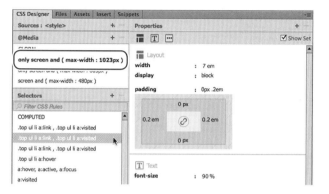

The width of the layout doesn't change when you select the rule, but note how the media query `screen and (max-width: 1023px)` is now highlighted. When you selected the rule, the CSS Designer identified the media query that contains it. This rule sets values only for width, padding, and font-size.

▶ **Tip:** Play close attention to the interrelation of the CSS Designer and the document display. Understanding how the two work together will pay dividends as you build webpages and troubleshoot your CSS.

8 Select the third copy of `.top ul li a:link, .top ul li a:visited` in the list. Examine the properties assigned to this rule.

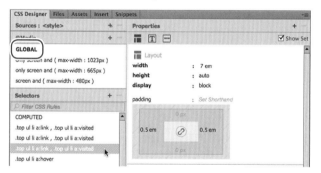

Once more, the layout doesn't change dimensions, but the @Media window in the CSS Designer highlights the GLOBAL media reference. This rule sets values for width, height, display, color, padding, font-size, line-height, and background-color.

The important points to take away from this investigation are: first, to notice how the CSS Designer reacts in different but important ways to both the screen dimensions and your cursor placement; and, second, to understand how media queries pass CSS styling to the page components, or not.

For example, the syntax used in all three media queries says "screen" and "max-width." Obviously, the media reference "screen" is meant to target all computer-based and mobile devices with *screens*. But the property "max-width" is a bit more complicated. It means that the styles contained within the media query are applied to all screen-based devices, starting at zero (0) width all the way up to and including the targeted dimension. Then, for all screens above that dimension, the styles are cancelled automatically and no longer apply at all.

To build this type of styling correctly, you start with the styling requirements for desktop screens, and then add media queries and additional rules only as needed to format the layout as the screen gets smaller. If designed properly, this method results in styling that uses the fewest number of media queries and rules.

The gray background color in the open menu was applied by the rule in the media query (`max-width: 665px`). The `<a>` or `<li>` element doesn't need a background color above this dimension, because the menu displays horizontally, and automatically inherits the background color assigned to the parent `<nav.top>` element.

9 Select `<style>` > `screen and (max-width: 665px)` > `.top ul li a:link, .top ul li a:visited`.
Change the `background-color` property to `#069`.

The background-color of the menu items changes to solid blue.

10 Move the cursor over each menu item, and observe the behavior.

As you move the cursor over each menu item, the solid background-color changes to a gradient background. The hover effect that appears in the (`max-width: 665px`) media query is the same one defined in the GLOBAL styles. As you can see, one rule is styling the menu across multiple media sizes.

11 Save the file.

12 Click the icon again to close the menu.

The icon is white, and doesn't match the site color scheme. You may think you know how to track down the styling for this element, but this element has a surprise in store for you.

Using Element Quick View

In certain circumstances, the tools you have learned how to use to troubleshoot your HTML structure and CSS styling do not work as expected. This is especially true when working with elements powered by JavaScript.

1 If necessary, open **mylayout.html** from the lesson06 folder in Live view.

2 Select `<style>` > `screen and (max-width: 665px)`.

At 665 pixels or less, the horizontal menu collapses to an icon. To match the site color scheme, you have to identify the icon element and the rule or rules that style it. Up until now, you have used the cursor to select elements and identify the CSS styling. Let's see how this technique works with this element.

3 Click the icon to select it.

Examine the tag selectors and the CSS Designer to identify the element and styling that creates the icon.

● **Note:** Since you cannot select the menu icon, your tag selector display may not match the screen shot.

When you click the icon, the menu opens, but something unusual happens. The tag selectors and the CSS Designer don't change. Let's try clicking it again.

4 Click the icon to select it again.

The menu closes, but there are no other changes in the tag selectors or CSS Designer. The JavaScript behavior seems to be interfering with the normal functionality of these tools. When you can't do something in Live view, you may need to switch to Design view.

5 Switch to Design view.

JavaScript is ignored in Design view. Unfortunately, so are some CSS properties—the icon has completely disappeared. And if you can't see it, you can't select it. In previous versions of the program, you would have to turn to Code view now, but Dreamweaver CC (2014 release) has more than a few tricks up its sleeve. Since you can't see the icon in Design view, let's try one more trick using Live view.

6 Switch to Live view.

7 Click the Element Quick View icon **</>**.
Examine the DOM diagram.

The Element Quick View diagram strips away all the content to show the raw HTML page structure. Depending on where your cursor is, the diagram may display the fully expanded menu structure and make it a simple matter to identify the button icon, or not.

▶ **Tip:** If the DOM structure is not fully expanded, click each element in turn to display its child structures until you find the one you're seeking.

8 Select the `button` element in the diagram.

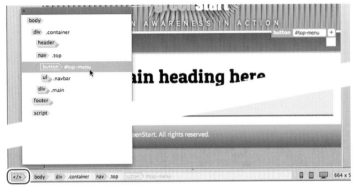

The tag selectors and CSS Designer finally display the structure and styling of the icon. Although you turned to Element Quick View as a last resort this time, don't be afraid to use it as your go-to tool at any time. The icon is formatted by the `#top-menu` rule.

9 In the CSS Designer, select `<style>` > `screen and (max-width: 665px)` > `#top-menu`.

10 Change the following properties:

```
border-color: #3AF
background-color: #3AF
```

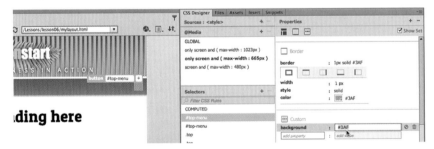

The icon changes to light blue to match the new site color scheme.

11 Save the file.

The basic layout is nearly finished. There's one last media query to check.

Adding rules to a media query

The final media query applies styles when the screen is 480 pixels or smaller. This one formats smartphone screens, for both portrait and landscape orientations. Let's check to see if it needs any modifications.

1 If necessary, open **mylayout.html** from the lesson06 folder in Live view.

2 In the CSS Designer, select `<style>` > `screen and (max-width: 480px)`.

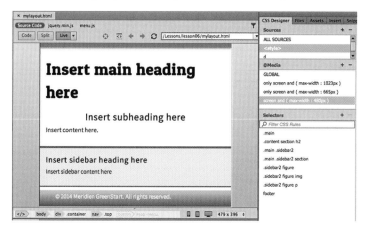

The layout displays at 480 pixels or less. The horizontal menu collapses to an icon. The main heading looks a bit too large, while everything else seems fine— at least on the surface. But don't forget to check the responsive menu.

3 Click the menu icon to open the menu.

The menu opens, showing the seven page placeholder links.

4 Position the cursor over each menu item, and observe the behavior.

Each item displays the rollover hover effect as the cursor passes over it.

5 Click the icon to close the menu.

Everything seems to look good and work as expected. Let's reduce the size of the main heading so that it fits the narrow screen better. It will require you to create a new CSS rule in this media query.

6 Insert the cursor in the text *Insert main heading here*.
Select the h1 tag selector.
Select `<style>` > `screen and (max-width: 480px)` > `.main`.

7 Create a new selector `.content h1`

8 Create the following properties for the new rule:

```
font-size: 200%
text-align: center
```

The heading resizes and centers. You have now addressed all the inconsistencies in the layout based on the default screen size provided by the predefined media queries. Unfortunately, this doesn't cover all contingencies.

Devices don't come in neat, predictable dimensions and orientations. It's a mixed bag of resolutions and sizes. Don't simply rely on the document preview generated by each media query. You need to review the layout at a variety of widths. You can start your testing regimen in Dreamweaver itself by using the program's responsive interface.

9 Select the GLOBAL media reference.

The screen resets to full size. You can now resize the screen manually to test the design on a range of screen sizes.

10 Drag the right edge of the document window to the left.
Observe how the content and structure adapt to various dimensions.

Everything seems to work fine until the screen gets smaller than 435 pixels. At that size, the motto breaks to two lines and overflows into the navbar. This small error is an example of the problems you could miss by relying only on the previews provided by using the media queries.

Let's adjust the text styling so that it remains in one line. But before you create a fix, it's important to first set the screen at the smallest anticipated width. For example, first-generation iPhones have a width of 320 pixels in portrait mode.

11 Drag the document window until the screen size is 320 pixels wide.

12 Insert the cursor into the text *GREEN AWARENESS IN ACTION* in the header.

13 Select `<style>` > `screen and (max-width: 480px)` > `.main`.
Create a new **header p** selector.

14 Create a new property `letter-spacing: .2em`

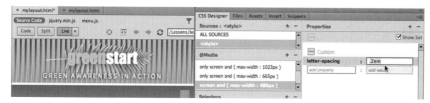

Using the new letter spacing, the text should now fit easily on one line even on the smallest smartphones. The adaptation of the layout for mobile devices is complete.

15 Save the file.

You may think you're finished styling and adapting a layout within Dreamweaver, yet you can't stop there. It's helpful to see pages within the program, but there's just no substitute for seeing a page on the device itself. However, testing pages on a dozen or more tablets and smartphones can be a huge challenge. Just the physical act of launching the device browser and typing in the URL of the test pages can waste hours of precious time. Fortunately, Adobe has a solution for that, too.

Edge Inspect

Another way to test your mobile design is to use a program named Adobe Edge Inspect, which is one of a new family of web-design tools available exclusively through Adobe Creative Cloud.

Edge Inspect is designed to mirror the screen display of your laptop or desktop browser on a variety of mobile devices, using Bluetooth along with a live Internet connection. At the moment, it only works with the Google Chrome browser. To use Edge Inspect, download and install the latest version of Chrome. Then, sign into your Creative Cloud account, download Edge Inspect to your computer, and install the app. Finally, you'll have to get the Inspect companion app for all your smartphones and tablets and install it on each device.

Once all the software is installed and ready, all you need to do is launch the Google Chrome browser on your desktop or laptop computer and activate the Inspect browser plug-in **In** . Then, launch Edge Inspect on one or more mobile devices, and sync them all to your computer by Bluetooth.

Note: Edge Inspect works only in Google Chrome (www.google.com/chrome) at the time of this writing.

Note: Depending on your operating system and mobile device, other applications may be required to work with Edge Inspect. See the link to the full installation instructions at the end of this section.

From this point on, whenever you load a page in the browser, you'll see the sample page mirrored on all your mobile devices. If you rotate the device, the appropriate media query will kick in and alter the display as specified. Edge Inspect supports pages hosted on the web and also those using a local web server that is online.

To learn more about Edge Inspect, check out https://creative.adobe.com/products/inspect.

For installation instructions, check out https://forums.adobe.com/docs/DOC-2535.

More information on media queries

To learn more about media queries and how to work with them, check out the following links:

- Adobe: http://tinyurl.com/adobe-media-queries
- W3C Consortium: http://tinyurl.com/w3c-media-queries
- Smashing Magazine: http://tinyurl.com/media-queries-smashing

Congratulations, you've successfully modified a predefined mobile-ready layout and adapted it to your site design requirements. Although it's hard to imagine what amazing new features may come along, one thing you can be sure of is that Dreamweaver will continue to be at the forefront of web development. With support for media queries and other responsive techniques, the program continues to innovate and be a leader in the industry.

Review questions

1 What are media queries?

2 How do media queries target a specific device or screen size?

3 What can you do with the screen resolution switchers?

4 Do you have to worry about CSS inheritance when using media queries?

5 In a mobile device, what happens to the webpage display if you rotate the device?

6 What function does Edge Inspect perform?

Review answers

1 Media queries are a CSS3 specification for loading style sheets interactively, based on the size and other characteristics of the device viewing the webpage.

2 Media queries include a logical expression that instructs the browser what style sheet to load, based on screen and device characteristics.

3 With screen resolution switchers, you can instantly switch the Dreamweaver document window to mobile, tablet, and desktop display sizes to test specific media queries.

4 Yes. But bear in mind that media queries can be written to format exclusively or in conjunction with other media queries or style sheets. By allowing a base set of styles to be inherited, you can save on the total amount of CSS that needs to be created by the designer and downloaded by the user.

5 By rotating the device, you are changing the width of the screen and its orientation. Both factors can be used to load various style sheets or rules to format the page components and content differently.

6 Edge Inspect is a new Creative Cloud app that allows you to instantly test mobile style sheets by linking your desktop computer to various mobile devices via Bluetooth.

7 WORKING WITH TEMPLATES

Lesson overview

In this lesson, you'll learn how to work faster, make updating easier, and be more productive. You'll learn how to do the following:

- Create a Dreamweaver template

- Insert editable regions

- Produce child pages

- Update templates and child pages

- Move an embedded style sheet to an external file

 This lesson will take about one hour to complete. If you have not already done so, download the project files for this lesson from the Lesson & Update Files tab on your Account page at www.peachpit.com, store them on your computer in a convenient location, and define a new site based on the lesson07 folder as described in the "Getting Started" section of this book. Your Account page is also where you'll find any updates to the lessons or to the lesson files. Look on the Lesson & Update Files tab to access the most current content.

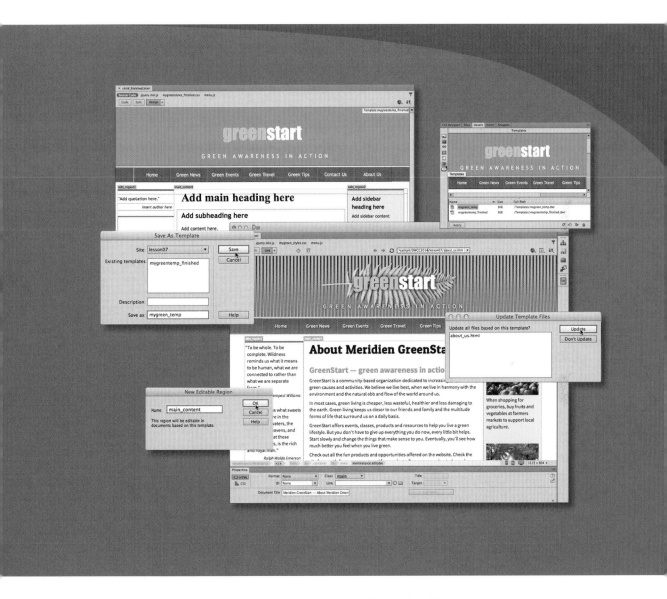

Dreamweaver's productivity tools and site-management capabilities are among its most useful features for a busy designer.

Previewing completed files

Note: If you have not already downloaded the project files for this lesson to your computer from your Account page, make sure to do so now. See "Getting Started" at the beginning of the book.

To better understand the topics in this lesson, let's preview the completed page in a browser.

1 Launch Adobe Dreamweaver CC (2014.1 release) or later.

2 If necessary, press F8 to open the Files panel.
   Select lesson07 from the site list drop-down menu.

3 Expand the lesson07 folder.
   Open **child_ finished.html** in Design view.
   Observe the design and structure of this page.

This page was created from a template; Dreamweaver displays the name of the parent file in the upper-right corner of the document window in Design view. The layout is identical to the page completed in Lessons 5 and 6, with some notable exceptions. If you look carefully, you'll see that the basic *visible* differences between your existing layout and the sample file are the three areas on the sample page displaying blue tabs and borders. These areas, or *editable regions*, are the biggest difference between a regular HTML page and a page based on a Dreamweaver template.

4 Move the cursor over the GreenStart banner in the header and the horizontal menu in Design view. Note the icon Dreamweaver displays.

The Locked icon ⊘ signifies that the area is locked and uneditable.

5 Insert the cursor anywhere in the main content.
Examine the tag selectors.

Note how the tag selectors on the left side are grayed out. This indicates that some of the elements in the file are not selectable, which in turn means they are also not editable. You will also see an unusual tag: `mmtinstance:editable`. This tag references the editable portion of the page. Tags to the left of it are in the locked portion of the page; the tags to the right are in the editable portion.

6 Select the placeholder *Add main heading here* in `article.content`.
Type **Get a fresh start with GreenStart** to replace the text.
Save the file.

The `<article>` element is contained in one of the blue editable areas labeled *main_content*, which allows you to select and change content within it.

7 Choose File > Preview in Browser, and select the default browser.

The browser display doesn't give you any clues as to how this page differs from the one you created earlier—that's the beauty of a template-based page. For all intents and purposes, a template-based page is just a normal HTML file. The extra code elements that enable its special features are basically comments added and read only by Dreamweaver and other web-aware applications, and should never affect the performance or display in a browser.

8 Close your browser, and return to Dreamweaver.
Close **child_ finished.html**.

For the last three lessons, you have been creating a layout similar to the one you just previewed. In the following exercises, you will turn that layout into a Dreamweaver template. But before you can create a template from it, there's still one major change to make.

Moving embedded CSS to an external file

Designers frequently use embedded style sheets to make the design and development phase of a new site faster and easier. That's because this way there's only one file to edit and preview in the browser—the content and styling are all stored in one page. But keeping the CSS embedded has a major downside, too. Any time you want to change the styling of an element, you have to modify the template and then update and upload every page in the website. By moving the CSS to an external file, it means all the webpages on a site can be reformatted by uploading a single file.

1 If necessary, open **mylayout.html**.
Switch to Code view.

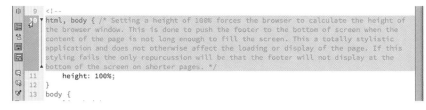

The style sheet is contained entirely within the `<style>`...`</style>` tags, starting around line 8. You will select the entire style sheet and move it to a new file.

2 Click the line number of the first rule in the style sheet, which should be `html`, `body` on line 10.

The contents of the first line should be highlighted. It's important that neither the `<style>`...`</style>` tags nor the comment `<!-- -->` markup are included in your selection. These notations are not valid CSS markup, and would cause the style sheet to malfunction if they appeared in the CSS file.

3 Scroll down to the closing `</style>` tag, around line 487.
Hold the Shift key, and click the line number of the last entry in the style sheet.

All the rules in the style sheet should now be selected, excluding the `<style>`...`</style>` tags and the comment `<!-- -->` markup.

4 Press Ctrl+X/Cmd+X to cut the code into memory.

```
 7   <title>Add Title Here</title>
 8   <style type="text/css" >
 9   <!--
10   -->
11   </style>
12   <!--[if lt IE 9]>
```

▶ **Tip:** If you accidentally copy the comment or mark up or `<style>` tags, don't worry. You can simply delete them in the CSS file. But, be sure to leave balanced markup in the HTML file.

Only the `<style>`...`</style>` tags and the comment `<!-- -->` markup should remain.

5 Choose File > New.

6 Select Blank Page > CSS in the New Document dialog.

7 Click Create.

A new CSS document appears in Dreamweaver.

8 Select the CSS comment markup `/* CSS Document */`, and press Ctrl+V/Cmd+V to paste the style sheet.

The CSS rules and markup replace the comment.

9 Choose File > Save.

Name the file **mygreen_styles.css**, and save it in the site root folder.

You have moved the style sheet from the layout to a new CSS file, but now you have to link the file to this page.

10 In **mygreen_styles.css**, choose File > Close.

11 Switch to Live view.

The layout is formatted now only by default HTML styling. You can relink the style sheet using the CSS Designer.

12 In the CSS Designer, click the plus-sign icon ➕ in the Sources window. Choose Attach Existing CSS File from the drop-down menu.

The Attach Existing CSS File dialog appears.

13 If necessary, select the Link option. Click Browse.

The Select Style Sheet File dialog appears.

14 If necessary, navigate to the site root folder. Select **mygreen_styles.css**, and click OK/Open.

15 In the Attach Existing CSS File dialog, click OK/Open.

If necessary, click the Refresh icon ⟳.

The layout should appear formatted as before. In the related files interface, you will see the filename **mygreen_styles.css**. In the CSS Designer, you should see references to the embedded `<style>` element and to **mygreen_styles.css**. There's no need to keep the embedded `<style>` element, so let's remove it.

16 In the Sources window, select the `<style>` reference.

Click the minus-sign icon ━ to delete the reference.

The reference in the CSS Designer and the corresponding code has been removed from the page.

17 Save the file.

You've separated the content from the style sheet. Now you're ready to convert the sample page into your site template.

Creating a template from an existing layout

A template is a type of master page from which related child pages are produced. Templates are useful for setting up and maintaining the overall look and feel of a website while providing a means for quickly and easily producing site content. A template is different from your completed pages; it contains areas that are editable and other areas that are not. Templates enable a workgroup environment, where page content is created and edited by several team members while the web designer controls the page design and the specific elements that must remain unchanged.

Although you can create a template from a blank page, converting an existing page into a template is far more practical, and also far more common. In this exercise, you'll create a template from your existing layout.

1 Launch Dreamweaver CC (2014.1 release) or later.

2 Open **mylayout.html** from the lesson07 folder.
Switch to Design view.

The first step in converting an existing page to a template is to save the page as a template. Most of the work creating a template must be completed in Design or Code view.

3 Choose File > Save as Template.

The Save As Template dialog appears.

▶ **Tip:** Adding the suffix "temp" to the filename helps to visually distinguish this file from others in the site folder display, but it's not a requirement.

4 If necessary, choose lesson07 from the Site pop-up menu.
Leave the Description field empty.
Type **mygreen_temp** in the Save As field.
Click Save.

Note: A dialog may appear, asking about saving the file without defining editable regions; just click Yes to save anyway. You'll create editable regions in the next exercise.

An untitled dialog appears, asking whether you want to update links.

Templates are stored in their own folder, Templates, which Dreamweaver automatically creates at the site root level.

5 Click Yes to update the links.

Since the template is saved in a subfolder, updating the links in the code is necessary so they will continue to work properly when you create child pages later. Dreamweaver automatically resolves and rewrites links as necessary when you save files anywhere in the site.

Although the page still looks exactly the same, you can identify that it's a template by the file extension .dwt displayed in the document tab, which stands for Dreamweaver template.

A Dreamweaver template is dynamic, meaning that the program maintains a connection to all pages within the site that are derived from the template. Whenever you add or change content within the dynamic regions of the page and save it, Dreamweaver passes those changes to all the child pages automatically, keeping them up to date. But a template shouldn't be completely dynamic. Some sections of the page should contain areas where you can insert unique content. Dreamweaver allows you to designate these areas of the page as *editable*.

Inserting editable regions

When you first create a template, Dreamweaver treats all the existing content as part of the master design. Child pages created from the template would be exact duplicates, and all the content would be locked and uneditable. This setup is great for repetitive features of the design, such as the navigation components, logos, copyright, contact information, and so on, but the downside is that it stops you from adding unique content to each child page. You get around this barrier by defining *editable regions* in the template. Dreamweaver creates one editable region automatically for the `<title>` element in the `<head>` section of the page; you have to create the rest.

First, give some thought to which areas of the page should be part of the template and which should be open for editing. At the moment, three sections of your current layout need to be editable: Sidebar 1, Sidebar 2, and the main content area.

1 Open **mylayout.html** from the lesson07 folder in Design view, if necessary.

2 Insert the cursor in the heading text *Insert main heading here.* Click the `.content` tag selector.

● **Note:** The template workflow currently works only in Design and Code views. You will not be able to perform any of these tasks in Live view.

Dreamweaver selects the entire `<article>` element.

3 Choose Insert > Template > Editable Region.

4 In the New Editable Region dialog, type **main_content** in the Name field. Click OK.

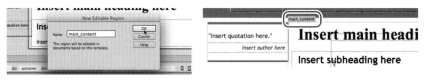

Each editable region must have a unique name, but no other special conventions apply. However, keeping them short and descriptive is a good practice. The name is used solely within Dreamweaver and has no other bearing on the HTML code. In Design view, you will see the new region name in a blue tab above the designated area, identifying it as an editable region.

You also need to add an editable region to Sidebar 1 and Sidebar 2. Each of these sidebar regions contains text placeholders that you can customize on each page.

5 Insert the cursor in Sidebar 1.
Click the .sidebar1 tag selector.

6 Choose Insert > Template > Editable Region.

7 In the New Editable Region dialog, type **side_region1** in the Name field. Click OK.

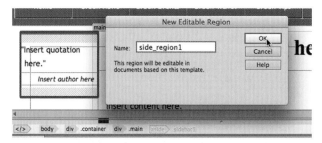

8 Insert the cursor in Sidebar 2.
Click the .sidebar2 tag selector.

9 Choose Insert > Template > Editable Region.

10 In the New Editable Region dialog, type **side_region2** in the Name field. Click OK.

11 Save the file.

Once you have set up the visible components of the template, you should turn your attention to areas that are hidden from most visitors.

Inserting metadata

A well-designed webpage includes several important components that users may never see. One such item is *metadata* that is often added to the <head> section of each page. Metadata is descriptive information about your webpage or the contents it contains that is often used by other applications, like the browser or a search engine. Adding metadata, for instance, a piece of metadata such as "*title*," is not only a good practice, it's vital to your ranking and presence in the various search engines. Each title should reflect the specific content or purpose of the page. But many designers also append the name of the company or organization, to help build more corporate or organizational awareness. By adding a title placeholder with the company name here in the template, you will save time typing it in each child page later.

1 If necessary, open **mygreen_temp.dwt** in Design view.

2 In the Document Title field of the Property inspector, select the placeholder text *Add Title Here*.

> **Tip:** The Document Title field is available only in the Property inspector when you are in Design or Code views.

Many search engines use the page title in the listings of a search result. If you don't supply one, the search engine will pick one of its own. Let's replace the generic placeholder with one geared for this website.

3 Type **Meridien GreenStart Association – Add Title Here** to replace the text. Press Enter/Return to complete the title.

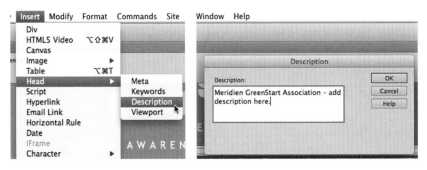

Along with the title, the other piece of metadata that usually appears in these search results is the page *description*. A description is a type of summary of a page that succinctly describes the contents in 25 words or less. Over the years, web developers have tried to drive more traffic to their sites by writing misleading titles and descriptions or outright lies. But be forewarned—most search engines have become wise to such tricks and will actually mark down sites that try to use these tactics.

To achieve the highest ranking with the search engines, make the description of the page as accurate as possible. In many cases, the contents of the title and the description metadata will appear verbatim in the results page of a search.

4 Choose Insert > Head > Description.

An empty Description dialog appears.

5 Type **Meridien GreenStart Association – add description here.** Click OK.

Dreamweaver has added the two metadata elements to the page. Unfortunately, only one of them was implemented properly in the template.

6 Switch to Code view. Locate and examine the `<title>` tag in the code and the surrounding markup.

In most cases, the `<title>` will appear around line 8. Notice how the title appears between two comments that delineate an "editable" portion of the template named `"doctitle"`.

7 Locate and examine the `<meta>` tag containing the "description" and the surrounding markup.

```
15   <!-- TemplateBeginEditable name="head" -->
16   <!-- TemplateEndEditable -->
17   <meta name="description" content="Meridien GreenStart Association –
     add description here.">
18   </head>
```

You should find the description near the end of the `<head>` section, around line 17. This element is not contained in an *editable* section of the template. What this means is that this metadata will be locked on all child pages, and you will not be able to customize it for that page.

Luckily, Dreamweaver comes to the rescue by providing an editable section designed for metadata just like this. In this case, it can't even get any more convenient—you'll find it just above the description delineated by the HTML comment markup `<!-- TemplateBeginEditable name="head" -->`. To make the description metadata editable, you'll need to move it into this section.

8 Click the line number containing the entire description, or select the entire `<meta>` element using the cursor.

The `<meta>` tag and its contents should occupy a single line of the markup.

9 Press Ctrl+X/Cmd+X to cut this code into memory.

10 Insert the cursor at the end of the comment `TemplateBeginEditable name="head"`. Press Enter/Return to insert a new line.

11 Click the line number of the new blank line.
Press Ctrl+V/Cmd+V to paste the description `<meta>` element.

● **Note:** The new line is simply intended to make the markup easier to read. It's otherwise unnecessary.

```
15   <!-- TemplateBeginEditable name="head" -->
16   <meta name="description" content="Meridien GreenStart Association –
     add description here.">
17   <!-- TemplateEndEditable -->
18   </head>
```

The description is now contained with the editable template region named `"head"`.

12 Choose File > Save.

You now have three editable regions—plus editable metadata for title and description—that you can change as needed when you create new child pages using this template.

◆ **Warning:** If you open a template in a text editor, all the code is editable, including the code for the noneditable regions of the page.

13 Choose File > Close All.

Now it's time to learn how to use your new template.

Producing child pages

Child pages are the *raison d'être* for Dreamweaver templates. Once a child page has been created from a template, only the content within the editable regions can be modified in the child page. The rest of the page remains locked within Dreamweaver. It's important to remember that this behavior is supported only within Dreamweaver and a few other HTML editors. Be aware: If you open the page in a text editor, like Notepad or TextEdit, the code is fully editable.

Creating a new page

The decision to use Dreamweaver templates for a site should be made at the beginning of the design process, so that all the pages in the site can be made as child pages of the template. In fact, that was the purpose of the layout you've built up to this point: to create the basic structure of your site template.

1 Launch Dreamweaver CC (2014.1 release) or later, if necessary.

2 Choose File > New, or press Ctrl+N/Cmd+N.

   The New Document dialog appears.

3 In the New Document dialog, select the Site Templates option.
   Select lesson07 in the Site list, if necessary.
   Select **mygreen_temp** in the Template For Site "lesson07" list.

4 Select the Update Page When Template Changes option, if necessary.
   Click Create.

Dreamweaver creates a new page based on the template. Typically, Dreamweaver defaults to the last document view (Code, Design, or Live) you were using for the new document. Note the name of the template file displayed in the upper-right corner of the document window. This will appear only in Design view. Before modifying the page, you should save it.

5 Choose File > Save.

   The Save As dialog appears.

6 In the Save As dialog, navigate to the site root folder.
Name the file **about_us.html**, and click Save.

The child page has been created. When you save the document in the site root folder, Dreamweaver updates all links and references to external files. The template makes it easy to add new content.

Adding content to child pages

When you create a page from a template, only the editable regions can be modified.

1 Open **about_us.html** in Design view, if necessary.

You'll find that many of the features and functionality of templates work properly only in Design view.

2 Position the cursor over each area of the page.

When the cursor moves over certain areas of the page, such as the header, horizontal menu, and footer, the Locked icon appears. These areas are uneditable regions that are locked and cannot be modified inside Dreamweaver. Other areas, like Sidebar 1, Sidebar 2, and the main content section, can be changed.

3 In the Title field, select the placeholder text *Add Title Here*.
Type **About Meridien GreenStart**, and press Enter/Return.

4 In the `main_content` region, select the placeholder text *Insert main heading here.* Type **About Meridien GreenStart** to replace the text.

5 Select the placeholder text *Insert subheading here.*
Type **GreenStart – green awareness in action!** to replace the text.

▶ **Tip:** To add a little editorial flair, use the command Insert > Character > Em-Dash to insert a long dash in the heading.

6 In the Files panel, double-click **aboutus.rtf** in the lesson07 resources folder to open the file.

Dreamweaver opens only simple, text-based file formats, like .html, .css, .txt, .xml, .xslt, and a few others. When Dreamweaver can't open the file, it will pass the file to a compatible program, such as Word, Excel, WordPad, TextEdit, and so on. The file contains content for the main content section.

7 Press Ctrl+A/Cmd+A to select all the text.
Press Ctrl+C/Cmd+C to copy the text.

8 Switch back to Dreamweaver.

9 Insert the cursor in the placeholder text *Insert content here.*
Select the p tag selector.

10 Press Ctrl+V/Cmd+V to paste the text.

The placeholder text is replaced by the new content. We can also add content to the sidebar elements.

11 Open **sidebars07.html** in Design view from the site root folder.

The file contains content for each sidebar.

12 Insert the cursor in the first paragraph, and examine the tag selectors.

The tag selectors indicate a structure identical to Sidebar 1 but unformatted by the CSS. Let's use this content to replace the existing sidebar.

13 Click the `.sidebar1` tag selector.
Press Ctrl+X/Cmd+X to cut the entire element into memory.

14 Select the **about_us.html** document tab.

The child page appears in the document window again.

15 Insert the cursor into Sidebar 1.
Select the `.sidebar1` tag selector.

16 Press Ctrl+V/Cmd+V to replace the sidebar placeholder.

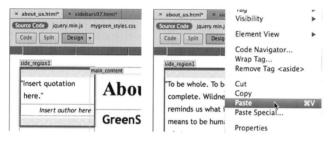

The replacement content appears, formatted by the external CSS file.

17 Select the **sidebars07.html** document tab.

18 Repeat steps 14–17 to replace the Sidebar 2 placeholder.

All three editable regions have now been populated with content.

19 Save the file.

20 Switch to Live view to preview the page.

As you can see, there is no indication that this template child page is any different from any other standard webpage. Editable regions don't limit the content you can insert into them; the regions can include text, images, tables, video, and so on.

21 Choose File > Close All. Do not save changes to any other file.

Once you have created child pages and added content, there will come a time when you need to add or change a menu item, update the header or footer, or otherwise modify the content in the base template.

Updating a template

Templates can automatically update any child pages made from that template. But only areas outside the editable regions will be updated. Let's make some changes in the template to learn how templates work.

▶ **Tip:** The Template category in the Assets panel does not appear when a document is open in Live view. Switch to Design or Code view, if necessary, to access this category.

1 Choose Window > Assets.

The Assets panel appears. If it appears floating freely in the document window, you can dock it with the CSS Designer panel. The Assets panel gives you immediate access to a variety of components and content available to your website.

2 In the Assets panel, click the Templates category icon ▦. If no templates appear in the list, click the refresh icon ↻.

The panel displays a list of site templates and a preview window. The name of your template appears in the list.

3 Right-click **mygreen_temp**, and choose Edit from the context menu.

Name	Size	Full Path
mygreen_temp	3KB	/Templates/mygreen_temp.dwt
mygreente		lates/mygreentemp_finished.dwt

Refresh Site List
Recreate site list

New Template
New from Template

Edit
Edit Original

Apply

The template opens.

4 In the horizontal menu, select the text *Home*.
Type **Green Home** to replace the text.

× mygreen_temp.dwt*

Source Code jquery.min.js   mygreen_styles.css   menu.js

Code Split Design ▼

| Green Home | Green News | Green Events | Green Travel |

5 In the vertical menu, select the text *Green News*.

Type **Headlines** to replace the text.

6 Select and replace the text *Insert* with the word **Add** wherever it appears in the main_content, side_region1, and side_region2 editable regions.

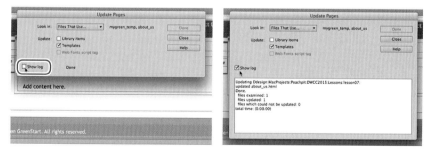

7 Save the file.

The Update Template Files dialog appears. The filename **about_us.html** appears in the update list.

8 Click Update.

The Update Pages dialog appears.

9 Select the Show Log option.

The window displays a report detailing which pages were successfully updated and which ones were not.

10 Close the Update Pages dialog.

Tip: If an open page has been changed during the update, it will show an asterisk in the document tab by its name.

11 Choose File > Open Recent > **about_us.html**.

Observe the page, and note any changes.

The changes made to the horizontal and vertical menus in the template are reflected in this file, but the changes to the sidebars and main content areas were ignored, and the content you added to both areas remain unaltered. As you can see, you can safely make changes and add content to the editable regions without worrying that the template will delete all your hard work. At the same time, the boilerplate elements of the header, footer, and horizontal menu all remain consistently formatted and up to date, based on the status of the template.

12 Click the document tab for **mygreen_temp.dwt** to switch to the template file.

13 Delete the word *Green* from the *Green Home* link in the horizontal menu. Change the word *Headlines* in the vertical menu back to **Green News**.

14 Save the template, and update related files.

15 Click the document tab for **about_us.html**.

Observe the page, and note any changes.

The horizontal menu has been updated. Dreamweaver even updates linked documents that are open at the time. The only concern is that the changes have not been saved; the document tab shows an asterisk, which means the file has been changed but not saved. If Dreamweaver or your computer were to crash at this moment, the changes would be lost; you would have to update the page manually or wait until the next time you make changes to the template to take advantage of the automatic update feature.

Tip: Always use the Save All command whenever you have multiple files open that have been updated by a template. In most cases, it's better to update when your files are closed so that they are saved automatically.

16 Choose File > Save All.

Dreamweaver's templates help you build and automatically update pages quickly and easily. In the upcoming lessons, you will use the newly completed template to create files for the project site. Although choosing to use templates is a decision you should make when first creating a new site, it's never too late to use them to speed up your workflow and make site maintenance faster and easier.

Review questions

1 How do you create a template from an existing page?

2 Why is a template dynamic?

3 What must you add to a template to make it useful in a workflow?

4 How do you create a child page from a template?

5 Can templates update pages that are open?

6 What are the disadvantages of using an embedded style sheet in a template?

Review answers

1 Choose File > Save as Template, and enter the name of the template in the dialog to create a .dwt file.

2 A template is dynamic because Dreamweaver maintains a connection to all pages created from it within a site. When the template is updated, it passes any changes to the locked areas of the child pages and leaves the editable regions unaltered.

3 You must add editable regions to the template; otherwise, unique content can't be added to the child pages.

4 Choose File > New, and in the New Document dialog, select Pages From Templates. Locate the desired template, and click Create. Or, right-click the template name in the Assets > Template category, and choose New From Template.

5 Yes. Open pages based on the template are updated along with files that are closed. The only difference is that files that are open are not automatically saved after being updated.

6 Leaving styles embedded in each page based on a template means you would have to upload every page whenever you make changes to any rule. When you use an external style sheet, you can update the entire site by uploading a single file.

8 WORKING WITH TEXT, LISTS, AND TABLES

Lesson overview

In this lesson, you'll create several web pages from your new template and work with headings, paragraphs, and other text elements to do the following:

- Enter heading and paragraph text
- Insert text from another source
- Create bulleted lists
- Create indented text
- Insert and modify tables
- Spellcheck your website
- Search and replace text

 This lesson will take about 3 hours and 30 minutes to complete. Before beginning, make sure you have copied the lesson08 files to your hard drive, and defined a site based on the lesson08 folder as described in the "Getting Started" section at the beginning of the book.

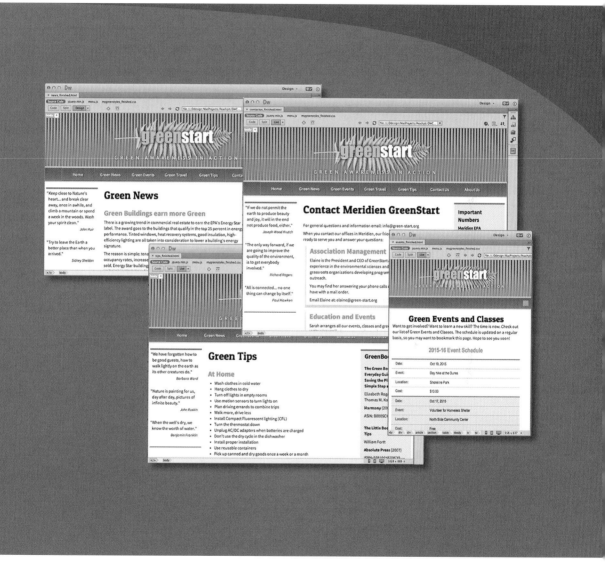

Dreamweaver provides numerous tools for creating, editing, and formatting web content, whether it's created within the program or imported from other applications.

Previewing the completed file

To get a sense of the files you will work on in the first part of this lesson, let's preview the completed pages in a browser.

1 Launch Adobe Dreamweaver CC (2014.1 release and later), if necessary. If Dreamweaver is already running, close any files currently open.

2 If necessary, define a new site for Lesson 8, as described in the "Getting Started" section at the beginning of the book. Name the new site **lesson08**.

3 If necessary, press F8 to open the Files panel.
Select lesson08 from the site drop-down list, and expand the site root folder.

Dreamweaver allows you to open one or more files at the same time.

4 Select **contactus_finished.html**. Press Ctrl/Cmd, and then select **events_ finished.html**, **news_finished.html**, and **tips_finished.html**.

By pressing Ctrl/Cmd before you click, you can select multiple non-consecutive files.

5 Right-click any of the selected files. Choose Open from the context menu.

All four files open. Tabs at the top of the document window identify each file.

● **Note:** Be sure to use Live view to preview each of the pages.

6 Click the **news_finished.html** tab to bring that file to the top, and switch to Live view, if necessary.

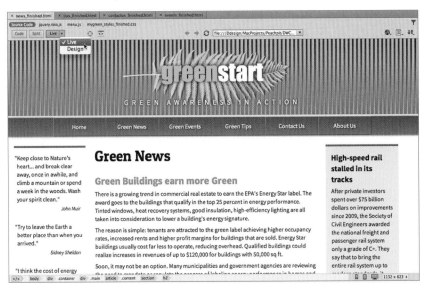

Note the headings and text elements used.

7 Click the **tips_finished.html** tab to bring that file to the top.

Note the bulleted list elements used.

8 Click the **contactus_finished.html** tab to bring that file to the top.

Note how text elements are indented and formatted.

9 Click the **events_finished.html** tab to bring that file to the top.

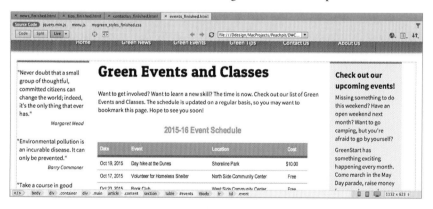

Note the two HTML-based tables used. The design employs techniques that allow the tables to adapt to tablets and smartphones.

10 Drag the right edge of the document window to the left.

As the screen narrows, the media queries apply styles to reformat the content and layout. Note how the tables themselves alter their appearance and structure drastically to fit the smaller screens.

11 Choose File > Close All.

In each of the pages, there is a variety of elements used, including headings, paragraphs, lists, bullets, indented text, and tables. In the following exercises, you will create these pages and learn how to format each of these elements.

Creating and styling text

Most websites are composed of large blocks of text with a few images sprinkled in for visual interest. Dreamweaver provides a variety of means of creating, importing, and styling text to meet any need. In the following exercises, you will learn a variety of techniques for working with and formatting text.

Importing text

In this exercise, you'll create a new page from the site template and then insert heading and paragraph text from a text document.

▶ **Tip:** The Assets panel may open as a separate, floating panel. To save screen space, feel free to dock the panel on the right side of the screen, as shown in Lesson 1, "Customizing Your Workspace."

1 Choose Window > Assets to display the Assets panel.
Select the Templates category icon 📃.
Right-click **mygreen_temp**, and choose New from Template from the context menu.

A new page is created based on the site template.

2 Save the file as **news.html** in the site root folder.

3 If necessary, choose Window > Properties to display the Property inspector.
In the Document Title field, select the placeholder text *Add Title Here*.
Type **Green News**, and press Enter/Return to complete the title.

4 In the Files panel, double-click **green_news.rtf** in the lesson08/resources folder.

Dreamweaver automatically launches a compatible program to open the file. The text is unformatted and features extra lines between each paragraph. These extra lines are intentional. For some reason, Dreamweaver swaps out single paragraph returns for <br> tags when you copy and paste them from another program. Adding a second return forces Dreamweaver to use paragraph tags instead.

This file contains four news stories. When you move the stories to the webpage, you're going to create your first semantic structures. As explained earlier, semantic web design attempts to provide a context for your web content so that it will be easier for users and web applications to find information and reuse it, as necessary. To aid in this goal, you'll move each story over to the web page one at a time and insert them into their own individual content structures.

5 In the text editor or word-processing program, insert the pointer at the beginning of the *Green Buildings earn more Green* text, and select all the text up to and including *Energy Waster?* (the first four paragraphs). Press Ctrl+X/Cmd+X to cut the text.

▶ **Tip:** When moving stories individually, cutting the text helps you keep track of which paragraphs have already been moved.

▶ **Tip:** When you use the clipboard to bring text into Dreamweaver from other programs, you must be in Design view if you want to honor the paragraph returns and other formatting.

6 Switch back to Dreamweaver.

Switch to Design view; select the placeholder heading *Add main heading here* in <article.content> and type **Green News** to replace it.

7 Insert the pointer in the placeholder heading *Add subheading here,* and note the tag selectors at the bottom of the document window.

The heading and the paragraph text are contained in one of the new HTML5 semantic elements: <section>. By inserting each news story into its own <section> element, you identify them as separate standalone content items that can be viewed independently of each other.

Note: Live view currently doesn't allow you to select more than one element at a time.

Tip: Using the <h2> tag selector will automatically select the placeholder text and the HTML tags, too.

8 Click the <h2> tag selector to select the element. Holding the Shift key, click at the end of the placeholder text *Add content here.*

The heading and paragraph placeholders are selected.

9 Press Ctrl+V/Cmd+V to paste the text from the clipboard and swap out the placeholder text.

The clipboard text appears in the layout. Now you're ready to move the next story.

10 Save the file.

Using a technique you learned earlier, you will create three new <section> elements and populate them with the remaining news stories.

Alternative HTML 4 workflow

The upcoming sections describe and build an HTML5 workflow using semantic elements and structures. If you are unable to use this type of structure and must still rely on HTML 4–compatible elements, never fear. You can build your pages using an equivalent HTML 4–compatible CSS layout and simply insert your content entirely in the <div.content> element that appears therein, or you can substitute generic <div> elements in place of the semantic elements described next. You can even create a quasi-semantic structure by adding an attribute such as class="section" to the containing <div> element.

Creating semantic structures

In this exercise, you will insert three HTML5 <section> elements to hold the remaining news stories. If you need to work in HTML 4, an alternative method would be to insert the stories into individual <div> elements and then assign them an attribute of class="section". But such a technique will not convey the same semantic weight as the HTML5 <section> element.

1 Switch to the text editor or word processor containing **green_news.rtf**. Select the next four paragraphs, beginning at *Shopping green saves energy* and ending at *in your own community*. Press Ctrl+X/Cmd+X to cut the text.

2 Switch to Dreamweaver. In Design view, insert the pointer anywhere in the existing news story, and click the `<section>` tag selector.

The entire `<section>` element and its contents are selected.

3 Press the right arrow key once to move the pointer after the closing `</section>` tag in the code.

Note: You won't be able to see the insertion point on the screen, but using this technique ensures it is in the correct position.

4 Choose Insert > Structure > Section.
Click OK to insert a new `<section>` element.

5 Press Ctrl+V/Cmd+V to paste the text from the clipboard and insert it into the new `<section>` element.

The second news story appears in the new `<section>` element, replacing the placeholder text.

6 Repeat steps 1–5 to create new `<section>` elements for the remaining two news stories.

When you're finished, you should have four `<section>` elements, one for each news story.

7 Close **green_news.rtf**. Do not save any changes.

8 Save **news.html**.

Note: By closing the file without saving the changes you have restored the original news stories to the file, in case you need them for later.

Creating headings

In HTML, the tags `<h1>`, `<h2>`, `<h3>`, `<h4>`, `<h5>`, and `<h6>` create headings. Any browsing device, whether it is a computer, a Braille reader, or a cell phone, interprets text formatted with any of these tags as a heading. In the Web, headings are used to introduce distinct sections with helpful titles, just as they do in books, magazine articles, and term papers.

Following the semantic meaning of HTML tags the news content begins with a heading *Green News*, formatted as an `<h1>`. The `<h1>` heading is considered the most important heading. To be semantically correct in HTML 4, only one such heading should be used per page. However, in HTML5, best practices have not yet been formalized. Some believe that we should continue the practice used in HTML 4. Others think that it should be permissible to use an <h1> in each semantic element or structure on a page; in other words, each <section>, <article>, <header>, or <footer> could have its own <h1> heading.

Until the new practice is codified we'll bend the rule a bit and continue the current practice by using one <h1> element per page as the primary page title. All other headings should therefore descend in order from the <h1>. Since each news story has equal importance, they all can begin with a second-level heading, or <h2>. At the moment, all the pasted text is formatted as <p> elements. Let's format the news headings as <h2> elements.

Tip: If the Format menu is not visible, select the HTML mode of the Property inspector.

1   In Design view, select the text *Green Buildings earn more Green*.
    Choose **Heading 2** from the Format menu in the Property inspector, or press Ctrl+2/Cmd+2.

The text is formatted as an <h2> element.

2   Repeat step 1 with the text *Shopping green saves energy*, *Recycling isn't always Green*, and *Fireplace: Fun or Folly?*

All the selected text should now be formatted as <h2> elements. Let's create a custom rule for this element to set it off from the other headings.

3   Insert the cursor in any of the newly formatted <h2> elements.
    Choose Window > CSS Designer to open the CSS Designer, if necessary.

4   Choose **mygreen_styles.css** > GLOBAL > .content h1.
    Click the Add Selector icon ✚.

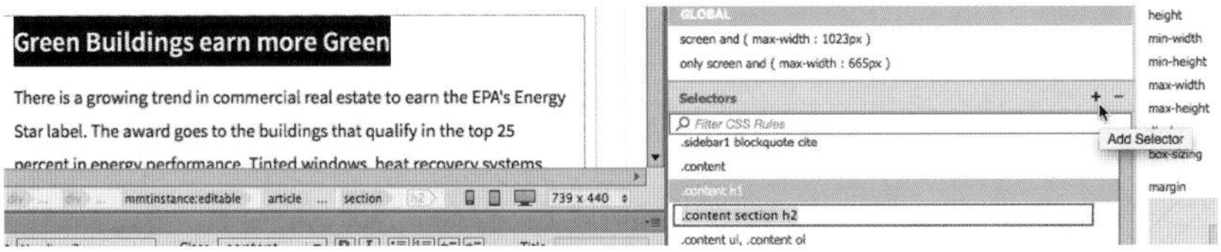

A new .content section h2 selector appears below the h1 rule.

Dreamweaver creates the name automatically based on your selection in the layout. This selector is a descendant selector, as described in Lesson 3, "CSS Basics," and will target its formatting only to <h2> elements that appear in a <section> element within <article.content>. This selector name is sufficiently specific for our purposes, but you can increase or decrease the specificity by pressing the up or down arrow keys.

5   Press the down arrow key two times. Observe the selector name each time.

Each time you press the down arrow, the selector becomes more specific. First the .main class is added, and then the .container class.

Since all the site content appears in div.container, it would be overkill to keep that class in the name. Keeping the .main class in the selector is not such an obvious choice. The div.main element is a structural element used to center the editorial content below the header and nav elements. Considering the current design structure, it will be rare to see <h2> elements appear outside div.main. So we'd be pretty safe in removing it from the selector name, too.

6   Press the up arrow two times to remove the .container and .main classes from the name, and then press Enter/Return to create the selector.

7   In the Properties window, create the following specifications:

```
top-margin: 15px
bottom-margin: 5px
color: #090
font-size: 170%
```

▶ **Tip:** A good designer carefully manages the naming and order of CSS rules. By first selecting an existing rule in the list you can determine the position of the new one. If the new rule doesn't appear in the proper location, just drag it to the desired position.

Note: By default, each heading tag—<h1>, <h2>, <h3>, and so on—is formatted smaller than the preceding tag. This formatting reinforces the semantic importance of each tag. Although size is an obvious method of indicating hierarchy, it's not a requirement; feel free to experiment with other styling techniques, such as color, indenting, borders, and background shading, to create your own hierarchical structure.

8   Save all files.

Adding other HTML structures

Descendant selectors are often sufficient for styling most elements and structures in a web page. But not all the structural elements are available from the Insert menu or panel. In this exercise, you will learn how to build a custom HTML structure using the Quick Tag Editor in two different ways.

1   Open **news.html** in Design view, if necessary.

2 In the Files panel, open **quotes08.txt**.

Since this is a plain text file, Dreamweaver should open it directly. The file contains quotations you will insert in the pages that will be created in this lesson.

3 Select the text of the first quotation, excluding the author name. Press Ctrl+X/Cmd+X to cut the text.

Note: When pasting text into existing HTML structures it is important not to accidentally delete or damage these structures.

4 Switch to **news.html**. Select the quotation placeholder text in sidebar 1. Press Ctrl+V/Cmd+V to paste the quotation. Observe the tag selector for the quotation.

The tag selector shows `aside.sidebar1 blockquote p` as the structure of the quotation.

5 Switch to **quotes08.txt**. Select and cut the author name, John Muir.

6 Switch to **news.html**. Select the *Author Name* placeholder text in sidebar 1. Paste the text, and observe the tag selector for the author name.

The tag selector shows `aside.sidebar1 blockquote cite.author` as the structure of the author name.

Now you should be prepared to create the other quotations.

7 Switch to **quotes08.txt**. Select and copy the entire next quotation and author.

8 In **news.html**, insert the cursor anywhere in the first quotation. Click the `blockquote` tag selector. Press the right arrow key.

The cursor should now appear after the `<blockquote>` element.

9 Press Ctrl+V/Cmd+V to paste the new quotation and author.

The text appears, but it is not styled properly.

10 Using the cursor and the tag selector interface, compare the structure of the two quotations, and note the differences.

The quotation and author name appear in two separate `<p>` elements. Part of the styling problem is due to the missing parent `blockquote` element. There's no menu option for adding this specific tag, but you can use the Quick Tag Editor to build all types of custom structures.

11 Drag to select the quotation text and the author name, Sydney Sheldon.

Tip: Press Ctrl+T/ Cmd+T to toggle between modes.

12 Press Ctrl+T/Cmd+T to activate the Quick Tag Editor.

The Quick Tag Editor appears. Since you have more than one element selected, it should default to Wrap mode.

13 Type `blockquote` and press Enter/Return twice to add the element as a parent to the two paragraphs.

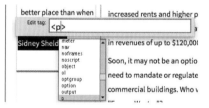

The quotation text is now formatted properly, but the author name needs one more tweak; we need to change the tag applied to it. As with `blockquote`, there's no menu option for the `<cite>` tag.

14 Insert the pointer in the author name, Sydney Sheldon.
Select the tag selector for the `<p>` element.
Press Ctrl+T/Cmd+T to activate the Quick Tag Editor.

The Quick Tag Editor appears. Since you have only one element selected, it should default to Edit mode.

15 Press the Backspace key to delete "p" from the selected tag.
Type `cite`, and press Enter/Return twice to complete the change.

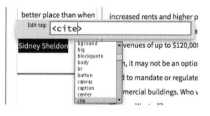

The author name now appears in a `<cite>` element and is styled identically to the other author.

16 Repeat steps 7-15 to move the third quotation from **quote08.txt** to sidebar 1 in **news.html**.

17 Save all files.

Creating lists

Formatting should add meaning, organization, and clarity to your content. One method of doing this is to use the HTML list elements. Lists are the workhorses of the web because they are easier to read than blocks of dense text; they also help users find information quickly. In this exercise, you will learn how to make an HTML list.

Note: The Template category is not visible in Live view. To create or edit Dreamweaver templates, you must switch to Design or Code views.

1   Choose Window > Assets to bring the Assets panel to the front.
    In the Template category, right-click **mygreen_temp**.
    From the context menu, choose New from Template.

    A new page is created based on the template.

2   Save the file as **tips.html** in the site root folder.

3   In the Property inspector, select the *Add Title Here* placeholder text.
    Type **Green Tips** to replace the text, and press Enter/Return.

4   In the Files panel, double-click **green_tips.rtf** in the resources folder of
    lesson08.

    The file will open outside of Dreamweaver. The content consists of three
    individual lists of tips on how to save energy and money at home, at work, and
    in the community. As in the news page, you will insert each list into its own
    `<section>` element.

5   In **green_tips.rtf**, select the text beginning with *At Home* and ending with
    Buy fruits and vegetables locally.
    Press Ctrl+X/Cmd+X to cut the text.

6   Switch back to Dreamweaver. In Design view, select the placeholder *Add main
    heading here* in `<article.content>`, and type **Green Tips** to replace it.

7   Select the placeholder heading *Add subheading here* and the paragraph text
    Add content here. Press Ctrl+V/Cmd+V to paste the text from the clipboard.

    The text for the first list section appears.

8   In **green_tips.rtf**, select and cut the text beginning with *At Work* and ending
    with *Buy natural cleaning products.*

9   In Dreamweaver, insert the pointer anywhere in the existing list of tips, and
    click the `<section>` tag selector.

    The entire `<section>` element and its contents are selected.

10 Press the right arrow key once to move the cursor after the closing `</section>`
    tag in the code.

11 Choose Insert > Structure > Section. Click OK in the Insert Section dialog to create a new `<section>` element.

The `<section>` element appears with placeholder text *Content for New Section Tag Goes Here* already selected.

12 Press Ctrl+V/Cmd+V to paste the text from the clipboard and replace the placeholder text in the new `<section>` element.

The second list appears in the new element. To create the last section, let's try using the Insert panel.

13 In **green_tips.rtf**, cut the list items for *In the community*.
You can close **green_tips.rtf**. Do not save any changes.

14 In Dreamweaver, insert the pointer anywhere in the second list.
Using the right arrow key as in step 10, move the cursor after the closing `</section>` tag.

15 Choose Window > Insert to open the Insert panel, if necessary.
In the Structure category, click the Section item to insert a new element.
In the Insert New Section dialog, click OK.

A new section appears with placeholder text.

16 Paste the list for *In the community*.

All three lists now appear in their own `<section>` elements.

As we did with the titles of the news stories, let's apply HTML headings to introduce the list categories.

17 Apply `<h2>` formatting to the text *At Home*, *At Work*, and *In the Community*.

The remaining text is currently formatted entirely as HTML paragraphs. Dreamweaver makes it easy to convert this text into an HTML list. Lists come in two flavors: ordered and unordered.

18 Select all the `<p>` elements under the heading At Home.
In the Property inspector, click the Ordered List icon ⊞.

An ordered list adds numbers automatically to the entire selection. Semantically, it prioritizes each item, giving them intrinsic values relative to one another. This list doesn't seem to be in any particular order; each item is more or less equal to the next one, so it's a good candidate for an unordered list—used when the items are in no particular order. Before you change the formatting, let's take a look at the markup.

19 Switch to Split view. Observe the list markup in the Code section of the document window.

```
52   <h2>At Home</h2>
53   <ol>
54   <li>Wash clothes in cold water</li>
55   <li>Hang clothes to dry</li>
56   <li>Turn off lights in empty rooms</li>
57   <li>Use motion sensors to turn lights on</li>
58   <li>Plan driving errands to combine trips</li>
```

The markup consists of two elements: <ol> and <li>. Note that each line is formatted as an <li> (list item). The <ol> parent element begins and ends the list and designates it as an ordered list. Changing the formatting from numbers to bullets is simple and can be done in Code or Design view.

Before changing the format, ensure that the formatted list is still entirely selected. You can use the <ol> tag selector, if necessary.

▶ **Tip:** The easiest way to select the entire list is to use the <ol> tag selector.

20 In the Property inspector, click the Unordered List icon ⊞.

```
52   <h2>At Home</h2>
53   <ul>
54   <li>Wash clothes in cold water</li>
55   <li>Hang clothes to dry</li>
56   <li>Turn off lights in empty rooms</li>
57   <li>Use motion sensors to turn lights on</li>
58   <li>Plan driving errands to combine trips</li>
```

mmtinstance:fileinstance </> body div .container div .main mmtinstance:editable article .content section

Properties				
<> HTML	Format None ▼	Class content ▼ **B** *I* ⊞	Title	
⊞ CSS	ID None ▼	Link ▼	Target ▼	
			Unordered List	
Document Title Meridian GreenStart -- Green Tips		Page Properties		

▶ **Tip:** You could also change the formatting by editing the markup manually in the Code view window. But don't forget to change both the opening and the closing parent elements.

All the items are now formatted as bullets.

If you observe the list markup, you'll notice that the only thing that has changed is the parent element. It now says <ul>, for *un*ordered list.

21 Select all the <p> formatted text under the heading *At Work*. In the Property inspector, click the Unordered List icon ⊞.

22 Repeat step 21 with all the text following the heading *In the Community*.

All three lists are now formatted with bullets.

23 In Dreamweaver, save all files.

Creating indented text

Some designers still use the `<blockquote>` element in Dreamweaver, and elsewhere, as an easy way to indent headings and paragraph text. Semantically, the `<blockquote>` element is intended to identify whole sections of text quoted from other sources. Visually, text formatted this way will appear indented and set off from the regular paragraph text and headings. But if you want to comply with web standards, you should leave this element for its intended purpose and instead use custom CSS classes when you want to indent text, as you will in this exercise.

1 Select Design view. Create a new page from the template **mygreen_temp**. Save the file as **contact_us.html** in the site root folder.

2 In the Property inspector, enter **Contact Meridien GreenStart** to replace the placeholder text *Add Title Here.*

3 In the Files panel, open **contact_us.rtf** from the Resources folder.

   The text consists of five department sections, including headings, descriptions, and email addresses for the managing staff of GreenStart. You will insert each department into its own `<section>` element.

4 In **contact_us.rtf**, select the first two introductory paragraphs, ending with *your questions:* and cut the text.

5 In Dreamweaver, enter **Contact Meridien GreenStart** to replace the placeholder heading *Add main heading here.*

6 Press Enter/Return to insert a new paragraph and paste the text.

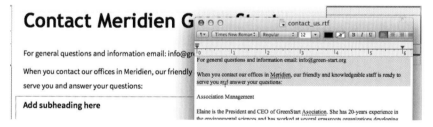

   The introductory text is inserted directly below the `<h1>` element. This text is not in the `<section>` element.

7 In **contact_us.rtf**, select the next four paragraphs that make up the *Association Management* section, and cut the text.

8 In Dreamweaver, in Design view, select the placeholder heading *Add subheading here* and the paragraph text *Add content here.*
   Press Ctrl+V/Cmd+V to paste the text.

9 Format the text *Association Management* as a Heading 2.

   The first section is completed.

10 In **contact_us.rtf**, select and cut the next four paragraphs that make up the *Education and Events* section.

11 Switch to Dreamweaver. Insert the cursor anywhere in the *Association Management* text, and click the `<section>` tag selector.
Move the cursor after the `<section>` element by pressing the right arrow key once.

Some Dreamweaver users prefer to make elements manually using the Quick Tag Editor.

12 Press Ctrl+T/Cmd+T to access the Quick Tag Editor.

The Quick Tag Editor appears.

With the cursor at its current position, Quick Tag Editor should default to Insert mode.

13 Type `<section>`, or double-click `section` in the hinting menu, and press Enter/Return to create the element.

You need to press Enter/Return a second time to close the Quick Tag Editor and create the element. Once created, you won't see any evidence of the new `<section>` element other than the tag selector display. Using this method, Dreamweaver creates the code but doesn't insert any placeholder text as it does with the Insert menu or panel options. To create content for the element, just start typing, or simply paste the text cut in step 10.

14 Paste the text from the clipboard.

15 Select the text *Education and Events*, and format it as a Heading 2.

16 Using any of the methods described above, create `<section>` elements for the remaining departments: *Transportation Analysis*, *Research and Development*, and *Information Systems.*

With all the text in place, you're ready to create the indent styling. If you wanted to indent a single paragraph, you would probably create and apply a custom class to the individual `<p>` element. In this instance, we want to indent the entire `<section>` element to produce the desired graphical effect.

First, let's assign a `class` attribute to the element. Since the class does not exist yet, you'll have to create it manually. This can be done in Live or Code views or in Design view using the Quick Tag Editor.

17 Insert the cursor anywhere in the *Association Management* `<section>` element. Click the `<section>` tag selector. Press Ctrl+T/Cmd+T.

The Quick Tag Editor appears, displaying the `<section>` tag. The cursor should appear at the end of the tag name.

18 Press the spacebar to insert a space.

The Code Hinting window appears, displaying the appropriate attributes for the `<section>` element.

19 Type **class** and press Enter/Return, or double-click the `class` attribute in the Code Hinting window.

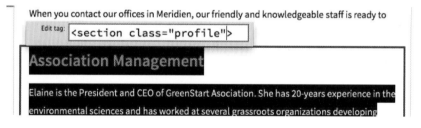

Note how Dreamweaver automatically creates the attribute markup and provides a list of any existing `class` attributes as you type. Since the class we want to use doesn't exist yet, you'll type the name yourself.

20 Type **profile** as the class name. Press Enter/Return as necessary to complete the attribute and close the Quick Tag Editor.

21 Select the new `.profile` tag selector.
Choose **mygreen_styles.css** > GLOBAL > `.content section h2`.
Click the Add Selector icon ➕.

The selector name `.main .content .profile` appears in the Selectors window.

22 Press the up arrow to remove `.main` from the selector name.
Press Enter/Return to complete the name.

The selector name should now appear as `.content .profile`.

23 Disable the Show Set option, if necessary.
Enter the following properties in the Properties window:

```
margin-right: 25px
margin-bottom: 15px
margin-left: 25px
```

Border specifications can be entered individually or all at once.

24 Click the Border category icon ☐.

25 Enter the following specifications for the left border:

```
border-left-width: 2px
border-left-style: solid
border-left-color: #cadaaf
```

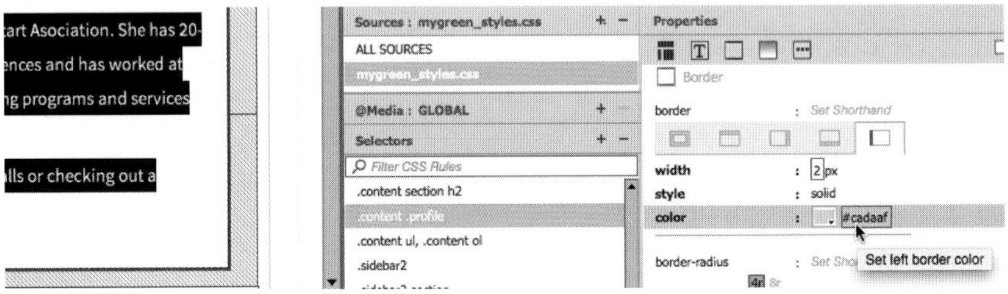

Entering the specifications all at once can often be faster and more efficient.

26 Select the Show Set option in the Properties window.

The window displays only properties that are set for the rule. It displays the specifications for the margins and the left border.

Tip: When creating specifications manually, enter the property name in the field and press tab. A value field will appear to the right. When Show Set is enabled no hinting appears in the values field.

27 Create the following shorthand property:
```
border-bottom: 10px solid #cadaaf
```

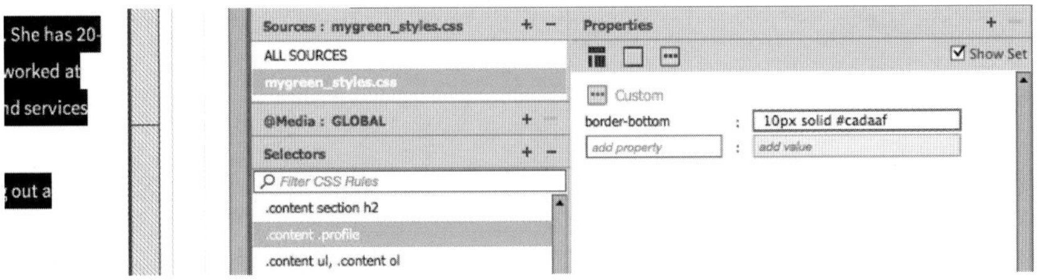

Borders appear on the left and bottom of the `section` element. The borders help to visually group the indented text under its heading.

28 Insert the cursor anywhere in the *Education and Events* section.
Click the `<section>` tag selector.

29 In the Properties inspector, choose **profile** from the Class menu.

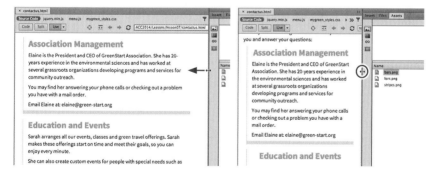

30 Repeat steps 28–29 to apply the `.profile` class to the remaining `<section>` elements.

Each section is indented and displays the custom border.

31 Save all files.

Whenever you add new components or styling to a site you need to make sure the elements and styling work well on all screen sizes and devices.

Making it responsive

In this exercise, you will test the new profile elements at multiple screen sizes and adapt them as needed.

1 If necessary, switch to Live view.

2 Drag the right edge of the screen to the left to make the document window narrower. Observe how the new components respond to the changing widths.

> **Tip:** When resizing the screen manually, make sure that no resolution switcher is currently selected. This will freeze the responsive function in the document window.

The `.profile` section looks fine until you get down to widths less than 480 pixels. At those sizes the left indent and border wastes too much space. You can fix this situation easily by simply adding alternate styling in the appropriate media query.

3 Restore the document window to its full width.

4 In the CSS Designer, choose `mygreen_styles.css` > `screen and (max-width: 480px)`

Create the following selector: `.content .profile`

5 Create the following properties in the new rule:

```
padding: 5px 0px 5px 0px
margin-top: 5px
border-top: 10px solid #cadaaf
border-bottom: 4px solid #cadaaf
border-left-style: none
```

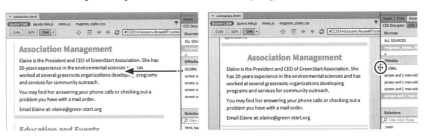

6 Save all files. Repeat steps 1–2 to test the new styling.

When the screen is smaller than 480 pixels, the `.profile` section expands to the full width of the screen and drops the indent and the left border. Remember to test all new components at every screen size and orientation and make changes to the styling as needed.

Creating and styling tables

Before the advent of CSS, HTML offered few tools to execute effective page designs. Instead, web designers resorted to using images and tables to create page layouts. Today, people steer clear of tables for page design and layout purposes for several reasons. Tables are hard to create, format, and modify. They can't adapt easily to different screen sizes or media types. And certain browsing devices and screen readers don't see the comprehensive page layouts; they only see tables for what they actually are: rows and columns of data.

When CSS debuted and was promoted as the preferred method for page design, some designers came to believe that tables were bad altogether. That was definitely an overreaction. Although tables are not good for page layout, they are very good, and necessary, for displaying many types of data, such as product lists, personnel directories, and timetables.

Dreamweaver enables you to create tables from scratch, to copy and paste them from other applications, or to create them instantly from data supplied by database or spreadsheet programs. You will learn how to create tables using several techniques in the following exercises.

Creating tables from scratch

Dreamweaver makes it easy to create tables from scratch.

1 Create a new page from the **mygreen_temp** template.
   Save the file as **events.html** in the site root folder.

2 Choose Modify > Page Properties.
   Enter **Green Events and Classes** to replace the *Title* placeholder text.

3 In Design view, select the *Add main heading here* placeholder heading, and type **Green Events and Classes** to replace it.

4 Press Enter/Return, and type the following text:
   Want to get involved? Want to learn a new skill? There's no time like the present. Check out our list of Green Events and Classes. The schedule is updated on a regular basis, so you may want to bookmark this page. Hope to see you soon!

5 Select the *Add subheading here* placeholder heading and the *Add content here* paragraph text. Press Delete.

6 Choose Insert > Table.

   The Table dialog appears.

   Some aspects of the table must be controlled and formatted by HTML attributes, but others can be controlled either by HTML or by CSS. Although you can use HTML avoid using it to format tables. As with text formatting, HTML is neither efficient nor flexible. The only advantage HTML has is that the attributes continue to be well supported by all popular browsers, both old and new. When you enter values in this dialog, Dreamweaver still applies them via HTML attributes.

> **Tip:** Whenever you select complete elements, it's a good practice to use the tag selectors.

7 Enter the following specification for the table:

Rows: **2**

Columns: **4**

Width: **500px**

Border thickness: **0**

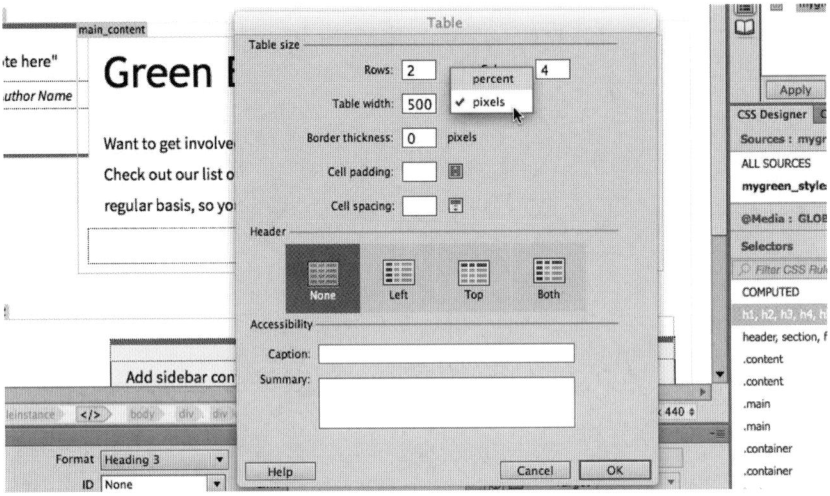

Tip: While in a table cell, pressing the Tab key moves the cursor to the next cell on the right. Hold the Shift key when pressing the Tab key to move to the left, or backward, through the table.

8 Click OK to create the table.

A four-column, two-row table appears below the main heading. Note that it is flush to the left side of the `<section>` element. The table is ready to accept input.

9 Insert the pointer in the first cell of the table.
Type **Date**, and press Tab to move into the next cell in the first row.

10 In the second cell, type **Event**, and press Tab.
Type **Location**, and press Tab.
Type **Cost**, and press Tab.

The cursor moves to the first cell of the second row.

11 In the second row, type **May 1** (in cell 1), **May Day Parade** (in cell 2), **City Hall** (in cell 3), and **Free** (in cell 4).

When the cursor is in the last cell, inserting additional rows in the table is easy.

12 Press Tab.

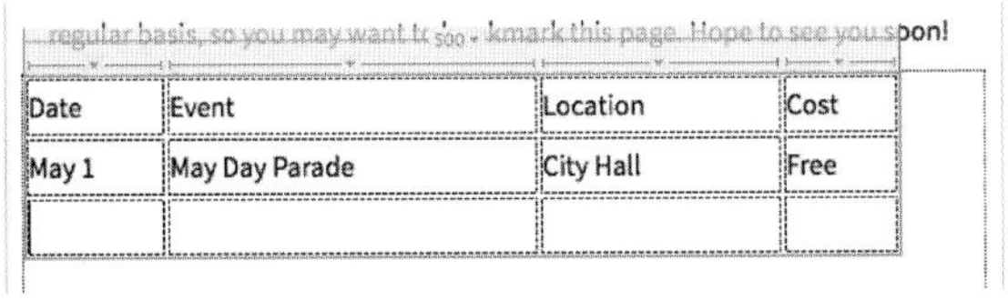

A new blank row appears at the bottom of the table. Dreamweaver also allows you to insert multiple new rows at once.

13 Select the `<table>` tag selector at the bottom of the document window.

The Property inspector displays the properties of the current table, including the total number of rows and columns.

14 Select the number 3 in the Rows field. Type **5**, and press Enter/Return to complete the change.

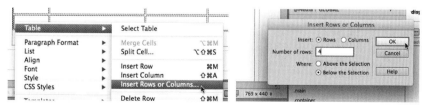

Dreamweaver adds two new rows to the table.

The fields in the Property inspector create HTML attributes to control various aspects of the table, including table width, width and height of cells, text alignment, and so on. You can also add rows and columns to the table interactively using the mouse.

15 Right-click the last row of the table. Choose Table > Insert Row from the context menu.

Another row is added to the table. The context menu can also insert multiple rows and/or columns at once.

16 Right-click on the last row of the table.
Choose Table > Insert Rows or Columns from the context menu.

The Insert Rows or Columns dialog appears.

17 Insert 4 rows below the selection, and click OK.

18 Save all files.

Copying and pasting tables

Although Dreamweaver allows you to create tables manually inside the program, you can also move tables from other HTML files or even other programs by using copy and paste.

1   Open the Files panel, and double-click **calendar.html** in the lesson08/resources folder to open it.

This HTML file opens in its own tab in Dreamweaver. Note the table structure—it has four columns and numerous rows.

2   Insert the cursor in the table.
Click the `<table>` tag selector.
Press Ctrl+C/Cmd+C to copy the table.

3   Click the **events.html** tab to bring that file to the front.

4   Insert the cursor in the table.
Select the `<table>` tag selector.
Press Ctrl+V/Cmd+V to paste the table.

The new table element completely replaces the existing table.

5   Save the file.

● **Note:** Dreamweaver allows you to copy and paste tables from some other programs, like Microsoft Word. Unfortunately, it doesn't work with every program.

Styling tables with CSS

Currently, all the formatting for the table is being supplied by HTML attributes. The table aligns to the left, touching the edge of the `<section>` element and stretching most of the way across it. CSS can also be used to format tables. CSS styles are more powerful than HTML-based formatting and will override them when they conflict. HTML attributes also have a disadvantage in that they must be applied to and edited for each table individually. On the other hand, CSS can control the formatting sitewide from a single style sheet. In the following exercise, you will create CSS rules to override the HTML styling.

1   If necessary, insert the pointer in the table.
Select the `table` tag selector.

2 In the CSS Designer, choose **mygreen_styles.css** > GLOBAL >
   `.content .profile`.
   Create a new selector `.content section table`.

3 In the CSS Designer Properties window, deselect the option Show Set,
   if necessary.

4 In the Type category, click to open the font-family property.
   Select Manage Fonts, and create the following custom font stack:

`"Arial Narrow", Arial, Verdana, sans-serif`

5 For the rule `.content section table` enter the following specifications:

```
width: 40em
margin-bottom: 2em
margin-left: 1em
font-family: "Arial Narrow", Arial, Verdana, sans-serif
font-size: 90%
border-bottom: 3px solid #060
```

The table resizes, moves away from the left edge of the `<section>` element,
and displays a dark green border at the bottom.

You have applied styling to one aspect of the table properties, but we can't stop there. The default formatting on the tags that comprise table markup is a hodgepodge of settings that are honored—or not—irregularly in various browsers. In other words, the default styling of a table can display differently in each browser that displays it.

One specific HTML attribute that may cause trouble is `cellspacing`, which produces a margin-like effect between individual cells. If you don't provide a specification for this attribute, some browsers may insert a small space between cells and may split any cell borders in two. In CSS, this attribute is address by the `border-collapse` property. If you don't want the table borders to be split inadvertently, you'll need to include this setting in the styling.

▶ **Tip:** Table styling may not appear properly in Design view. Switch to Live view to see the full effect of your CSS.

6 In the CSS Designer, select the rule `.content section table`
Select the Border category, and set the following property:

`border-collapse: collapse`

In Design view, you won't see any difference in how the tables are displayed, but don't let that dissuade you from the need for this attribute.

7 Save all files.

It's important to remember that the rule `.content section table` you just created will format the overall structure of tables inserted into the `<section>` element on any page using this style sheet throughout the site. Now we need to turn our attention to the inner workings of the tables. For example, you'll find that the widths of the individual columns are not controlled by the `<table>` element.

Styling table cells

Just as for tables, column styling can be applied by HTML attributes or CSS rules, with the same advantages and disadvantages discussed earlier. Formatting for columns is applied through two elements that create the individual cells: `<th>` for table header and `<td>` for table data.

It's a good idea to create a generic rule to reset the default formats of the `<th>` and `<td>` elements. Later, you will create custom rules to apply more specific settings.

1 Insert the cursor into any cell of the table.
In the CSS Designer, choose **mygreen_styles.css** > GLOBAL > `.content section table`.

2 Create a new selector `.content section td, .content section th`

This simplified selector will work fine.

3 In the Properties window, select the Show Set option.

4 Create the following properties for the rule `.content section td, .content section th`

```
padding: 5px
text-align: left
border-top: 1px solid #090
```

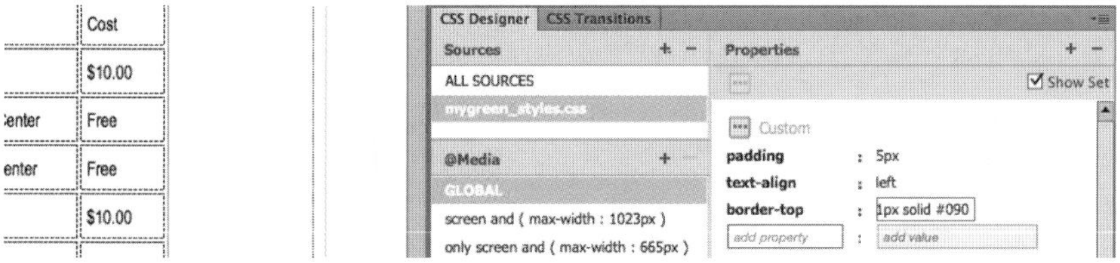

A thin green border appears above each row of the table, making the data easier to read. You may not be able to see the border properly unless you use Live view.

Long columns and rows of undifferentiated data can be tedious to read and hard to decipher. Headers are often used to help the reader identify data. By default, the text in header cells is formatted in bold and centered to help it stand out from the normal cells, but some browsers do not honor this default styling. So, don't count on it. You can make the headers stand out by giving them a touch of color of your own.

Note: Remember that the order of the rules can affect the style cascade as well as how and what styling is inherited.

5 Choose **mygreen_styles.css** > GLOBAL > `.content section td, .content section th`.

Create a new rule `.content section th`

6 Create the following properties in the `.content section th` rule:

```
color: #FFC
text-align: center
border-bottom: 6px solid #060
background-color: #090
```

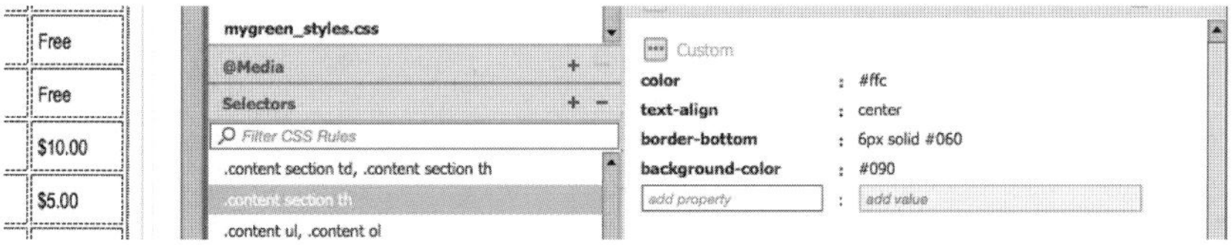

Note: Make sure that the standalone <th> rule for the <th> element appears after the rule styling th and td elements or some of its formatting will be reset.

The rule is created, but it still needs to be applied. Dreamweaver makes it easy to convert existing <td> elements into <th> elements.

<mark>Note:</mark> You cannot select more than one cell at a time in Live view.

7   In Design view, insert the cursor into the first cell of the first row of the table. In the Property inspector, select the Header option. Note the tag selector.

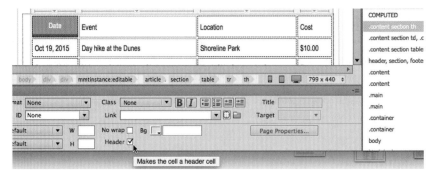

The cell background is filled with green.

When you click the Header checkbox, Dreamweaver automatically rewrites the markup, converting the existing `<td>` tags to `<th>` and thereby applying the CSS formatting. This functionality will save you lots of time over editing the code manually. You can also convert multiple cells at one time.

8   Insert the cursor into the second cell of the first row. Drag to select the remaining cells in the first row. Or, you can select an entire row at once by positioning the cursor at the left edge of the table row and clicking when you see the black selection arrow appear.

9   In the Property inspector, select the Header option to convert the table cells to header cells.

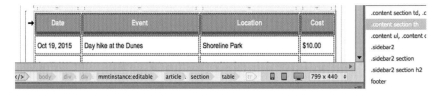

The whole first row is filled with green as the table cells are converted to header cells.

10 Save all files.

Controlling table display

Unless you specify otherwise, empty table columns will divide the available space between them equally. But once you start adding content to the cells, all bets are off—tables seem to get a mind of their own and divvy up the space in a different way. In most cases, they'll award more space to columns that contain more data, but that's not guaranteed to happen.

Allowing the table to decide for itself probably won't achieve acceptable spacing results; many designers resort to HTML attributes or custom CSS classes to control the width of the individual columns. This is especially important when you throw mobile devices into the mix. When you create custom styles to format column widths, you can base the rule names either on the width value itself or on the content, or subject, of the column. To provide the highest level of control, for the purposes of making the tables responsive, we'll assign unique classes to the cells in each column.

● **Note:** In HTML 4, rule names can't start with numerals or punctuation characters. In HTML5, these restrictions have been mostly relaxed. But it's probably still a good idea not to use periods (.) or hash marks (#) in your selector names.

1 Choose **mygreen_styles.css** > GLOBAL > `.content section th`.
   Create the following new rules:

   ```
   .content section .date
   .content section .event
   .content section .location
   .content section .cost
   ```

Four new rules appear in the Selectors window but contain no styling information. Even without styling, the classes can be assigned to each column. Dreamweaver makes it easy to apply classes to an entire column.

2 Position the pointer above the first column of the table until you see a black arrow. Click to select the entire column.

3 Choose `date` from the Class menu in the Property inspector.

   The cells in the first column should display `th.date` or `td.date` in the tag selector interface.

4 Repeat steps 2 and 3 to apply the appropriate classes to each column.

   Controlling the width of a column is quite simple. Since the entire column must be the same width, you only have to apply a width specification to one cell. If cells in a column have conflicting specifications, typically the largest width wins. Since you just applied a class to the entire Date column, settings will affect every cell at once. This will make it easier to get the table to adapt to any screen.

5 Add the following property to the rule `.content section .date`

```
width: 7em
```

The Date column resizes, although the change may not be visible in Design view. The remaining columns automatically divvy up the space left over. Column styling can also specify text alignment as well as width. Let's apply styling to the contents of the Cost column.

6 Add the following properties to the rule `.content section.cost`

```
width: 5em
text-align: center
```

The Cost column resizes to a width of 5 ems and the text aligns to the center. Now if you want to control the styling of the columns individually, you have the ability to do so. Note the tag selector shows the class names with each element, such as

`<th.cost>` or `<td.cost>`.

7 Save all files.

Inserting tables from other sources

In addition to creating tables by hand, you can also create them from data exported from databases and spreadsheets. In this exercise, you will create a table from data that was exported from Microsoft Excel to a comma-separated values (CSV) file. As with the other content models, you will first create a `<section>` element in which to insert the new table.

1 In Design view, insert the pointer anywhere in the existing table.
Select the `<section>` tag selector.
Press the right arrow key.

The cursor moves after the closing `</section>` tag.

2 Using any of the methods described earlier, insert a new `<section>` element.

3 Without moving the cursor, choose File > Import > Tabular Data.

The Import Tabular Data dialog appears.

4 Click the Browse button, and select **classes.csv** from the lesson08/resources folder. Click Open.

Comma should be automatically selected in the Delimiter menu.

5 Select the following options in the Import Tabular Data dialog:
Table width: **500 pixels**
Border: **0**

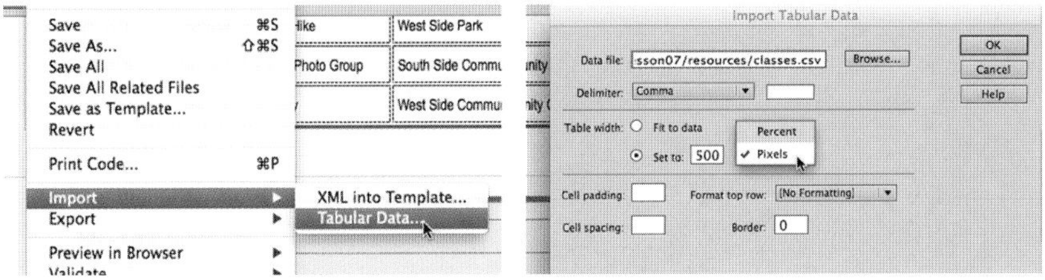

The table width will actually be controlled by the table rule created earlier, but HTML attributes will be honored in browsers or devices that do not support CSS. Because this is the case, make sure that the HTML attributes you use don't break the layout.

6 Click OK.

A new table—containing a class (course) schedule—appears below the first. The new table consists of five columns with multiple rows. The first row contains header information but is still formatted as normal table cells.

7 Select the first row of the Class schedule.
In the Property inspector, select the Header option.

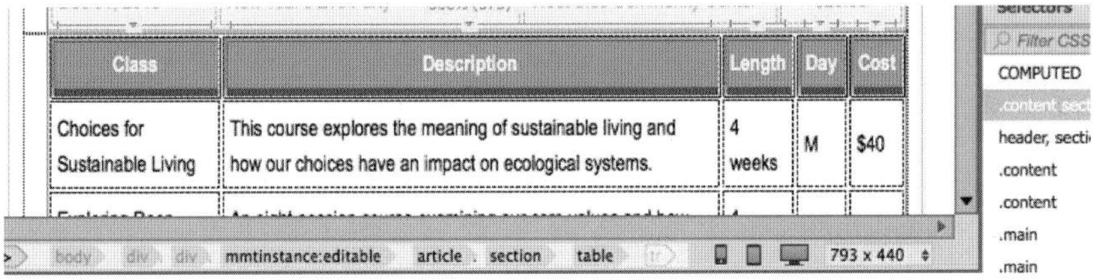

The background of the first row instantly fills with green and with reversed text. You'll notice that the text data is wrapping awkwardly in the last three columns. You will use the .cost class created earlier for the Cost column in the new table, but the other two will need custom classes of their own.

8 Select the entire Cost column as you did in the previous exercise.
In the Property inspector, choose cost from the Class menu.

The two Cost columns are now the same width.

9 In the CSS Designer, right-click the rule .content section .cost. Choose Duplicate from the context menu.

10 Enter `.content section .day` in the new Selector Name field.
Press Enter/Return to create the new rule.

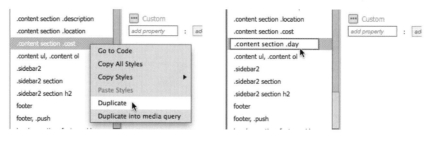

11 Repeat step 8 to apply the day class to the Day column in the Classes table.

12 Duplicate the rule `.content section .day`.
Enter `.content section length` as the new rule name.
Apply the `length` class to the Length column in the Classes table.

By creating custom classes for each column, you have the means to modify each column individually. We need to make two more rules: one to format the Class column and the other to format the Description column.

13 Duplicate the rule `.content section .date`.
Enter `.content section .class` as the new rule name.
Change the width to `10em`.

14 Duplicate the rule `.content section .event`.
Enter .content section `.description` as the new rule name.

15 Apply the `class` class to the Class column.
Apply the `description` class to the Description column.

All columns in both tables now have classes assigned to them.

16 Save all files.

Adjusting vertical alignment

If you study the content of the Classes table, you will notice that many of the cells contain paragraphs that wrap to multiple lines. When cells in a row have differing amounts of text in them, by default the shorter content is aligned vertically to the middle of the cell. Many designers find this behavior unattractive and prefer to have the text align to the tops of the cells. As with most of the other attributes, vertical alignment can be applied by HTML attributes or CSS. To control the vertical alignment with CSS, you can add the specification to one of our newly created rules.

1 In the Sources window, select **mygreen_style.css**.
Select the `.content section th, .content section td` rule.

The <th> and <td> elements style the text stored in the table cells.

2 In the Properties window, create the following property:

`vertical-align: top`

All the text in both tables now aligns to the top of the cells.

3 Save all files.

Adding and formatting caption elements

The two tables you inserted on the page contain different information but don't feature any differentiating labels or titles. To help users distinguish between the two sets of data, let's add a title to each and a bit of extra spacing. The `<caption>` element was designed to identify the content of HTML tables. This element is inserted as a child of the `<table>` element itself.

1 Insert the cursor in the first table. Select the `<table>` tag selector. Switch to Code view.

By selecting the table first in Design view, Dreamweaver automatically highlights the code in Code view, making it easier to find.

2 Locate the opening `<table>` tag. Insert the cursor directly after this tag. Type `<caption>` or select it from the code-hinting menu when it appears.

3 Type **2015-16 Event Schedule**, and then type `</` to close the element.

```
        you soon!</p>
52   <section>
53   <table>
54   <caption>2015-16 Event Schedule</caption>
55   <tr>
56   <th class="date">Date</th>
57   <th class="event">Event</th>
58   <th class="location">Location</th>
```

4 Switch to Design view.

The caption is complete and inserted as a child element of the table.

5 Repeat steps 5-16 for the second table.
Type **2013-14 Class Schedule** and then type `</` to close the element.

6 Switch to Design view.

The captions are relatively small, and they're lost against the color and formatting of the table. Let's beef them up a bit with a custom CSS rule.

7 Select the rule `.content section table`.

Create a new selector `.content section caption`.

8 Create the following properties for the rule `.content section caption`:

```
margin-top: 20px
padding-bottom: 20px
color: #090
font-weight: bold
font-size: 160%
line-height: 1.2em
```

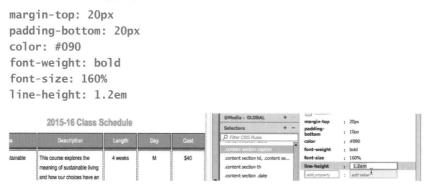

9 Save all files.

10 Examine your work using Live view or a browser.

Formatting the tables and the captions with CSS has made them much easier to read and understand. Feel free to experiment with the size and placement of the caption and specifications affecting the tables.

Making tables responsive

The tables are finished and ready to go. They should work fine for normal desktop displays, but the underlying page design is built to work seamlessly all the way down to smartphones. Tables are notoriously ill-suited for smaller screens because they don't naturally adapt to them. To understand this concept, let's see how they function on a smaller screen.

1 If necessary, open **events.html** in Dreamweaver.

Design view doesn't provide an accurate rendition of the tables; Live view would be a better choice, but the best option is to actually view the page in a browser.

2 Choose File > Preview in Browser. Choose your favorite browser from the list.

The page opens in the browser, displaying all the colors, fonts, background images, and other CSS specifications set by the style sheet. To see how the tables will react to a smaller screen, just resize the browser window.

3 Drag the right edge of the browser window to the left to make it narrower. Watch carefully how the tables respond, or not, to the changing environment.

As the screen becomes narrower, the media queries will kick in and reformat the page and components to adapt to the smaller screen. Everything seems to work fine in the desktop and tablet sizes down to about 810 pixels, just before the last media query kicks in for smartphones. At that point, the screen starts to cut off the right edge of the tables. If you keep dragging the edge of the window, you'll see it happen again after the last media query kicks in and the screen gets narrower than 620 pixels.

Unlike the headline text, which adapts by wrapping or resizing to fit the changing window, the tables simply stick to their original widths and become truncated. There are several approaches for making tables more responsive. Some use JavaScript or jQuery to apply structural or stylistic changes. Others rely solely on CSS to reformat and restyle the tables. We'll take the latter approach.

We could use the existing media queries to format the tables, but from the tests we just conducted it was obvious that the tables started to break before the last media query kicked in. In this case, we can add a new media query geared to format only tables whenever the screen is 810 pixels wide or smaller.

4 In CSS Designer, select **mygreen_styles.css** in the Sources window.

5 Click the Add Media Query icon ➕ in the @Media window.

6 Create the following media query and click OK:

```
media: screen AND
max-width: 810 px
```

Media queries can be written to work exclusively or in tandem. The current style sheet formats four different conditions: general appearance, screens 1024 pixels wide and smaller, screens 665 pixels wide and smaller, and screens 480 pixels and smaller. Settings added to this new specification will override the general styles and those in the first media query whenever they conflict, but not those in the remaining media queries. Since the tables seem to have trouble only when the screen dips below 811 pixels, you'll only need to add styles to the new media query to fix the problems entirely. The new media query shouldn't interfere with any of the styling provided by the existing rules.

To start, we'll need to change the nature of the elements that comprise tables so we can display them in a completely different way. In some cases, it will be easier to work in the CSS Designer; at other times you may enter the settings directly in Code view. Feel free to use whichever method feels more comfortable to you.

7 Switch to Live view and open the CSS Designer, if necessary.
Choose **mygreen_styles.css** > `screen and (max-width:810px)`.
Create a new selector `table, thead, tbody, tr, th, td, caption`.

8 Add the `display: block` property to the new rule.

The cells are now displayed vertically, stacking one atop the other. This rule resets the default behavior of the table elements so that we can control their appearance on smaller screens. Some cells appear narrower than others because formatting is still being inherited from other parts of the style sheet. You'll have to create additional rules to override these specifications.

Note: Be sure that all subsequent rules and properties are added only to the new media query for max-width 810 pixels, created in step 6. For specific instructions, refer back to the sidebar "Rules of order" in Lesson 5, "Creating a Page Layout."

9 Create a new rule `.content section table` with the following properties:

```
width: 95%
margin-right: auto
margin-left: auto
```

This rule resets the width of the table to be flexible. It will now scale with the rest of the page elements. With the data stacking vertically, it doesn't make much sense now to have a header row. We could set the header row to use the `display:none` property to hide it, but that's not recommended for accessibility standards. The next best thing would be to simply format it to take up no space.

10 Create a new rule `.content section th` with the following properties:

```
height: 0px;
margin: 0px;
padding: 0px;
border: none;
overflow: hidden;
```

The header rows disappear visually, but are still accessible to visitors using screen readers or other assistive devices. But now that they are invisible, we have to address the fact that there are no headers describing the data being displayed. For this purpose, we'll resort to a new CSS3 property that can actually create labels based on the CSS class applied to the cell. Some of the latest CSS3 properties are not directly supported in the CSS Designer, but you can enter them manually in the Properties window or in Code view, and Dreamweaver may provide hinting support for them, as well.

11 Create the new `td.date:before` rule.

12 Enable the Show Set option in the Properties window.

Enter the following custom property:value combo:

```
content:"Date:"
```

Notice how the label "Date:" appears in all the cells styled by the `.date` class. You need to make a similar rule for each of the data elements.

13 Repeat steps 11 and 12 to create the following rules and properties:

Rule	Property:Value
`td.event:before`	`content: "Event:"`
`td.location:before`	`content: "Location:"`
`td.cost:before`	`content: "Cost:"`
`td.class:before`	`content: "Class:"`
`td.description:before`	`content: "Description:"`
`td.day:before`	`content: "Day:"`
`td.length:before`	`content: "Length:"`

Each data cell now shows the appropriate labels. CSS can also style the data and labels.

Note: Although the formatting is identical for these rules at this point, you may want to adjust the styling for one or more items later. Keeping the rules separate can add flexibility even though it adds to the amount of code that has to be downloaded.

14 Create the following rules:

```
.content section .date
.content section .event
.content section .location
.content section .cost
.content section .class
.content section .description
.content section .length
.content section .day
```

As long as the styling for all the data cells is identical, feel free to combine all the rules into a single selector, separated by commas. Remember to mind the punctuation and spelling carefully. Even a tiny error in the code can cause the formatting to fail. Next, let's apply some styling to the labels themselves to help make them stand out more distinctly.

15 Apply the following properties to each rule or in the compound rule:

```
width: auto
display: block
padding-left: 30%
position: relative
text-align: left
```

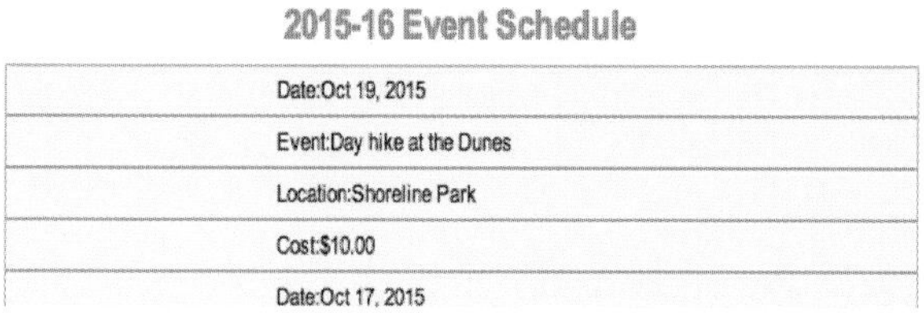

2015-16 Event Schedule

Date:Oct 19, 2015
Event:Day hike at the Dunes
Location:Shoreline Park
Cost:$10.00
Date:Oct 17, 2015

The event and class entries are now indented, and all appear at the same width.

16 Create a new rule `td:before` with the following properties:

```
width: 25%
display: block
padding-right: 10px
position: absolute
top: 6px
left: 1em
color: #060
font-weight: bold
white-space: nowrap
```

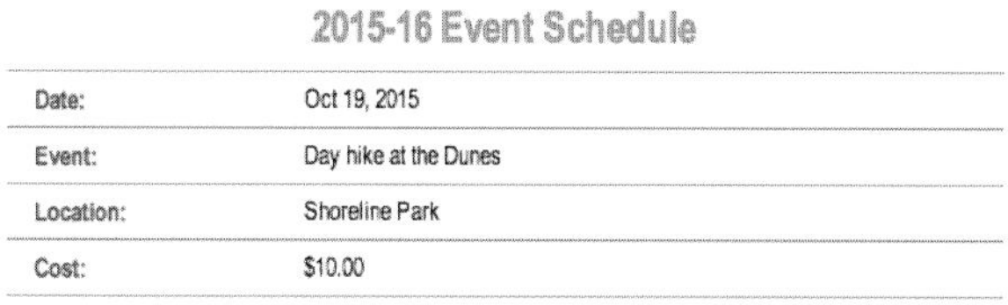

2015-16 Event Schedule

Date:	Oct 19, 2015
Event:	Day hike at the Dunes
Location:	Shoreline Park
Cost:	$10.00

The labels now appear separately from the data and are styled in boldface and dark green. The only thing left to do now is to differentiate one record from the next. One way is to simply add a darker border between each table row.

17 Create a new rule `.content section tr` with the following property:
`border-bottom: 2px solid #060`

Using a CSS3 selector will add a little more pizazz to the table.

18 Create a new rule `tr:nth-of-type(odd)` with the following property:
`background-color: #d4ead4`

This CSS3-based selector actually applies the background only on odd rows of the table.

Both tables are now slickly styled and responsive to any changes in the screen size. But, although they look good in Live view, don't get complacent, it's vital to test the design in a variety of browsers and mobile devices, too.

19 Save all files. Preview the page in the default browser. Test the media queries and the responsive table styling by changing the size of the browser window.

Congratulations! You've learned not only how to insert HTML tables into your web pages but also how to make them adapt to almost any screen environment. It's very likely that everything you tried in this exercise worked perfectly in both Dreamweaver and any browser you tested it in. But you have to remember that CSS3 is still fairly new and has not been fully adopted within the industry. The good news is that most of the mobile devices we're targeting should support the various settings used in this exercise. And you can be sure Dreamweaver will stay current with the latest updates.

Spellchecking web pages

It's important to ensure that the content you post to the web is error free. Dreamweaver includes a robust spellchecker capable of identifying commonly misspelled words and creating a custom dictionary for nonstandard terms that you might use on a regular basis.

Note: Spellcheck will run only in Design view. If you are in Code view, Dreamweaver will switch to Design view automatically. If you are in Live view, the command will be unavailable.

1 Click the **contact_us.html** tab to bring that document to the front, or open it from the site root folder.

2 Switch to Design view. Insert the pointer at the beginning of the main heading *Contact Meridien GreenStart* in `<article.content>`.
Choose Commands > Check Spelling.

Spellchecking starts wherever the pointer has been inserted. If the pointer is located lower on the page, you will have to restart the spellcheck at least once to examine the entire page. It also does not check content locked in noneditable template regions.

The Check Spelling dialog highlights the word *Meridien*, which is the name of the fictional city where our GreenStart association is located. You could click Add To Personal to insert the word into your custom dictionary but, for now, we will skip over other occurrences of the name during this check.

3 Click Ignore All.

Dreamweaver's spellchecker highlights the word *GreenStart*, which is the name of the association. If GreenStart was the name of your own company, you'd want to add it to your custom dictionary. However, you don't want to add a fictional company name to your dictionary.

4 Click Ignore All again.

Dreamweaver highlights the domain for the email address *info@greenstart.org*.

5 Click Ignore All.

Dreamweaver highlights the word *Asociation*, which is missing an "s."

6 To correct the spelling, locate the correctly spelled word (Association) in the Suggestions list, and double-click it.

7 Continue the spellcheck to the end.
Correct any misspelled words and ignore proper names, as necessary.
If a dialog prompts you to start the check from the beginning, click Yes.

Dreamweaver will start spellchecking from the top of the file to catch any words it may have missed.

8 Click OK when the spellcheck is complete. Save the file.

It's important to point out that spellcheck is only designed to find words that are *spelled* incorrectly. It will not find words that are *used* incorrectly. In those instances, nothing takes the place of a careful reading of the content.

Finding and replacing text

The ability to find and replace text is one of Dreamweaver's most powerful features. Unlike other programs, Dreamweaver can find almost anything, anywhere in your site, including text, code, and any type of whitespace that can be created in the program. You can search the entire markup, or you can limit the search to just the rendered text in Design view or to just the underlying tags. Advanced users can enlist powerful pattern-matching algorithms called *regular expressions* to perform sophisticated find-and-replace operations. And then Dreamweaver takes it one step further by allowing you to replace the targeted text or code with similar amounts of text, code, and whitespace.

In this exercise, you'll learn some important techniques for using the Find and Replace feature.

1 Click the **events.html** tab to bring that file to the front, or open the file from the site root folder.

There are several ways to identify the text or code you want to find. One way is simply to type it in the Find field. In the Events table, the name *Meridien* was spelled incorrectly as *Meridian*. Since *Meridian* is an actual word, the spellchecker won't flag it as an error and give you the opportunity to correct it. So, you'll use find and replace to make the change instead.

2 Switch to Design view, if necessary.
Insert the pointer in the *Green Events and Classes* heading.
Choose Edit > Find and Replace.

The Find and Replace dialog appears. The Find field is empty.

3 Type **Meridian** in the Find field. Type **Meridien** in the Replace field.
Choose Current Document from the Find In menu, and choose Text from the Search menu.

4 Click Find Next.

Dreamweaver finds the first occurrence of *Meridian*.

5 Click Replace.

Dreamweaver replaces the first instance of *Meridian* and immediately searches for the next instance. You can continue to replace the words one at a time, or you can choose to replace all occurrences.

6 Click Replace All.

If you replace the words one at a time, Dreamweaver inserts a one-line notice at the bottom of the dialog that tells you how many items were found and how many were replaced. When you click Replace All, Dreamweaver closes the Find and Replace dialog and opens the Search report panel, which lists all the changes made.

7 Right-click the Search report tab, and select Close Tab Group from the context menu.

Another method for targeting text and code is to select it *before* activating the command. This method can be used in either Design or Code view.

8 In Design view, locate and select the first occurrence of the text *Burkeline Mountains Resort* in the Location column of the Events table. Choose Edit > Find and Replace.

The Find and Replace dialog appears. The selected text is automatically entered into the Find field by Dreamweaver. This technique is even more powerful when used in Code view.

9 Close the Find and Replace dialog. Switch to Code view.

10 With the pointer still inserted in the *Burkeline Mountains Resort* text, click the `<tr>` tag selector at the bottom of the document window.

11 Choose Edit > Find and Replace. The Find and Replace dialog appears.

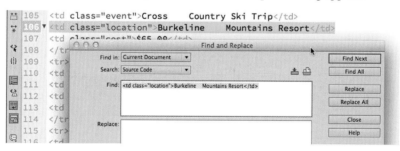

Observe the Find field. The selected code is automatically entered into the Find field by Dreamweaver in its entirety, including the line breaks and other whitespace. The reason this is so amazing is that there's no way to enter this type of markup in the dialog manually.

12 Select the code in the Find field. Press Delete to remove it. Type `<tr>`, and press Enter/Return to insert a line break. Observe what happens.

Pressing Enter/Return did not insert a line break; instead, it activated the Find command, which finds the first occurrence of the `<tr>` element. In fact, you can't manually insert any type of line break within the dialog.

You probably don't think this is much of a problem, since you've already seen that Dreamweaver inserts text or code when it's selected first. Unfortunately, the method used in step 8 doesn't work with large amounts of text or code.

13 Close the Find and Replace dialog box. Click the `<table>` tag selector.

The entire markup for the table is selected.

14 Choose Edit > Find and Replace. Observe the Find field.

This time, Dreamweaver didn't transfer the selected code into the Find field. To get larger amounts of text or code into the Find field, and to enter large amounts of replacement text and code, you need to use copy and paste.

15 Close the Find and Replace dialog. Select the table again, if necessary. Right-click the selected code, and choose Copy from the context menu.

16 Press Ctrl+F/Cmd+F to activate the Find and Replace command. Right-click the Find field, and choose Paste from the context menu.

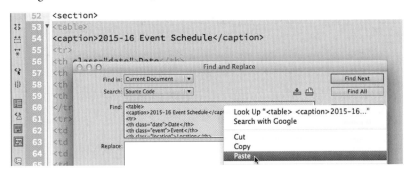

The entire `<table>` selection is pasted into the Find field.

17 Insert the cursor into the Replace field, and press Ctrl+V/Cmd+V.

The entire selection is pasted into the Replace field. Obviously, the two fields contain identical markup, but it illustrates how easy it would be to change or replace large amounts of code.

18 Close the Find and Replace dialog. Save all files.

In this lesson, you created four new pages and learned how to import text from multiple sources. You formatted text as headings and lists, and then styled it using CSS. You inserted and formatted tables, added captions to each one, and styled them to make them responsive. And you reviewed and corrected text using Dreamweaver's spellcheck and Find and Replace tools.

Superpowerfindelicious!

Note the options in the Find In and Search menus. The power and flexibility of Dreamweaver shines brightest here. The Find and Replace command can search in selected text, the current document, all open documents, in a specific folder, in selected files of the site, or the entire current local site. But as if those options weren't enough, Dreamweaver also allows you to target the search to the source code, text, advanced text, or even a specific tag.

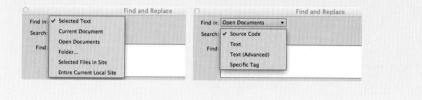

Optional self-paced exercise

At the end of the lesson, the four pages created are only partially completed. Before proceeding to the next lesson, go ahead and finish each page using the resources in the files **quotes08.txt** and **sidebar2_08.txt**, located in the resources folder. If you have any questions about how the content should be created or formatted, check out the finished files with the same names, within the site root folder for lesson08. Be sure to save all your changes when you are finished.

Review questions

1 How do you format text to be an HTML heading?

2 Explain how to turn paragraph text into an ordered list and then an unordered list.

3 Describe two methods for inserting HTML tables into a web page.

4 What element controls the width of a table column?

5 What items will not be found by Dreamweaver's spellcheck command?

6 Describe three ways to insert content in the Find field.

Review answers

1 Use the Format field menu in the Property inspector to apply HTML heading formatting, or press Ctrl+1/Cmd+1, Ctrl+2/Cmd+2, Ctrl+3/Cmd+3, and so on.

2 Highlight the text with the cursor, and click the Ordered List button in the Property inspector. Then click the Unordered List button to change the numbered formatting to bullets.

3 You can copy and paste a table from another HTML file or a compatible program. Or, you can insert a table by importing the data from a delimited file.

4 The width of a table column is controlled by the widest <th> or <td> element that creates the individual table cell within the specific column.

5 The spellcheck command finds only words *spelled* incorrectly, not the ones *used* incorrectly.

6 You can type text into the Find field; you can select text before you open the dialog and then allow Dreamweaver to insert the selected text; or you can copy the text or code and then paste it into the field.

9

WORKING WITH IMAGES

Lesson overview

In this lesson, you'll learn how to work with images to include them in your web pages in the following ways:

- Inserting an image

- Using Photoshop Smart Objects

- Copying and pasting an image from Photoshop and Fireworks

 This lesson will take about 1 hour and 30 minutes to complete. If you have not already done so, download the project files for this lesson from the Lesson & Update Files tab on your Account page at www.peachpit.com, and store them on your computer in a convenient location, and define a site based on the lesson09 folder as described in the "Getting Started" section of this book. Your Account page is also where you'll find any updates to the lessons or to the lesson files. Look on the Lesson & Update Files tab to access the most current content.

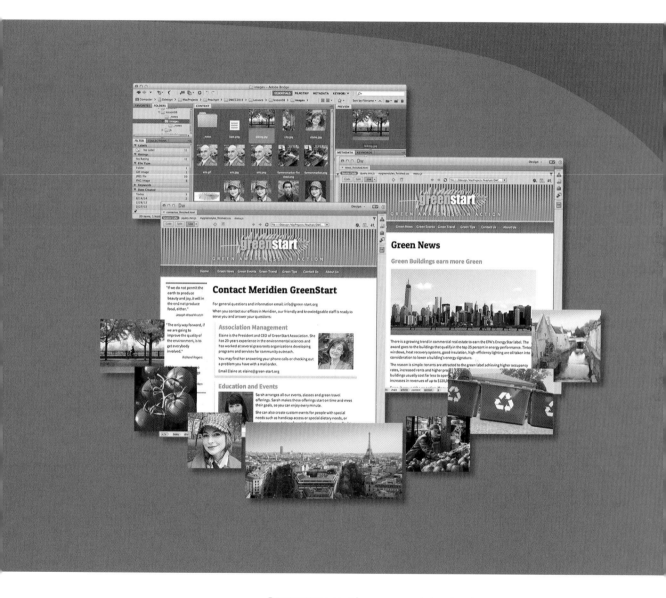

Dreamweaver provides many ways to insert and adjust graphics, both within the program and in tandem with other Creative Suite tools such as Adobe Fireworks and Adobe Photoshop.

Web image basics

● **Note:** If you have not already downloaded the project files for this lesson to your computer from your Account page, make sure to do so now. See "Getting Started" at the beginning of the book.

Vector graphic formats excel in line art, drawings, and logo art. Raster technology works better for storing photographic images.

The web is not as much a place as it is an experience. And essential to that experience are the images and graphics—both still and animated—that populate most websites. In the computer world, graphics fall into two main categories: *vector* and *raster*.

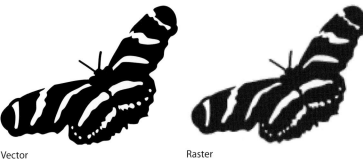

Vector   Raster

Vector graphics

Vector graphics are created by math. They act like discrete objects, which you can reposition and resize as many times as you want without affecting or diminishing their output quality. The best application of vector art is wherever geometric shapes and text are used to create artistic effects. For example, most company logos are built from vector shapes.

Vector graphics are typically stored in the AI, EPS, PICT, or WMF file formats. Unfortunately, most web browsers don't support these formats. The vector format that is supported is SVG (scalable vector graphic). The simplest way to get started with SVG is to create a graphic in your favorite vector-drawing program—like Adobe Illustrator or CorelDRAW—and then export it to this format. If you are a good programmer, you may want to try creating SVG graphics using XML (Extensible Markup Language). To find out more about creating SVG graphics, check out www.w3schools.com/svg.

Raster graphics

Although SVG has definite advantages, web designers primarily use raster-based images in their web designs. Raster images are built from *pixels*, which stands for *picture elements*. Pixels have three basic characteristics:

- They are perfectly square in shape.
- They are all the same size.
- They display only one color at a time.

Raster-based images are composed of thousands, even millions, of pixels arranged in rows and columns, in patterns that create the illusion of an actual photo, painting, or drawing. It's an illusion, because there is no real photo on the screen, just a bunch of pixels that fool your eyes into seeing an image. And as the quality of the image increases, the more realistic the illusion becomes. Raster-image quality is based on three factors: resolution, size, and color.

The inset image shows an enlargement of the flowers, revealing the pixels that comprise the image itself.

Resolution

Resolution is the most well known of the factors affecting raster image quality. It is the expression of image quality, measured in the number of pixels that fit in one inch (ppi). The more pixels you can fit in one inch, the more detail you can depict in the image. But better quality comes at a price. An unfortunate byproduct of higher resolution is larger file size. That's because each pixel must be stored as bytes of information within the image file—information that has real overhead in computer terms. More pixels mean more information, which means larger files.

Note: Printers and printing presses use round "dots" to create photographic images. Quality on a printer is measured in dots per inch, or dpi. The process of converting the square pixels used in your computer into the round dots used on the printer is called screening.

Resolution has a dramatic effect on image output. The web image on the left looks fine in the browser but doesn't have enough quality for printing.

72 ppi

300 ppi

Luckily, web images only have to appear, and look their best, on computer screens, which are based mostly on a resolution of 72 ppi. This is low compared to other applications or output—like printing, where 300 dpi is considered the lowest acceptable quality. The lower resolution of the computer screen is an important factor in keeping most web image files down to a reasonable size for downloading from the Internet.

Size

Size refers to the vertical and horizontal dimensions of the image. As image size increases, more pixels are required to create it, and therefore the file becomes larger. Since graphics take more time to download than HTML code, many designers in recent years have replaced graphical components with CSS formatting to speed up the web experience for their visitors. But if you need or want to use images, one method to ensure snappy downloads is to keep image size small. Even today, with the proliferation of high-speed Internet service, you won't find too many websites that depend on full-page graphics.

Although these two images share the identical resolution and color depth, you can see how image dimensions can affect file size.

500KB

1.6MB

Color

Color refers to the color space, or *palette*, that describes each image. Most computer screens display only a fraction of the colors that the human eye can see. And different computers and applications display varying levels of color, expressed by the term *bit depth*. Monochrome, or 1-bit color, is the smallest color space, displaying only black and white, with no shades of gray. Monochrome is used mostly for line-art illustrations, for blueprints, and to reproduce handwriting.

The 4-bit color space describes up to 16 colors. Additional colors can be simulated by a process called *dithering*, where the available colors are interspersed and juxtaposed to create an illusion of more colors. This color space was created for the first color computer systems and game consoles. Because of its limitations, this palette is seldom used today.

The 8-bit palette offers up to 256 colors or 256 shades of gray. This is the basic color system of all computers, mobile phones, game systems, and handheld devices. This color space also includes what is called the *web-safe* color palette. Web-safe refers to a subset of 8-bit colors that are supported on both Mac and Windows computers. Most computers, game consoles, handheld devices and even phones now support higher color palettes, so 8-bit is not as important any more. Unless you need to support non-computer devices, you can probably disregard the web-safe palette altogether.

Today, a few older cell phones and handheld games support the 16-bit color space. This palette is called *high color* and sports a grand total of 65,000 colors. Although this sounds like a lot, 16-bit color is not considered good enough for most graphic design purposes or professional printing.

The highest color space is 24-bit color, which is called *true color*. This system generates up to 16.7 million colors. It is the gold standard for graphic design and professional printing. Several years ago, a new color space was added to the mix: 32-bit color. It doesn't offer any additional colors, but it provides an additional eight bits of data for an attribute called *alpha transparency*.

Alpha transparency enables you to designate parts of an image or graphic as fully or even partially transparent. This trick allows you to create graphics that seem to have rounded corners or curves, and can even eliminate the white bounding box typical of raster graphics.

Here you can see a dramatic comparison of three color spaces and what the total number of available colors means to image quality.

24-bit color   8-bit color   4-bit color

As with size and resolution, color depth can dramatically affect image file size. With all other aspects being equal, an 8-bit image is over seven times larger than a monochrome image. And the 24-bit version is over three times larger than the 8-bit image. The key to effective use of images on a website is finding the balance of resolution, size, and color to achieve the desired optimal quality.

Raster image file formats

Raster images can be stored in a multitude of file formats, but web designers have to be concerned with only three: GIF, JPEG, and PNG. These three formats are optimized for the Internet and compatible with most browsers. However, they are not equal in capability.

GIF

GIF (graphic interchange format) was one of the first raster image file formats designed specifically for the web. It has changed only a little in the last 20 years. GIF supports a maximum of 256 colors (8-bit palette) and 72 ppi, so it's used mainly for web interfaces—buttons and graphical borders and such. But it does have two interesting features that keep it pertinent for today's web designers: index transparency and support for simple animation.

JPEG

JPEG, also written JPG, is named for the Joint Photographic Experts Group that created the image standard back in 1992 as a direct reaction to the limitations of the GIF file format. JPEG is a powerful format that supports unlimited resolution, image dimensions, and color depth. Because of this, most digital cameras use JPEG as their default file type for image storage. It's also the reason most designers use JPEG on their websites for images that must be displayed in high quality.

This may sound odd to you, since "high quality" (as described earlier) usually means large file size. Large files take longer to download to your browser. So why is this format so popular on the web? The JPEG format's claim to fame comes from its patented user-selectable image compression algorithm, which can reduce file size as much as 95 percent. JPEG images are compressed each time they are saved and then decompressed before they are opened and displayed.

Unfortunately, all this compression has a downside. Too much compression damages image quality. This type of compression is called *lossy*, because it loses quality. In fact, the loss in quality is great enough it can potentially render the image totally useless. Each time designers save a JPEG image, they face a trade-off between image quality and file size.

Here you see the effects of different amounts of compression on the file size and quality of an image.

Low quality
High compression
130K

Medium quality
Medium compression
150K

High quality
Low compression
260K

PNG

PNG (portable network graphics) was developed in 1995 because of a looming patent dispute involving the GIF format. At the time, it looked as if designers and developers would have to pay a royalty for using the .gif file extension. Although that issue blew over, PNG has found many adherents and a home on the Internet because of its capabilities.

PNG combines many of the features of GIF and JPEG, and adds a few of its own. For example, it offers support for unlimited resolution, 32-bit color, and full alpha and index transparency. It also provides lossless compression, which means you can save an image in PNG format and not worry about losing any quality when you save the file.

The only downside to PNG is that its most important feature—alpha transparency—is not fully supported in older browsers. As these browsers are retired year after year, this issue is not much of a concern to most web designers.

But, as with everything on the web, your own needs may vary from the general trend. Before using any specific technology, it's always a good idea to check your site analytics and confirm which browsers your visitors are actually using.

Previewing the completed file

To get a sense of the files you will work on in this lesson, let's preview the completed pages in the browser.

1 Launch Adobe Dreamweaver CC (2014.1 release or later).

2 If necessary, select lesson09 from Site dropdown menu in the Files panel.

3 Open **contactus_finished.html** from the lesson09 folder.
  Preview the page in your favorite browser.

  The page includes several images, as well as a Photoshop Smart Object.

4 Drag the right edge of the browser to resize the window.
  Observe how the layout and images adapt to the changing screen size.

Note: If you have not already downloaded the project files for this lesson to your computer from your Account page, make sure to do so now. See "Getting Started" at the beginning of the book.

The images align alternately to the left and the right down the page and are small enough to fit any size screen, but they move within the text as the screen narrows. When the browser window gets to the size of a smartphone, the images move to a separate line and center above the text.

5 Open **news_finished.html** from the lesson09 folder.
  Preview the page in your favorite browser.

6 Drag the right edge of the browser to resize the window.
Observe how the layout and images adapt.

The first image stretches across the main content area. As the screen gets smaller, the image scales along with it to match the width of the area. As the screen gets wider, the picture fills the space again.

7 Close your browser and return to Dreamweaver.

The sample files display images of varying sizes and composition. Some images are small enough to fit any size screen; others scale responsively as the size of the page changes. In the following exercises, you will insert these images into these pages using a variety of techniques and format them to work on any screen.

Inserting an image

Note: When working with images in Dreamweaver, you should be sure that your site's default images folder is set up according to the directions in the "Getting Started" section at the beginning of the book.

Images are key components of any web page, both for developing visual interest and for telling stories. Dreamweaver provides numerous ways to populate your pages with images, using built-in commands and even using copy and paste from other Adobe apps. Let's start with some of the tools built into Dreamweaver itself, such as the Assets panel.

1 In the Files panel, open **contact_us.html** in Design view.

2 Insert the cursor at the beginning of the first paragraph under the heading *Association Management* in `<section.profile>` and before the name *Elaine*.

3 Choose Window > Assets to display the Assets panel, if necessary. Click the Images category icon ![icon] to display a list of all images stored within the site.

4 Locate and select **elaine.jpg** in the list.

A preview of **elaine.jpg** appears in the Assets panel. The panel lists the image's name, dimensions in pixels, and file type, as well as its full directory path.

5 Note the dimensions of the image: 150 pixels by 150 pixels.

Note: The Images window shows all images stored anywhere in the defined site—even ones outside the site's default images folder—so you may see listings for images stored in the lesson subfolders, too.

6 At the bottom of the panel, click the Insert button.

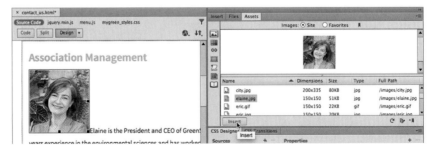

The image appears at the current cursor location.

7 In the Alt text field in the Property inspector, enter
Elaine, Meridien GreenStart President and CEO as the alternate text.

Note: Alt text provides descriptive metadata about images that may be seen if the image doesn't load properly in the browser, or may be accessed by individuals with visual disabilities.

8 Choose File > Save.

You inserted Elaine's picture in the text, but it doesn't look very nice at its current position. In the next exercise, you will adjust the image position using a CSS class.

Adjusting image positions with CSS classes

The <img> element is an inline element by default. That's why you can insert images into paragraphs and other elements. When the image is taller than the font size, the image will increase the vertical space for the line in which it appears. In the past, you could adjust its position using either HTML attributes or CSS, but the HTML-based attributes have been deprecated recently from the language as well as from Dreamweaver. Now you must rely completely on CSS-based techniques.

Note: Selecting the style sheet, media reference, and rule this way ensures that the new rule is inserted in the proper location in the style sheet.

If you want all the images to align in a certain fashion, you can create a custom rule for the <img> tag to apply specific styling. In this instance, the employee photos will alternate from right to left going down the page and have the text wrap around the image to use the space more effectively. To do this, you'll create a custom class to provide options for left and right alignment.

1 If necessary, open **contact_us.html** in Design view.

2 In the CSS Designer, choose **mygreen_styles.css** > GLOBAL > `.content .profile`.
Create a new selector `.flt_rgt`

The name is short for "float right," hinting at what command you're going to use to style the images.

3 If necessary, select the Show Set option, and create the following properties:
`float: right`
`margin-left: 10px`

You can apply the new class from the Property inspector.

4 In the layout, select the image **elaine.jpg**.
From the Class menu in the Property inspector, choose `flt_rgt`.

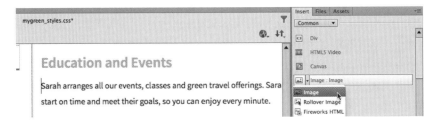

As you learned in Lesson 3, applying a float to the image removes it from the normal flow of the HTML elements, although it still maintains its width and height. The image moves to the right side of the section element; the text wraps around on the left. The margin setting keeps the text from touching the edge of the image itself. You will create a similar rule to align images to the left in the next exercise.

Working with the Insert panel

The Insert panel duplicates key menu commands and has a number of options that make inserting images and other code elements both quick and easy.

1 In Design view, insert the cursor at the beginning of the first paragraph under the heading *Education and Events* and before the name *Sarah*.

2 Choose Window > Insert to display the Insert panel, if necessary.

3 In the Insert panel, choose the Common category.
Click the Image drop-down menu.

The menu offers three options: Image, Rollover Image, and Fireworks HTML.

4 From the pop-up menu, choose Image.

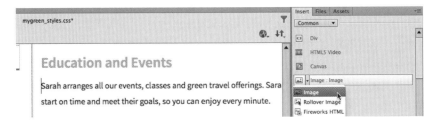

The Select Image Source dialog appears.

5 Select **sarah.jpg** from the site images folder. Click OK/Open.

6 In the Property inspector, enter **Sarah, GreenStart Events Coordinator** in the Alt text field.

7 In the CSS Designer, choose **mygreen_styles.css** > GLOBAL > `.flt_rgt`. Create a new selector `.flt_lft`

The name is short for "float left."

8 Create the following properties:

```
float: left
margin-right: 10px
```

9 Apply the `flt_left` class to the **sarah.jpg** image.

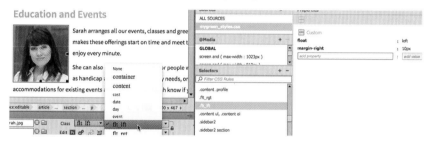

The image drops down into the paragraph on the left side, with the text wrapping on the right.

10 Save the file.

Another way to insert images in your web page is by using the Insert menu.

Using the Insert menu

The Insert menu duplicates all the commands you'll find in the Insert panel. Some users find the menu faster and easier to use. Others prefer the ready nature of the panel, which allows you to focus on one element and quickly insert multiple copies of it at once. Feel free to alternate between the two methods as desired. In this exercise, you will use the Insert menu to add images.

1 Insert the cursor at the beginning of the first paragraph under the heading *Transportation Analysis*, before the name *Eric*.

2 Choose Insert > Image > Image, or press Ctrl+Alt+I/Cmd+Optiont+I.

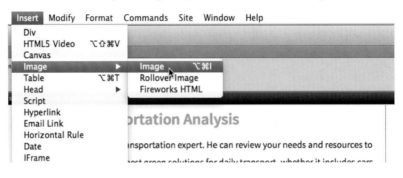

The Select Image Source dialog opens.

3 Navigate to the site's default images folder in lesson09.
Select the file **eric.png**.

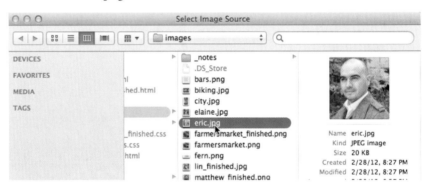

4 Click Open.

The **eric.png** image appears in the Dreamweaver layout at the last position of the cursor.

5 In the Property inspector, type **Eric, Transportation Research Coordinator** in the Alt text field.

6 Apply the `flt_rgt` class to this image.

7 Save all files.

So far, you have inserted web-compatible image formats. But Dreamweaver is not limited to the file types GIF, JPEG, and PNG; it can work with other file types, too. In the next exercise, you will learn how to insert a Photoshop document (PSD) into a webpage.

Inserting non-web file types

Although most browsers will display only the web-compliant image formats described earlier, Dreamweaver also allows you to use other formats; the program will then automatically convert the file to a compatible format on the fly.

1 Insert the cursor at the beginning of the first paragraph, under the heading *Research and Development* and before the name *Lin*.

2 Choose Insert > Image > Image.
Navigate to the resources folder in the lesson09 folder.
Select **lin.psd**.

3 Click OK/Open to insert the image.

The image appears in the layout, and the Image Optimization dialog opens; it acts as an intermediary that allows you to specify how and to what format the image will be converted.

4 Observe the options in the Preset and Format menus.

The presets allow you to select predetermined options that have a proven track record for web-based images. The Format menu allows you to specify your own settings from among five options: GIF, JPEG, PNG 8, PNG 24, and PNG 32.

5   Choose JPEG High For Maximum Compatibility from the Presets menu. Note the Quality setting.

This Quality setting produces a high-quality image with a moderate amount of compression. If you lower the Quality setting, you automatically increase the compression level and reduce the file size; increase the Quality setting for the opposite effect. The secret to effective design is to select a good balance between quality and compression. The default setting for the JPEG High preset is 80, which is sufficient for your purposes.

● **Note:** When an image has to be converted this way, Dreamweaver usually saves the converted image into the site's default images folder. This is not the case when the images inserted are web-compatible. So before you insert an image, you should be aware of its current location in the site and move it to the proper folder first, if necessary.

6   Click OK to convert the image.

The Save Web Image dialog appears with the name *lin* entered in the Save As field. Dreamweaver will add the .jpg extension to the file automatically. Be sure to save the file to the default site images folder. If Dreamweaver does not automatically point to this folder, navigate to it before saving the file.

7   Click Save.

The Save Web Image dialog closes. The image in the layout is now linked to the JPEG file saved in the default images folder.

8   Enter **Lin, Research and Development Coordinator** in the Alt text field.

The image appears in Dreamweaver at the cursor position. The image has been resampled to 72 ppi but still appears at its original dimensions, so it's larger than the other images in the layout. You can resize the image in the Property inspector.

9 If necessary, click the Toggle Size Constrain icon 🔒 to display the closed lock. Change the Width value to **150px** and press Enter/Return.

Note: Whenever you change HTML or CSS properties, you may need to press Enter/ Return to complete the modification.

When the lock icon appears closed, the relationship between width and height is constrained, and the two change proportionally to each other: Change one, they both change. The change to the image size is only temporary at the moment, as indicated by the Reset ⊘ and Commit ✔ icons. An exclamation mark appears in the upper-left corner of the image, indicating that the image has been modified but the changes have not been committed. In other words, the HTML attributes specify the size of the image as 150 pixels by 150 pixels, but the JPEG file holds an image that's still 300 pixels by 300 pixels—four times as many pixels as it needs to have.

10 Click the Commit icon ✔.

A dialog appears warning that the change will be permanent.

11 Click OK.

The image resizes to 150 by 150 pixels. The linked image, stored in the Images folder, is now permanently resized. The exclamation mark on the image disappears.

12 Apply the flt_lft class to this image. Save the file.

The image now appears like the other images in the layout, but something is different about it. An icon appears in the upper-left corner that identifies this image as a Photoshop Smart Object.

Right size, wrong size

Until the latest mobile devices appeared on the scene, deciding what size and resolution to use for web images was pretty simple. You picked a specific width and height, and saved the image at 72 pixels per inch. That's all you needed to do.

But today, web designers want their sites to work well for all visitors, no matter what type or size device they want to use. So the days of picking one size and one resolution may be gone forever. But what's the answer? At the moment, there isn't one perfect solution.

One trend simply inserts an image that is larger or higher resolution, and resizes it using CSS. This allows the image to display more clearly on high-resolution screens, like Apple's Retina display. The downside is that lower-resolution devices are stuck downloading an image that's larger than they need. This not only slows the loading of the page for no reason, but it can incur higher data charges for smartphone users.

Another idea is to provide multiple images optimized for different devices and resolutions and to use JavaScript to load the proper image as needed. But many users object to using scripts for such basic resources as images.

Others want a standardized solution. So W3C is working on another technique using a new element named `<picture>` that will not require JavaScript at all. Using this new element, you would select several images and declare how they should be used, and then the browser would load the appropriate image. Unfortunately, this element is so new that Dreamweaver doesn't support it yet, and few browsers even know what it is.

Implementing a responsive workflow for images is outside the scope of this course. For the purposes of these lessons, you will simply learn how to adapt standard web images to the current responsive template using CSS and media queries.

Working with Photoshop Smart Objects (optional)

Note: Dreamweaver and Photoshop can work only with the existing quality of an image. If your initial image quality is unacceptable, you may not be able to fix it in Photoshop. You will have to re-create the image or pick another.

Unlike other images, Smart Objects maintain a connection to their original Photoshop (PSD) file. If the PSD file is altered in any manner and then saved, Dreamweaver identifies those changes and provides the means to update the web image used in the layout. The following exercise can be completed only if you have Photoshop installed on your computer with Dreamweaver.

1   If necessary, open **contact_us.html** in Design view.
    Scroll down to the **lin.jpg** image in the *Research and Development* section. Observe the icon in the upper-left corner of the image.

The icon indicates that the image is a Smart Object. The icon appears only within Dreamweaver itself; visitors see the normal image in the browser. If you want to edit or optimize the image, you can simply right-click the image and choose the appropriate option from the context menu.

To make substantive changes to the image, you will have to open it in Photoshop. (If you don't have Photoshop installed, copy lesson09 > resources > smartobject > **lin.psd** into the lesson09 > resources folder to replace the original image, and then skip to step 6.) In this exercise, you will edit the image background using Photoshop.

2   Right-click the **lin.jpg** image.
    Choose Edit Original With > Photoshop CC 2014 from the context menu.

Note: The exact name of the apps appearing in the menu may differ depending on what version of Photoshop you have installed and your operating system.

Photoshop CC 2014 launches—if it is installed on your computer—and loads the file.

3   In Photoshop, choose Window > Layers to display the Layers panel, if necessary. Observe the names and states of any existing layers.

The image has two layers: Lin and New Background. New Background is turned off.

4   Click the eye icon  for the New Background layer to display its contents.

The background of the image changes to show a scene from a park.

5 Save the Photoshop file.

6 Switch back to Dreamweaver.
Position your cursor over the Smart Object icon.

A tool tip appears indicating that the original image has been changed. You don't have to update the image at this time, and you can leave the out-of-date image in the layout for as long as you want. Dreamweaver will continue to monitor its status as long as it's in the layout. But for this exercise, let's update the image.

7 Right-click the image, and choose Update From Original from the context menu.

Before (Left)   After (Right)

This Smart Object, and any other instances of it, change to reflect the new background. You can check the status of the Smart Object by positioning the pointer over the image. A tool tip will appear showing that the image is synced. You can also insert the same original PSD image multiple times in the site using different dimensions and image settings under different file names. All the Smart Objects will stay connected to the PSD and will allow you to update them as the PSD changes.

8 Save the file.

As you can see, Smart Objects have several advantages over a typical image work-flow. For frequently changed or updated images, using a Smart Object can simplify updates to the website in the future.

Copying and pasting images from Photoshop

As you build your website, you will need to edit and optimize many images before you use them in your site. Adobe Photoshop is an excellent program for performing these tasks. A common workflow is to make the needed changes to the images and then manually export the optimized GIF, JPEG, or PNG files to the default images folder in your website. But sometimes simply copying images and pasting them directly into your layout is faster and easier.

1 Launch Adobe Photoshop, if necessary.
Open **matthew.tif** from the lesson09 > resources folder.
Observe the Layers panel.

● **Note:** You should be able to use any version of Photoshop for this exercise. But, Creative Cloud subscribers can download and install the latest version at any time.

The image has only one layer. In Photoshop, by default you can copy only one layer at a time to paste into Dreamweaver. To copy multiple layers, you will have to merge or flatten the image first, or you will have to use the command Edit > Copy Merged to copy images with multiple active layers.

2 Press Ctrl+A/Cmd+A to select the entire image.
Press Ctrl+C/Cmd+C to copy the image.

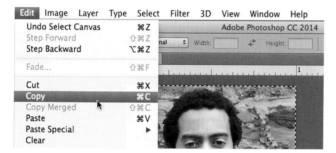

3 Switch to Dreamweaver. Scroll down to the Information Systems section in **contact_us.html**. Insert the cursor at the beginning of the first paragraph in this section and before the name *Matthew*.

4 Press Ctrl+V/Cmd+V to paste the image from the clipboard.

The image appears in the layout, and the Image Optimization dialog opens.

5   Choose the preset PNG24 for Photos (Sharp Details), and choose PNG 24 from the Format menu. Click OK.

The Save Image dialog appears.

6   Name the image **matthew.png**, and select the default site images folder, if necessary. Click Save.

7   Enter **Matthew, Information Systems Manager** in the Alt text field in the Property inspector.

The **matthew.png** image appears in the layout. As in the earlier exercise, the PNG image is larger than the other images.

8   In the Property inspector, change the image dimensions to **150px** by **150px**. Click the Commit icon ✔ to apply the change permanently.

9   Apply the class flt_rgt to **matthew.png**.

Information Systems

Matthew is our do-it-all guy. He takes care of the business end of things. He maintains this web site, the online store and reservation system. He's also experienced at helping people complete their orders and can step in to help when everyone else is busy.

Even though Matthew is good with numbers, he's also an avid biker

The image appears in the layout at the same size as the other images and aligned to the right. Although this image came from Photoshop, it's not "smart" like a Photoshop Smart Object, and can't be updated automatically. It does, however, give you an easy way to load the image into Photoshop or another image editor to perform any modifications.

10 In the layout, right-click the **matthew.png** image. Choose Edit With > Photoshop CC 2014 from the context menu.

The program launches and displays the PNG file from the site images folder. If you make changes to this image, you merely have to save the file to update the image in Dreamweaver.

11 In Photoshop, press Ctrl+L/Cmd+L to open the Levels dialog. Adjust the brightness and contrast of the image. Save and close the image.

Note: This exercise is geared specifically to Photoshop, but the changes can be made in most image editors.

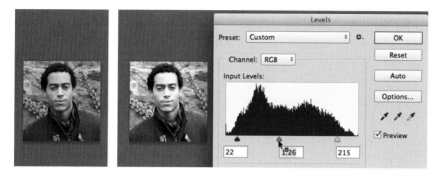

12 Switch back to Dreamweaver. Scroll down to view the **matthew.png** image in the Information Systems section.

The image should be updated in the layout automatically. Since you saved the changes under the original filename, no other action is necessary. This method saves you several steps and avoids any potential typing errors.

Note: Although Dreamweaver automatically reloads any modified file, most browsers won't. You will have to refresh the browser display before you see any changes.

13 Save all the files.

Today, the modern web designer has to contend with a multitude of visitors using different browsers and devices. Depending on the size of the images and how they are inserted, you may need to use several different strategies to get them to work effectively in your page design.

For example, the images used on the *Contact Us* page are small enough that they should be usable all the way down to the size needed on a smartphone, but they'll need some work to make them look better on smaller screens.

Adapting images to smaller screens

Making images work in a truly responsive way is not a simple task. It involves much more than making images resize to fit the available screen space. Today, the Internet is being accessed by a multitude of different types of devices, from cells phones and tablets all the way to desktop computers and televisions. Besides the obvious matter of screen size, you also have to contend with pixel resolution, bandwidth, device memory, and much more. The subject could easily consume the remaining pages of this book and is outside the scope of learning how to use Dreamweaver. Instead, we will forego all the other considerations and concentrate on creating a scheme that simply allows the images to adapt to the screen size.

As you will see, you can get the current images to make the most of the available space as the pages respond to the size of the screen by creating a few specific rules in the appropriate media queries. The first step is to observe how images adapt to the current design, and then create an effective strategy for reformatting them.

1 Open **contact_us.html**. Preview the page in the default browser.

2 Resize the width of the browser window as necessary to engage each of the existing media queries. Observe how the images adapt to the different designs.

The images are small enough that they adapt well to desktop and tablet screen sizes. On the smallest screens, the text doesn't look good wrapping around the edge of the images. One fix would be to remove the float and center the images, instead.

3 In CSS Designer, choose **mygreen_styles.css** > `screen and (max-width:468px)`.
Create a new rule `.flt_lft, .flt_rgt`

4 Add the following properties to the new rule:

```
max-width: 95%
display: block
margin: 0px auto
float: none
```

Tablet and desktop (left) Smartphone (right)

These new settings put the images on their own line and center them. The `max-width` property makes sure that larger images automatically scale down with the screen. In the next exercise, you will insert a much larger image that will have to use a different responsive strategy.

Inserting images by drag and drop

Most of the programs in the Creative Suite offer drag-and-drop capabilities. Dreamweaver is no exception.

1 Open **news.html** from the site root folder in Live view.

2 Choose Window > Assets to display the Assets panel, if necessary.

The Assets panel is no longer opened by default in the Dreamweaver workspace. You can leave it as a floating dialog or dock it to keep it out of the way.

3 Drag the Assets panel to dock it beside the Files tab.

4 In the Assets panel, click the Images icon 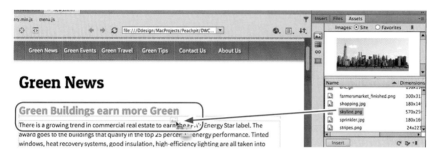.

5 Drag **skyline.png** from the panel to the layout so that the image is inserted between the heading *Green Buildings earn more Green* and the first paragraph.

► **Tip:** If you don't see specific image files listed in the Assets panel, click the Refresh icon **C** to reload site images. You may also have to select the Site option in the Assets panel to see all images in the site.

Note the green smart guide that appears, indicating where the image will be inserted when you release the mouse button. You need a steady hand and a little practice to perfect your drag-and-drop technique, but it's a good way to get images into your layout quickly.

6 Enter **Green buildings are top earners** in the Property inspector's Alt text field.

Unlike the images used in the previous exercises, **skyline.png** was inserted between the `<heading>` and the `<p>` elements. HTML images are inline by default, and normally would be used within a block element. As an inline element, **skyline.png** will need some custom styling to fit in with the current page design.

7 In the CSS Designer, choose **mygreen_styles.css** > GLOBAL > `.content .profile`.
Create a new selector `.content .full`.

This class can be applied to any image you wish to fit the width of the content section.

8 Create the following properties for the new rule:

```
display: block
margin-left: 15px
```

9 Select the **skyline.png** in the layout, if necessary.

When an element or section of text is selected in Live view, the Element view interface appears. You can use this interface to add or edit classes or ids, among other tasks.

10 Click the + icon in the Element View interface.

You can add a new class or id, or select from a list of ones already defined in the layout or any referenced style sheet.

11 Type a period (.) to display a list of classes already defined in this workflow.

The new .full class should appear in the list of classes.

12 Select .full from the list of classes.

The styling created in step 8 is now applied to the image. The image now conforms to the layout on desktop screens. But what happens if the screen gets smaller? You can check the behavior in Live view, or you can preview the page in a browser window.

13 Save all files.

14 Drag the right edge of the document window to the left, and observe how the image adapts to the changes to the layout.

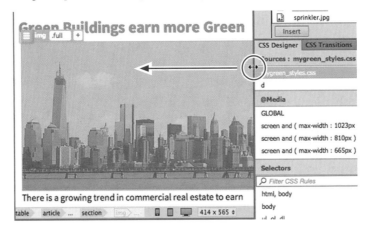

The image remains at its original size as the window gets smaller. In the finished file, previewed at the beginning of the lesson, this image scaled automatically as the document window changed sizes. To make this image responsive, we need to tweak an existing CSS rule and create some additional ones.

Making images responsive

In this exercise, you will adapt the image styling so that it scales with the size of the layout and the device window.

1 If necessary, open **news.html** in Live view.

2 In the CSS Designer, choose **mygreen_styles.css** > GLOBAL > `.content .full`.

Create the following properties in the selected rule:

```
height: auto
max-width:95%
```

These specifications will force the image to scale with the layout.

3 Drag the right edge of the document window to the left, and observe how the image adapts to the changes to the layout.

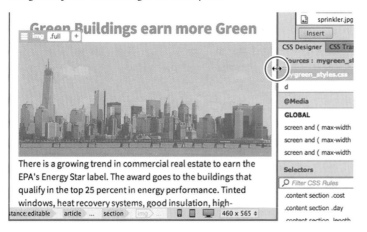

This time, the image scales with the layout. However, at sizes narrower than 468 pixels, the image appears slightly off-center. You can fix this by adding a new rule in the appropriate media query.

4 In the CSS Designer, choose **mygreen_styles.css** > `screen and (max-width:468px)`

Create the following selector:

`.content .full`

5 Create the property `margin: 0px auto` in the new rule.

This new margin setting will center the image any time the screen is 468 pixels wide or smaller. You can apply the `.full` class to any image that needs to stretch across the entire content element. Smaller images can continue to use the `.flt_rgt` or `.flt_left` class. As you add images to this or other sites, be prepared to create additional CSS rules to deal with other such situations.

Optimizing images with the Property inspector

Optimized web images try to balance image dimensions and quality against file size. Sometimes you may need to optimize graphics that have already been placed on the page. Dreamweaver has built-in features that can help you achieve the smallest possible file size while preserving image quality. In this exercise, you'll use tools in Dreamweaver to scale, optimize, and crop an image for the web.

1   If necessary, open **news.html** in Design view.

2   Insert the cursor at the beginning of the *Shopping green saves energy* heading. Choose Insert > Image > Image.
   Insert **farmersmarket.png** from the site images folder.

3   Enter **Buy local to save energy** in the Alt text field.

4   Apply the class flt_rgt to the image.

   The image is too large and could use some cropping. To save time, you can use tools in Dreamweaver to fix the image composition.

5   If necessary, choose Window > Properties to display the Property inspector.

   Whenever an image is selected, image-editing options appear to the right of the image source field in the Property inspector. The buttons here allow you to edit the image in Photoshop or Fireworks, or to adjust various settings in place. See the sidebar "Dreamweaver's graphic tools" for an explanation of each button.

   There are two ways to reduce the dimensions of an image in Dreamweaver. The first method changes the size of the image temporarily by imposing user-defined dimensions.

6   Select **farmersmarket.png**. If necessary, click the Toggle Size Constrain icon 🔒 in the Property inspector to lock the image proportions.
   Change the image width to **350 pixels**.

   When the Size Constraint is locked, the height automatically conforms to the new width. Note that Dreamweaver indicates that the new size is not permanent by displaying the current specifications in bold and also by displaying the Reset ⊘ and Commit ✔ icons.

7 Click the Commit icon ✔ .

A dialog appears that indicates the change will be permanent.

8 Click OK.

Dreamweaver can also crop images.

9 With the image still selected, click the Crop icon ⊠ in the Property inspector.

A dialog appears indicating that the action will permanently change the image.

10 Click OK.

Crop handles appear slightly inset from the edges of the image. We want to crop the width, but not the height.

11 Drag the crop handles to set the image to a width of 300 pixels and a height of 312 pixels.

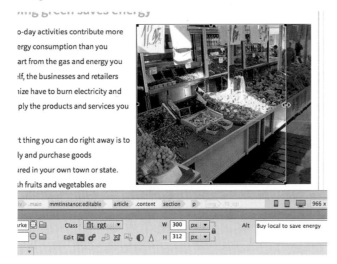

12 Press Enter/Return or double-click the image to apply the change.

13 Save all files.

Most designers will edit and resize images prior to bringing them into Dreamweaver, but it's nice to know that these tools are available for any last-minute changes or fast turnarounds.

In this lesson, you learned how to insert images and Smart Objects into a Dreamweaver page, copy and paste from Photoshop, and use the Property inspector to edit images.

There are numerous ways to create and edit images for the web. The methods examined in this lesson show but a few of them, and are not meant to recommend or endorse one method over another. Feel free to use whatever methods and workflow you desire based on your own situation and expertise.

Dreamweaver's graphic tools

All Dreamweaver's graphic tools appear in the Property inspector when an image is selected. Here are the seven tools:

 Edit—Opens the selected image in the defined external graphics editor if you have them installed. You can assign a graphics-editing program to any given file type in the File Types/Editors category of the Preferences dialog. The button's image changes according to the program chosen. For example, if Fireworks is the designated editor for the image type, a Fireworks icon is shown; if Photoshop is the editor, you'll see a Photoshop icon .

 Edit Image Settings—Opens the Image Optimization dialog, allowing you to apply user-defined optimization specifications to the selected image.

 Update from Original—Updates the placed Smart Object to match any changes to the original source file.

Crop—Permanently removes unwanted portions of an image. When the Crop tool is active, a bounding box with a series of control handles appears within the selected image. You can adjust the bounding box size by dragging the handles. When the box outlines the desired portion of the image, double-click the graphic to apply the cropping.

Resample—Permanently resizes an image. The Resample tool is active only when an image has been resized.

Brightness and Contrast—Offers user-selectable adjustments to an image's brightness and contrast; a dialog presents sliders for each value that can be adjusted independently. A live preview is available so that you can evaluate adjustments before committing to them.

Sharpen—Affects the enhancement of image details by raising or lowering the contrast of pixels on a scale from 0 to 10. As with the Brightness and Contrast tool, Sharpen offers a real-time preview.

You can undo most graphics operations by choosing Edit > Undo until the containing document is closed or you quit Dreamweaver.

Review questions

1 What are the three factors that determine raster image quality?

2 What file formats are specifically designed for use on the web?

3 Describe at least two methods for inserting an image into a web page using Dreamweaver.

4 True or false: All graphics have to be optimized outside of Dreamweaver.

5 What is the advantage of using a Photoshop Smart Object over copying and pasting an image from Photoshop?

Review answers

1 Raster image quality is determined by resolution, image dimensions, and color depth.

2 The compatible image formats for the web are GIF, JPEG, PNG, and SVG.

3 One method to insert an image into a web page using Dreamweaver is to use the Insert panel. Another method is to drag the graphic file into the layout from the Assets panel. Images can also be copied and pasted from Photoshop and Fireworks.

4 False. Images can be optimized even after they are inserted into Dreamweaver by using the Property inspector. Optimization can include rescaling, changing format, or fine-tuning format settings.

5 A Smart Object can be used multiple times in different places on a site, and each instance of the Smart Object can be assigned individual settings. All copies remain connected to the original image. If the original is updated, all the connected images are immediately updated as well. When you copy and paste all or part of a Photoshop file, however, you get a single image that can have only one set of values applied to it.

10

WORKING WITH NAVIGATION

Lesson overview

In this lesson, you'll apply several kinds of links to page elements by doing the following:

- Creating a text link to a page within the same site

- Creating a link to a page on another website

- Creating an email link

- Creating an image-based link

- Creating a link to a location within a page

 This lesson will take about 1 hour and 45 minutes to complete. If you have not already done so, download the project files for this lesson from the Lesson & Update Files tab on your Account page at www.peachpit.com, and store them on your computer in a convenient location, as described in the "Getting Started" section of this book. Your Account page is also where you'll find any updates to the lessons or to the lesson files. Look on the Lesson & Update Files tab to access the most current content. Before you begin this lesson, define a new site based on the lesson10 folder using the method described in the "Getting Started" section at the beginning of the book.

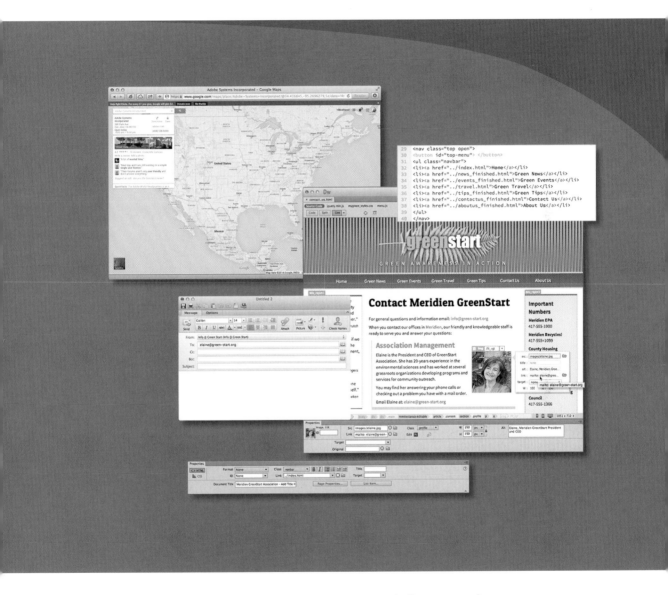

Dreamweaver can create and edit many types of links—from text-based links to image-based links—and does so with ease and flexibility.

Hyperlink basics

The World Wide Web, and the Internet in general, would be a far different place without the hyperlink. Without hyperlinks, HTML would simply be ML (markup language). The *hypertext* in the name refers to the functionality of the hyperlink. So what is a hyperlink?

A hyperlink, or *link*, is an HTML-based reference to a resource available on the Internet or within the computer hosting a web document. The resource can be anything that can be stored on and displayed by a computer, such as a web page, image, movie, sound file, PDF—in fact, almost any type of computer file. A hyperlink creates an interactive behavior specified by HTML and CSS, or the programming language you're using, and is enabled by a browser or other application.

An HTML hyperlink consists of the anchor <a> element and one or more attributes.

Internal and external hyperlinks

The simplest hyperlink—an internal hyperlink—takes the user to another part of the same document or to another document stored in the same folder or hard drive on the web server that hosts the site. An external hyperlink is designed to take the user to a document or resource outside your hard drive, website, or web host.

Internal and external hyperlinks may work differently, but they have one thing in common: They are enabled in HTML by the <a> *anchor* element. This element designates the address of the destination, or *target*, of the hyperlink, and can then specify how it functions using several attributes. You'll learn how to create and modify the <a> element in the exercises that follow.

Relative vs. absolute hyperlinks

A hyperlink address can be written in two ways. When you refer to a target by where it is stored in relation to the current document, it is called a *relative* link. This is like telling someone that you live next door to the blue house. If she were driving down your street and saw the blue house, she would know where you live. But those directions don't really tell her how to get to your house, or even to your neighborhood. A relative link frequently will consist of the resource name and perhaps the folder it is stored within, such as `logo.jpg` or `images/logo.jpg`.

Sometimes, you need to spell out precisely where a resource is located. In those instances, you need an *absolute* hyperlink. This is like telling someone you live at 123 Main Street in Meridien. This is typically how you refer to resources outside your website. An absolute link includes the entire uniform resource locator, or URL, of the target, and may even include a filename—such as http://forums.adobe.com/index.html—or just a folder within the site.

Both types of links have advantages and disadvantages. Relative hyperlinks are faster and easier to write, but they may not work if the document containing them is saved in a different folder or location in the website. Absolute links always work no matter where the containing document is saved, but they can fail if the targets are moved or renamed. A simple rule that most web designers follow is to use relative links for resources within a site and absolute links for resources outside the site. Of course, whether you follow this rule or not, it's important to test all links before deploying the page or site.

Previewing the completed file

To see the final version of the file you will work on in this lesson, let's preview the completed page in the browser.

1 Launch Adobe Dreamweaver CC (2014.1 release or later).

2 If necessary, press F8 to open the Files panel. Select lesson10 from the site list.

3 In the Files panel, expand the lesson10 folder.

4 In the Files panel, right-click **aboutus_finished.html**. Choose Preview in Browser from the context menu.

Note: Before beginning this exercise, download the project files and define a new site based on the lesson10 folder using the instructions in the "Getting Started" section at the beginning of the book.

The **aboutus_finished.html** file appears in your default browser. This page features only internal links in the horizontal menu.

5 Position the cursor over the horizontal navigation menu. Hover over each button, and examine the behavior of the menu.

The menu is the same one created and formatted in Lesson 5, "Creating a Page Layout."

6 Click the *Green News* link.

The browser loads the finished *Green News* page.

▶ **Tip:** Most browsers will display the destination of a hyperlink in the status bar at the bottom of the browser window. In some browsers, this status bar may be turned off by default.

7 Position the cursor over the *About Us* link. Observe the browser to see if it's displaying the link's destination anywhere on the screen.

Typically, the browser shows the link destination in the status bar.

8 Click the *Contact Us* link.

The browser loads the finished *Contact Us* page, replacing the *Green News* page. The new page includes internal, external, and email links.

9 Position the cursor over the Meridien link in the second paragraph of the main content area. Observe the status bar.

The status bar displays the http://maps.google.com link.

10 Click the Meridien link.

A new browser window appears and loads Google Maps. The link is intended to show the visitor where the Meridien GreenStart Association offices are located. If desired, you can even include address details or the company name in this link so that Google can load the exact map and directions.

Note that the browser opens a separate window or document tab when you click the link. This is a good behavior to use when directing visitors to resources outside your site. Since the link opens in a separate window, your own site is still open and ready to use. This practice is especially helpful if your visitors are unfamiliar with your site and may not know how to get back to it once they click away.

11 Close the Google Maps window.

The *Contact Us* page is still open. Note that each employee has a link applied to their email address.

12 Click an email link for one of the employees.

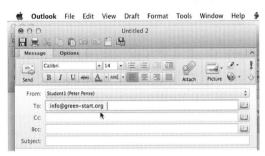

Note: Many web visitors don't use email programs installed on their computers. They use web-based services like AOL, Gmail, Hotmail, and so on. For these visitors, email links like the one you tested won't work. The best option is to create a web-hosted form on your site that sends the email to you via your own server.

The default mail application launches on your computer. If you have not set up this application to send and receive mail, the program will usually start a wizard to help you set up this functionality. If the email program is set up, a new message window, similar to the one pictured in the screen shot, appears with the email address of the employee automatically entered in the To field.

13 Close the new message window, and exit the email program.

14 Scroll down to the *Education and Events* section. Click the *events* link.

The browser loads the *Green Events and Classes* page. The browser focuses on the table containing the list of upcoming events at the top of the page.

15 In the horizontal menu, click the *Contact Us* link.

The *Contact Us* page loads again.

16 Scroll down to the *Education and Events* section. Click the *classes* link.

The browser loads the *Green Events and Classes* page again, but this time the browser focuses on the table containing the list of upcoming classes at the bottom of the page.

17 Click the *Return to top* link that appears above the class schedule. You may need to scroll up or down the page to see it.

The browser jumps back to the top of the page.

18 Close the browser and switch to Dreamweaver, if necessary.

You have tested a variety of different types of hyperlinks: internal, external, relative, and absolute. In the following exercises, you will learn how to build each type.

Creating internal hyperlinks

Creating hyperlinks of all types is easy with Dreamweaver. In this exercise, you'll create relative text-based links to pages in the same site, using a variety of methods. You can create links in Design view, Live view, and Code view.

Creating relative links in Design view

You may spend a significant amount of time in Design view creating the structure and content of your page. Dreamweaver provides several methods for creating and editing links in Design view.

1 Open **about_us.html** from the site root folder in Design view.

2 In the horizontal menu, position the cursor over the Home text in the horizontal menu. Observe the type of cursor that appears.

The "slash" icon indicates that this section of the page is locked. The horizontal menu was not added to an editable region in Lesson 7, "Working with Templates," so it's considered part of the template and is locked. To add a hyperlink to this menu item, you'll have to open the template.

3 Choose Window > Assets. In the Assets panel Template category, right-click **mygreen_temp**, and choose Edit from the context menu.

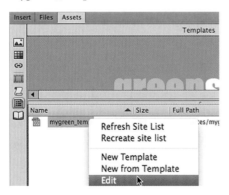

4 Switch to Design view, if necessary.

In the horizontal menu, insert the cursor in the Home text.

The horizontal menu is editable in the template.

Tip: When editing or removing an existing hyperlink, you don't need to select the entire link; you can just insert the cursor anywhere in the link text. Dreamweaver assumes you want to change the entire link by default.

5 If necessary, choose Window > Properties to open the Property inspector. Examine the contents of the Link field in the Property inspector.

To create links, the HTML tab must be selected in the Property inspector. The Link field shows a hyperlink placeholder (#). The home page doesn't exist yet, but the link can be created by typing the name of the file or resource into this field.

6 In the Link field, select and delete the hash mark (#).

Type `../index.html`, and press Enter/Return to complete the link.

Note: The link won't have the typical hyperlink appearance because of the special formatting you applied to this menu in Lesson 5, "Creating a Page Layout."

You've created your first text-based hyperlink. Since the template is saved in a subfolder, you need to add the path element notation (../) to the filename so that the link properly resolves once the template pages are updated. This notation tells the browser or operating system to look in the parent directory of the current folder. Dreamweaver rewrites the link when the template is applied to a page, depending on where the containing page is saved.

At any time, you may insert a link by typing it manually, just this way. But, you don't always have to type the link. Entering links by hand can introduce a variety of errors that can break the very link you are trying to create. If you want to link to a file that already exists, Dreamweaver also offers interactive ways to create links.

7 In the horizontal menu, select the *About Us* text.

8 Click the Browse for File icon 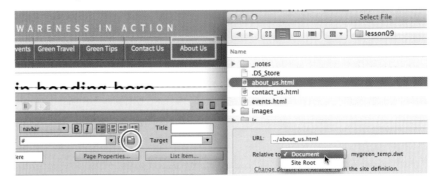, adjacent to the Link field.
In the Select File dialog, select **about_us.html** from the site root folder.
Make sure that the Relative To menu is set to Document.
Click OK/Open.

The hyperlink placeholder is replaced by the text *../about_us.html*. By setting the Relative to Document option, Dreamweaver writes the link based on the file's location *relative* from one to the other. The Relative to Site Root option writes the link from the site's root folder, which would create an absolute link.

Now, let's try making a link using a more visual approach.

9 In the horizontal menu, select the *Contact Us* text.

10 Click the Files tab to bring the panel to the top, or choose Window > Files.

11 In the Property inspector, drag the Point to File icon ⊕—next to the Link field—to **contact_us.html** in the site root folder displayed in the Files panel.

▶ **Tip:** If a folder in the Files panel contains a page you want to link to, but the folder is not open, drag the Point to File icon over the folder, and hold it in place to expand that folder so that you can point to the desired file.

Dreamweaver enters the filename and any necessary path information into the Link field.

12 Insert the cursor into the *Green News* link text in the horizontal menu.

13 Change the # placeholder to **../news.html**

14 Modify the rest of the menu as follows:

Green Events: **../events.html**

Green Travel: **../travel.html**

Green Tips: **../tips.html**

Note: The travel.
html page will be
created later.

For files that have not been created, you will always have to enter the link manually. Remember that all the links added to the template pointing to files in the site root folder must include the **../** notation so that the link resolves properly. Remember also that Dreamweaver will modify the link as needed once the template is applied to the child page.

Creating a home link

Most websites display a logo or company name, and this site is no different. The GreenStart logo appears in the header element—a product of two background graphics, a gradient, and some text. Frequently, such logos are used to create a link back to the site home page. In fact, this practice has become a virtual standard on the web. Since the template is still open, it's easy to add such a link to the GreenStart logo.

1 Select the `GreenStart` text in the `h1` element in `<header>`.

The text component of the logo is highlighted. Dreamweaver keeps track of links you create in each editing session until you close the program.

2 In the Property inspector, open the Link field, and choose `../index.html` from the drop-down menu.

Note: You can select
any range of text to
create a link, from one
character to an entire
paragraph or more;
Dreamweaver will add
the necessary markup
to the selection.

This selection will create a link to the home page you will create later. The `<a>` tag now appears in the tag selector interface, and the logo has changed color to match the default styling of hyperlinks supplied by the main style sheet. Although you may want normal hyperlinks to be styled this way, it's not desirable to allow the logo to look like this. It's a simple fix with CSS.

3 In the CSS Designer, choose **mygreen_styles.css** > GLOBAL > header p. Create the following selector: `header h2 a:link, header h2 a:visited`

This selector will target the "default" and "visited" states of the link within the logo.

4 Add the following properties to the new rule:

```
color: inherit
text-decoration: none
```

Note: Design view will not render all the styling properly, but it will appear correctly in Live view and in a browser.

These properties will cancel the hyperlink styling and return the text to its original appearance. By using `inherit` for the color value, the color applied by the `header h2` rule will be passed automatically to the text. That way, any time the color in the `header h2` rule changes, the hyperlink will be styled in turn without any additional work.

So far, all the links you've created and the changes you've made are only on the template. The whole purpose of using the template is how easy it makes it to update pages in your site.

Updating links in child pages

To apply the links you've created to all the existing pages based on this template, all you have to do is save it.

1 Choose File > Save.

The Update Template Files dialog appears. You can choose to update pages now or wait until later. You can even update the template files manually, if desired.

2   Click Update.

Dreamweaver updates all pages created by this template. The Update Pages dialog appears, and displays a report listing the updated pages.

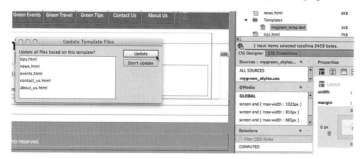

3   Close the Update Pages dialog. Close **mygreen_temp.dwt**.

Note the asterisk in the document tab for **about_us.html**, which indicates that the changed page hasn't been saved.

4   Save **about_us.html**, and preview it in the default browser. Position the cursor over the *About Us* and *Contact Us* text.

● **Note:** When you close templates or web pages, Dreamweaver may ask you to save changes to mygreen_styles.css. Whenever you see these warnings, always save the changes; otherwise you could lose all your newly created rules and properties.

You can see the links applied to each item in the browser status bar. When the template was saved, it updated the locked regions of the page, adding the hyperlinks to the horizontal menu. Pages that are closed at the time of updating are automatically saved. Open pages must be saved manually or you will lose changes applied by the template.

5   Click the *Contact Us* link.

The *Contact Us* page loads to replace the *About Us* page in the browser.

6   Click the *About Us* link.

The *About Us* page loads to replace the *Contact Us* page. The links were added even to pages that weren't open at the time.

7   Close the browser, and switch to Dreamweaver.

▷ **Tip:** Thoroughly test every link you create on every page.

You learned three methods for creating hyperlinks with the Property inspector: typing the link manually, using the Browse for File function, and using the Point to File tool.

Creating an external link

The pages you linked to in the previous exercise were stored within the current site. You can also link to any page—or other resource—stored on the web if you know the URL.

Creating an absolute link in Live view

In the previous exercise, you used Design view to build all your links. As you build pages and format content, you'll use Live view frequently to preview the styling and appearance of your elements. Although some aspects of content creation and editing are limited in Live view, you can still create and edit hyperlinks. In this exercise, you'll apply an external link to some text using Live view.

1   Click the document tab for **contact_us.html** to bring it to the top, or open it from the site root folder.

2   In the second <p> element in the MainContent region, note the word *Meridien*.

    You'll link this text to the Google Maps site.

▶ **Tip:** For this exercise you can use any search engine or web-based mapping application.

3   Launch your favorite browser. In the URL field, type **maps.google.com**, and press Enter/Return.

    Google Maps appears in the browser window.

● **Note:** In some browsers, you can type the search phrase directly in the URL field.

4   Type **Adobe Systems, San Jose, CA** into the search field, and press Enter/Return.

● **Note:** We're using Adobe's headquarters in place of the fictional city of Meridien. Feel free to use another search term.

Adobe headquarters in San Jose appears on a map in the browser. In Google Maps, somewhere on the screen you should see a settings icon; it typically looks like a gear sprocket.

5   Open the settings interface as appropriate for your chosen mapping application.

Search engines and browsers may display their link sharing and embedding interface slightly differently than the one pictured. Google Maps, MapQuest, and Bing usually offer at least two separate code snippets: one for use within a hyperlink and the other to generate an actual map that you can embed in your site. Note how the link contains the entire URL of the map, making it an *absolute* link. The advantage of using absolute links is that you can copy and paste them anywhere in the site without worrying whether the link will resolve properly.

6 Select and copy the link.

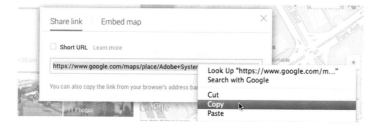

7 Switch to Live view in Dreamweaver.
Select the word *Meridien.*

In Live view, you can select an entire element or insert the cursor within the element to edit or add text, as needed. When an element or section of text is selected, the Element view interface appears. You can use this interface to add classes or ids to the selection, apply bold and italics, or (as in this case) apply hyperlinks.

8 Click the Hyperlink icon 🔗 in the Element view interface.
Insert the cursor in the Link field, and press Ctrl+-V/Cmd+V to paste the link.

> For general questions and infor... ...rt.org
> **B** *I* 🔗 lxd1a50d4e8ddac319 🖿
> When you contact our offices in Meridien, our friendly and knowledgeable staff is ready to serve you and answer your questions:

The selected text displays the default formatting for a hyperlink. You can repeat this procedure at any time to link to a custom map.

9 Save the file, and preview it in the default browser. Test the link.

When you click the link, the browser takes you to the opening page of Google Maps, assuming you have a connection to the Internet. But there is a problem: Clicking the link replaced the *Contact Us* page in the browser; it didn't open a new window as in the earlier example. To make the browser open a new window, you need to add a simple HTML attribute to the link.

10 Switch to Dreamweaver. Select the *Meridien* link in Live view.

For general questions and information email: info@green-start.org

When you contact our offices in Meridien, our friendly and knowledgeable staff is ready to serve you and answer your questions:

The Element view interface appears. The Property inspector displays the properties of the existing link.

Tip: You can access the Target attribute in the Property inspector in Live, Design, and Code views whenever a link is selected.

11 Choose _blank from the Target field menu.

12 Save the file, and preview the page in the default browser again. Test the link.

This time when you click the link, the browser opens a new window.

13 Close the browser windows, and switch back to Dreamweaver.

As you can see, Dreamweaver makes it easy to create links to internal or external resources.

Setting up email links

Tip: The Email Link menu cannot be accessed in Live view. But you can use the menu in Design view or Code view or just create the links by hand in Live view.

Another type of link is the email link, which instead of taking the visitor to another page, opens the visitor's email program. It can create automatic, pre-addressed email messages from your visitors for customer feedback, product orders, or other important communications. The code for an email link is slightly different from the normal hyperlink, and—as you probably guessed already—Dreamweaver can create the proper code for you automatically.

1 If necessary, open **contact_us.html** in Design view.

2 Select the email address (info@green-start.org) in the first paragraph underneath the heading, and press Ctrl+C/Cmd+C to copy the text.

3 Choose Insert > Email Link.

The Email Link dialog appears. The text selected in the document window is automatically entered into the Text field.

4 Insert the cursor in the Email field, and press Ctrl+V/Cmd+V to paste the email address.

▶ **Tip:** If you select the text before you access the dialog, Dreamweaver enters the text in the field for you automatically.

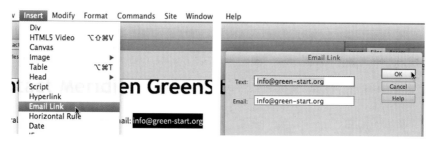

5 Click OK. Examine the Link field in the Property inspector.

Dreamweaver inserts the email address into the Link field and also enters the `mailto:` notation, which creates a link that will automatically launch the visitors' default email program.

6 Save the file, and preview it in the default browser. Test the email link.

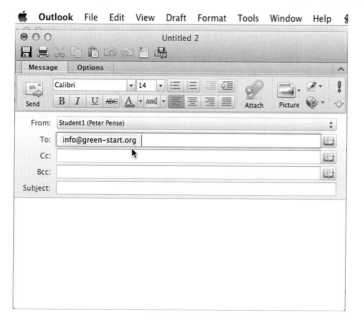

If your computer has a default email program installed, it will launch and create a new email message using the email address provided in the link. If there is no default email program, your computer's operating system may ask you to identify one.

7 Close any open email program, related dialogs, or wizards. Switch to Dreamweaver.

You can also create email links by hand.

8   Switch to Live view. Select and copy the email address for Elaine.

9   Using the Element View interface, create a new link, and enter `mailto:`
    Paste Elaine's email address directly after the colon.

You may find her answering your phone calls or checking out a
problem you ha[...] **B** *I* **8** mailto:elaine@green 📇
Email Elaine at: elaine@green-start.org

The text `mailto:elaine@green-start.org` appears in the Element view link
field. You can use this same technique to add links to images.

Creating an image-based link

Image-based links work like any other hyperlinks, and can direct users to internal
or external resources. You can use the Insert menu or apply links and other attribute using the Element View interface.

Creating image-based links using Element View

In this exercise, you will create and format an image-based link using the email
addresses of each GreenStart employee in Element View.

1   If necessary, open **contact_us.html** in Live view from the site root folder.

2   Select the image of Elaine in the *Association
    Management* section.

    The Element View interface for images looks
    slightly different from that of other types of
    elements. To access the hyperlink option, you
    must first open the Element View image menu.

3   In the Element View interface, click the
    Menu icon ▤.

The menu opens and displays options for the image attributes `src`, `title`, `alt`,
`link`, `target`, `width`, and `height`.

4 If the email address is still in memory from the previous exercise, simply enter `mailto:` and paste the address.

Otherwise, enter `mailto:elaine@green-start.org` in the link field.

The hyperlink that is applied to the image will launch the default email program in the same fashion as it did with the text-based link earlier.

5 Select and copy the email address for Sarah.

Repeat steps 2–4 to create an email link for Sarah's image.

6 Create image links for the remaining employees using the appropriate email address for each.

All the image-based links on the page are complete. You can also create text-based links using Element View.

Creating text links using Element View

In this exercise, you will create text-based email links as needed for the remaining employees.

1 If necessary, open **contact_us.html** in Live view.

2 Select and copy the email address for Sarah.

The Element View appears around the selected text.

3 Click the Link icon 🔗.

A link field appears. A folder icon displays on the right side of the link field. If you were linking to a file on the website, you could click the folder to target the file. In this case, we're creating an email link.

4 Insert the cursor in the link field.

Enter `mailto:` and paste Sarah's email address.

5 Using Element view, create email links for the remaining email addresses displayed on the page.

6 Save all files.

> **Note:** Normally, an image formatted with a hyperlink displays a blue border, similar to the blue underscore that text links get. But the predefined CSS that came with the layout includes an `img` rule, which sets this default border to None.

Attack of the killer robots

While on the surface it sounds like a good idea to add email links to make it easier for your customers and visitors to communicate with you and your staff, email links are a two-edged sword. The Internet is awash with bad actors and unethical companies that use intelligent programs, or *robots*, to constantly search for live email addresses that they can flood with unsolicited email and spam. Putting a plain email address on your site as shown in these exercises is like putting a sign on your back that says "kick me."

In place of active email links, many sites use a variety of methods for limiting the amount of spam they receive. One technique uses images to display the email addresses, since robots can't read data stored in pixels (yet). Another leaves off the hyperlink attribute and types the address with extra spaces, like this:

elaine @ green-start .org

However, both of these techniques have drawbacks; if visitors try to use copy and paste, it forces them to type your email address from memory or go out of their way to remove the extra spaces. Either way, the chances of you receiving any communication decreases with each step the user has to accomplish without additional help.

At this time, there is no foolproof way to prevent someone from using an email address for nefarious purposes. Coupled with the fact that fewer users actually have a mail program installed on their computers any more, the best method for enabling communication for your visitors is to provide a means built into the site itself. Many sites create web-hosted forms that collect the visitor's information and message and then pass it along using server-based email functionality.

Targeting page elements

As you add more content, the pages get longer, and navigating to that content gets more difficult. Typically, when you click a link to a page, the browser window loads the page and displays it starting at the very top. But it can be very helpful when you provide convenient methods for users to link to a specific point on a page.

HTML 4.01 provided two methods to target specific content or page structures: a *named anchor* and an id attribute. However, the named anchor method has been deprecated in HTML5 in favor of ids. Named anchors won't suddenly cease to function the day HTML5 is fully adopted, but you should start practicing now.

Creating internal targeted links

In this exercise, you'll work with id attributes to create the target of an internal link. You can add ids in Live, Design, or Code view.

1   Open **events.html** in Live view.

2 Scroll down to the table containing the class schedule.

When users move down this far on the page, the navigation menus are out of sight and unusable. The farther they read down the page, the farther they are from the primary navigation. Before users can navigate to another page, they have to use the browser scroll bars or the mouse scroll wheel to get back to the top of the page. Adding a link to take users back to the top can vastly improve their experience on your site. Let's call this type of link an internal, *targeted* link.

Internal targeted links have two parts: the link itself and the target. Which one you create first doesn't matter.

3 Insert the cursor in the Class table.
Press the up arrow key once.

The `<table>` element highlights, showing that it is selected.

4 Press the up arrow key again.

The `<section>` element highlights.

5 Open the Insert panel, and select the Structure category.
Click the Paragraph icon.

The position assist window opens.

6 Click the Before icon.

A new paragraph element appears in the layout, with the placeholder text *This is the content for Layout P Tag.*

7 Select the placeholder text, and type **Return to top** to replace it.

The text is inserted between the two tables, formatted as a `<p>` element. The text would look better centered.

8 In the CSS Designer, choose **mygreen_styles.css** > GLOBAL > `.content .profile`.

Create a new selector `.ctr`.

9 Create the following property for the `.ctr` rule:

`text-align: center`

Classes can also be assigned in the Element View interface.

10 In Live view, select the element containing the text *Return to top.*

The Element View interface appears, displaying the p tag. Click the plus sign (+) to add a class to the element.

11 Type a period (.) to display a list of all defined classes.
Choose .ctr from the list.

.container	Halloween Haunted Hike	West Side Park
.content		
.cost	Nature Photography Photo Group	South Side Community (
.ctr		
.date	New Year's Eve Party	West Side Community C
.day		
.event		
.flt_lft		

Return to top

The *Return to top* text is aligned to the center. The tag selector now displays `p.ctr`.

12 Select the text *Return to Top.*
Click the Link icon and type `#top` in the Link field.

B I [icon] #top

Return to top

By using `#top`, you have created a link to a target within the current page. When users click the *Return to top* link, the browser window jumps to the position of the target. This target doesn't exist yet. For this link to work properly, you need to insert the destination as high on the page as possible.

13 Switch to Design view.

14 Scroll to the top of **events.html**. Position the cursor over the header element.

The mouse icon indicates that this part of the page (and its related code) is uneditable, because the header and horizontal navigation menu are based on the site template. Putting the target at the very top is important, or a portion of the page may be obscured when the browser jumps to it. Since the top of the page is part of an uneditable region, the best solution is to add the target directly to the template.

Creating a link destination using an id

By adding a unique id to the template, you will be able to access it automatically throughout the site wherever you want to add a link back to the top of a page.

1 Open the template **mygreen_temp** in Design view.

2 Insert the cursor in the h2 element in the <header>.
Select the h2 tag selector.
In the Property inspector, type **top** in the ID field.

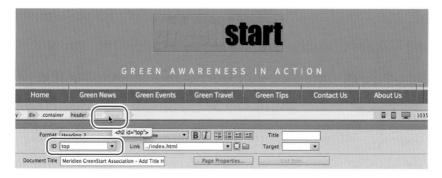

▶ **Tip:** When applying classes or ids, you can insert the cursor in the element or select the tag selector. The attribute will automatically be applied to the first containing element.

● **Note:** An id can be created and applied to any HTML element. They don't have to be referenced in the style sheet at all.

The tag selector changes to h2#top; otherwise, the page shows no visible difference. The big difference is in how the page reacts to the internal hyperlink.

3 Save the file and update all template child pages. Close the template.

4 Switch to or open **events.html**, if necessary.
Save the file, and preview it in the default browser.

5 Scroll down to the Class table. Click the *Return to top* link.

The browser jumps back to the top of the page.

Now that the id has been inserted in every page of the site by the template, you can copy the *Return to top* link and paste it anywhere in the site you want to add this functionality.

6 Switch to Dreamweaver.
Select and copy the <p> element containing the text and *Return to top* link.

7 Scroll down to and insert the cursor in the Class table.
Using the tag selector, select the <table> element.
Press the right arrow key once to move the cursor after the closing </table> tag.
Press Ctrl+V/Cmd+V to paste the paragraph and link.

The p.ctr element and link appear at the bottom of the page.

8 Save the file, and preview it in the browser. Test both *Return to top* links.

Both links can be used to jump back to the top of the document. In the next exercise, you'll learn how to create link targets using element attributes.

Creating a destination link in Element View

There's no need to add any extra elements to create hyperlink destinations if you can add an id attribute to a handy element nearby. In this exercise, you will use the Element view interface to add an id to an existing element.

1 If necessary, open **events.html** in Live view.
Insert the cursor in the Events table.
Press the up arrow key once to select the `<table>` element.

The Element View interface and the Property inspector display the attributes currently applied to the Events table. You can add an id using either tool.

Note: When creating ids, remember that they have to be unique names. They are case-sensitive, so look out for typos.

2 Click the plus sign (+) in the Element View interface.
Type a hash mark (#).

If any ids were defined in the style sheet but unused on the page, a list would appear. Since nothing appears, it means that there are no unused ids. Creating a new one is easy.

Note: If you add the id to the wrong element, simply delete it, and try again.

3 Type `calendar`, and press Enter/Return.

The tag selector now displays `table#calendar`. Since ids are unique identifiers, that makes them perfect for targeting specific content on a page. We also need to create an id for the Class table.

4 Select the Class table as in step 1.
In the Element View interface, type `#classes` in the field.

The tag selector now displays `table#classes`.

5 Save all files.

You'll learn how to link to these ids in the next exercise.

Targeting id-based link destinations

By adding unique ids to both tables, you have provided an ideal target for internal hyperlinks to navigate to a specific section of your web page. In this exercise, you will create a link to each table.

1 If necessary, open **contact_us.html** in Live view.
Scroll down to the *Education and Events* section.

2 Select the word *events* in the first paragraph of the section.

3 Using the Element View interface, create a link to the file **events.html**.

This link will open the file, but you're not finished. You now have to direct the browser to navigate down to the Events table.

4 Type `#calendar` at the end of the filename to complete the link.

Tip: You can select single words by double-clicking on them.

Note: Hyperlinks cannot contain spaces; make sure the id reference follows the filename immediately.

The word *events* is now a link targeting the Events table in the **events.html** file.

5 Select the word *classes*, and create a link to the **events.html** file.
Type `#classes` to complete the link.

6 Save the file, and preview the page in a browser.
Test the links to the Events and Class tables.

The links open the *Events* page and navigate to the appropriate tables.

Checking your page

Dreamweaver can check your page automatically for valid HTML, accessibility, and broken links. In this exercise, you'll check your links and learn what you can do in case of a browser compatibility problem.

1 If necessary, open **contact_us.html** in Design view.

2 Choose Site > Check Links Sitewide.

A Link Checker panel opens. The Link Checker panel reports broken links to the files **index.html** and **travel.html** you created for nonexistent pages. You'll make these pages later, so you don't need to worry about fixing these broken links now. The Link Checker will find broken links to external sites, should you have any.

3 Right-click the Link Checker tab, and choose Close Tab Group from the context menu.

You've made big changes to the appearance of the pages in this lesson by creating links to specific positions on a page, to email, and to an external site. You also created a link that uses images as the clickable item. Finally, you checked your page for broken links.

Adding destination links to the same page (optional)

Using the skills you have just learned, open **events.html**, and create destination links for the words *Events* and *Classes* that appear in the first paragraph.

Remember, the words will link to the tables on the same page. Can you figure out how to construct these links properly? If you have any trouble, check out the **events_finished.html** file for the answer.

Review questions

1 Describe two ways to insert a link into a page.

2 What information is required to create a link to an external web page?

3 What's the difference between standard page links and email links?

4 What attribute is used to create destination links?

5 What limits the usefulness of email links?

6 Can links be applied to images?

7 How can you check to see if your links will work properly?

Review answers

1 Select text or a graphic, and then, in the Property inspector, click the Browse for File icon next to the Link field, and navigate to the desired page. A second method is to drag the Point to File icon to a file within the Files panel.

2 Link to an external page by typing or copying and pasting the full web address (a fully formed URL) in the Link field of the Property inspector or the Element view interface.

3 A standard page link opens a new page or moves the view to a position somewhere on the page. An email link opens a blank email message window if the visitor has an email application installed.

4 You can apply unique id attributes to any element to create a link destination.

5 Email links may not be very useful because many users do not use built-in email programs, and the links will not automatically connect with Internet-based email services.

6 Yes, links can be applied to images and used in the exact same way text-based links are.

7 Run the Link Checker report to test links on each page individually or sitewide. You should also test them in a browser.

11

ADDING INTERACTIVITY

Lesson overview

In this lesson, you'll add Web 2.0 functionality to your webpages by doing the following:

- Using Dreamweaver behaviors to create an image rollover effect

- Inserting a jQuery accordion widget

 This lesson will take about 1 hour and 30 minutes to complete. If you have not already done so, download the project files for this lesson from the Lesson & Update Files tab on your Account page at www.peachpit.com, store them on your computer in a convenient location, and define a new site based on the lesson11 folder as described in the "Getting Started" section of this book. Your Account page is also where you'll find any updates to the lessons or to the lesson files. Look on the Lesson & Update Files tab to access the most current content.

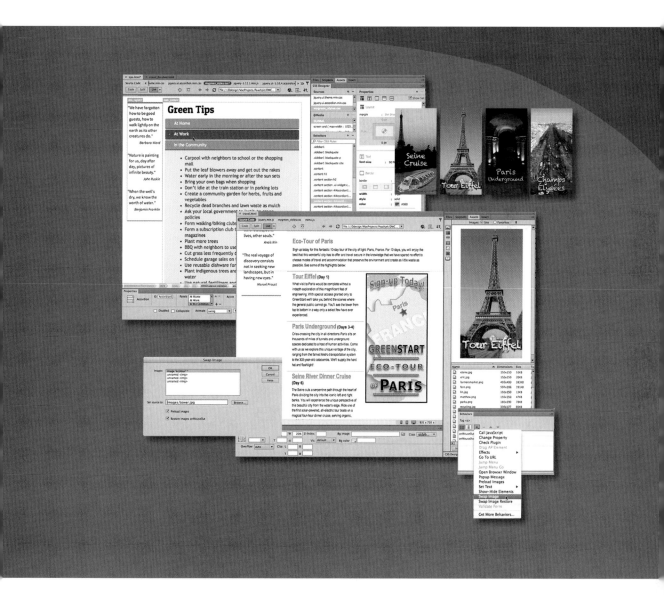

Dreamweaver can create sophisticated interactive effects with behaviors and accordion panels using Adobe's jQuery framework.

Learning about Dreamweaver behaviors

Note: If you have not already downloaded the project files for this lesson to your computer from your Account page, make sure to do so now. See "Getting Started" at the beginning of the book.

Note: To access the Behaviors panel and menu, you must have a file open.

The term *Web 2.0* was coined to describe a major change in the user experience on the Internet—from mostly static pages, featuring text, graphics, and simple links, to a new paradigm of dynamic webpages filled with video, animation, and interactive content. Dreamweaver has always led the industry in providing a variety of tools to drive this movement, from its tried-and-true collection of JavaScript behaviors and jQuery widgets to the latest support for jQuery Mobile. This lesson explores two of these capabilities: Dreamweaver behaviors and jQuery UI widgets.

A Dreamweaver *behavior* is predefined JavaScript code that performs an action—such as opening a browser window or showing or hiding a page element—when it is triggered by an event, such as a mouse click. Applying a behavior is a three-step process:

1 Create or select the page element that you want to trigger the behavior.

2 Choose the behavior to apply.

3 Specify the settings or parameters of the behavior.

The triggering element often involves a hyperlink applied to a range of text or to an image. In some cases, the behavior is not intended to load a new page, so it employs a dummy link enabled by the hash sign (#), similar to ones that you used in Lesson 10, "Working with Navigation." The Swap Image behavior you will use in this lesson does not require a link to function, but keep this in mind when you work with other behaviors.

Dreamweaver offers more than 16 built-in behaviors, all accessed from the Behaviors panel (Window > Behaviors). Hundreds of other useful behaviors can be downloaded from the Internet for free or a small fee. Some are available from the online Adobe Add-ons website, which can be added to the program by clicking the Add Behavior icon ✚ in the Behaviors panel and choosing Get More Behaviors from the pop-up menu or by choosing Window > Browse Add-ons.

When the Adobe Add-ons page loads in the browser, click the link to download the plug-in, extension, or other add-on. Often you can simply double-click the add-on to install it.

The following are some examples of the functionality available to you using the built-in Dreamweaver behaviors:

• Opening a browser window

• Swapping one image for another to create what is called a *rollover effect*

• Fading images or page areas in and out

• Growing or shrinking graphics

• Displaying pop-up messages

- Changing the text or other HTML content within a given area

- Showing or hiding sections of the page

- Calling a custom-defined JavaScript function

Not all behaviors are available all the time. Certain behaviors become available only in the presence and selection of certain page elements, such as images or hyperlinks. For example, the Swap Image behavior must be applied to an image.

Each behavior invokes a unique dialog that provides relevant options and specifications. For instance, the dialog for the Open Browser Window behavior enables you to open a new browser window; set its width, height, and other attributes; and set the URL of the displayed resource. After the behavior is defined, it is listed in the Behaviors panel with its chosen triggering action. As with other behaviors, these specifications can be modified at any time.

Behaviors are extremely flexible, and multiple behaviors can be applied to the same trigger. For example, you could swap one image for another and change the text of the accompanying image caption—and do it all with one click. Although some effects may appear to happen simultaneously, behaviors are actually triggered in sequence. When multiple behaviors are applied, you can choose the order in which the behaviors are processed.

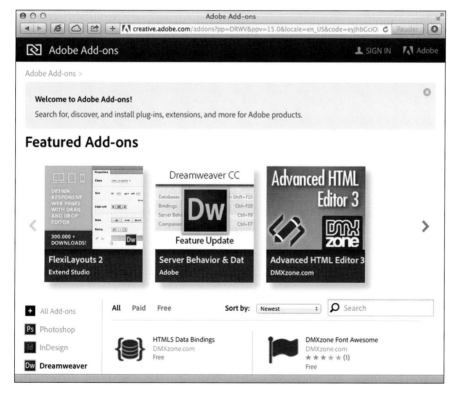

Adobe add-ons offer tons of resources for many of the applications in Creative Cloud, including both free and paid add-ons.

Previewing the completed file

In the first part of this lesson, you'll create a new page for GreenStart's travel services. Let's preview the completed page in a browser.

1   Launch Adobe Dreamweaver CC (2014.1 release) or later.
    If necessary, define a site based on the lesson11 folder.
    Name the site **lesson11**.

2   Open **travel_finished.html**, and preview the page in the default browser.

    The page includes Dreamweaver behaviors.

3   If Microsoft Internet Explorer is your default browser, a message may appear
    in the browser window indicating that it has prevented scripts and ActiveX
    controls from running. If so, click Allow Blocked Content.

    This message appears only when the file is previewed from your hard drive.
    It doesn't appear when the file is actually hosted on the Internet.

4   Position the cursor over the *Tour Eiffel* heading.
    Observe the image to the right of the text.

    The existing image swaps for one of the Eiffel Tower.

5   Move the pointer to the *Paris Underground* heading.
    Observe the image to the right of the text.

    As the pointer moves off the *Tour Eiffel* heading, the image reverts to the Eco-
    Tour ad. Then, as the pointer moves over the heading *Paris Underground*, the ad
    image swaps for one of underground Paris.

6   Pass the pointer over each <h3> heading, and observe the image behavior.

    The image alternates between the Eco-Tour ad and images of each of the tours.
    This effect is the Swap Image behavior.

7   When you're finished, close the browser window, and return to Dreamweaver.

In the next exercise, you'll learn how to work with Dreamweaver behaviors. Close
travel-finished.html.

Working with Dreamweaver behaviors

Adding Dreamweaver behaviors to your layout is a simple point-and-click operation. But before you can add the behaviors, you have to create the travel page.

1 Choose File > New.

In the New Document dialog, select the **Site Templates** category. Select **mygreen_temp** from lesson11, and click Create.

A new document window opens based on the template.

2 Switch to Design view, if necessary.

Save the new document as **travel.html** in the site root folder.

3 Open **sidebars.html** in Design view from the lesson11 resources folder.

Insert the cursor into the first paragraph.

Examine the tag selectors for the current insertion point.

The paragraph is a child of a `<blockquote>` within a `.sidebar1` element. The structure is identical to the `.sidebar1` element in the template file.

4 Select the `.sidebar1` tag selector.

5 Copy `.sidebar1` from **sidebars.html**.

6 Switch to **travel.html**.

Insert the cursor into the `.sidebar1` placeholder text.

Select the `.sidebar1` tag selector.

7 Paste the new content to replace the existing `.sidebar1`.

8 Repeat steps 4–7 to replace the placeholder content in sidebar 2 with the appropriate content from **sidebars.html**. Close **sidebars.html**.

9 Open **travel-text.html** in Design view from the lesson11 resources folder.

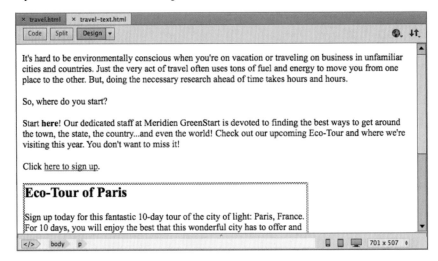

The **travel-text.html** file contains a table and text for the travel page. Note that the text and table are unformatted.

10 Select and copy all the contents within the page. Close **travel-text.html**.

11 Select the main heading placeholder *Add main heading here* in **travel.html**. Type **Green Travel** to replace the text.

12 Select the heading placeholder *Add subheading here*. Type **Eco-Touring** to replace it.

13 Select the p tag selector for the *Add content here* text. Press Ctrl+V/Cmd+V to paste the travel text.

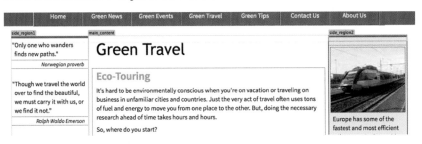

The content from **travel-text.html** appears, replacing the placeholder text. It assumes the default formatting for text and tables applied by the style sheet you created in Lesson 8, "Working with Text, Lists, and Tables."

Let's insert the Eco-Tour ad, which will be the base image for the Swap Image behavior.

14 Double-click the *SideAd* placeholder.

Navigate to the site images folder, and select **ecotour.png**.
Click OK/Open.

The placeholder is replaced by the Eco-Tour ad. But before you can apply the Swap Image behavior, you have to identify the image you want to swap. You do this by giving the image an id.

15 If necessary, select **ecotour.png** in the layout.

In the Property inspector, select the existing id SideAd.
Type ecotour, and press Enter/Return.
Enter **Eco-Tour of Paris** in the Alt field.

▶ **Tip:** Although it takes more time, giving all your images unique ids is a good practice.

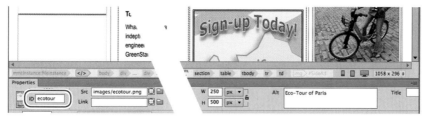

16 Save the file.

Next, you'll create a Swap Image behavior for **ecotour.png**.

Applying a behavior

As described earlier, many behaviors are context sensitive, based on the elements or structure present. A Swap Image behavior can be triggered by any document element, but it affects only images displayed within the page..

1 Choose Window > Behaviors to open the Behaviors panel.

2 Insert the cursor in the *Tour Eiffel* text, and select the <h3> tag selector.

3 Click the Add Behavior icon **+**.
Choose Swap Image from the behavior list.

The Swap Image dialog lists any images on the page that are available for this behavior. This behavior can replace one or more of these images at a time.

● **Note:** Items listed as unnamed <img> are images without id attributes. If you wish to swap them too, you'll have to first give them ids.

4 Select the image "ecotour" item, and click Browse.

5 In the Select Image Source dialog, select **tower.jpg** from the site images folder. Click OK/Open.

● **Note:** The Preload Images option forces the browser to download all images necessary for the behavior when the page loads. That way, when the user clicks the trigger, the image swap occurs without any lags or glitches.

6 In the Swap Image dialog, select the Preload Images option, if necessary, and click OK.

A Swap Image behavior is added to the Behaviors panel with an attribute of onMouseOver. Attributes can be changed, if desired, using the Behaviors panel.

7 Click the onMouseOver attribute to open the pop-up menu, and examine the other available options.

The menu provides a list of trigger events, most of which are self-explanatory. For now, however, leave the attribute as onMouseOver.

8 Save the file, and click Live view to test the behavior.
Position the cursor over the *Tour Eiffel* text.

When the cursor passes over the text, the Eco-Tour ad is replaced by the image of the Eiffel Tower. But there is a small problem. When the cursor moves away from the text, the original image doesn't return. The reason is simple: You didn't tell it to. To bring back the original image, you have to add another command—Swap Image Restore—to the same element.

Applying a Swap Image Restore behavior

In some instances, a specific action requires more than one behavior. To bring back the Eco-Tour ad once the mouse moves off the trigger, you have to add a restore function.

1 Switch to Design view.
Insert the cursor in the *Tour Eiffel* heading, and examine the Behaviors panel.

The inspector displays the currently assigned behavior. You don't need to select the element completely; Dreamweaver assumes you want to modify the entire trigger.

2 Click the Add Behavior icon ➕▾.

Choose Swap Image Restore from the pop-up menu.

Click OK in the Swap Image Restore dialog to complete the command.

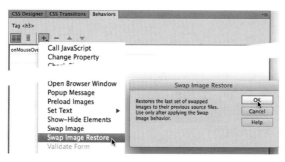

The Swap Image Restore behavior appears in the Behaviors panel with an attribute of onMouseOut.

3 Switch to Code view, and examine the markup for the *Tour Eiffel* text.

The trigger events—onMouseOver and onMouseOut—were added as attributes to the <h3> element. The rest of the JavaScript code was inserted in the document's <head> section.

4 Save the file, and switch to Live view to test the behavior.

Test the text trigger *Tour Eiffel*.

When the pointer passes over the text, the Eco-Tour image is replaced by the one of the Eiffel Tower, and then reappears when the pointer is withdrawn. The behavior functions as desired, but nothing is visibly "different" about the text. There is nothing here to prompt a user to roll their pointer over the heading. The end result will be that many users will miss the swap image effect altogether.

Users sometimes need to be encouraged or directed to these types of effects. Many designers use hyperlinks for this purpose, since users are already familiar with how they function. Let's replace the current effect with one based on a hyperlink.

Removing applied behaviors

Before you can apply a behavior to a hyperlink, you need to remove the current Swap Image and Swap Image Restore behaviors.

1 Switch to Design view. Open the Behaviors panel, if necessary.

Insert the cursor in the *Tour Eiffel* text.

The Behaviors panel displays the two applied events. Which one you delete first doesn't matter.

2 Select the Swap Image event.
In the Behaviors panel, click the Remove Event icon —.

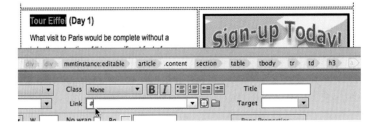

3 Select the Swap Image Restore event.
In the Behaviors panel, click the Remove Event icon.

Both events are now removed. Dreamweaver also removes any unneeded JavaScript code.

4 Save the file, and check the text in Live view again.

The text no longer triggers the Swap Image behavior. To reapply the behavior, you need to add a link or link placeholder to the heading.

Adding behaviors to hyperlinks

Behaviors can be added to hyperlinks, even if the link doesn't load a new document. For this exercise, you'll add a link placeholder (#) to the heading to support the desired behavior.

1 Select the *Tour Eiffel* text within the <h3> element.
Type # in the Property inspector Link field.
Press Enter/Return to create the link placeholder.

The text displays with the default hyperlink styling.

2 Insert the cursor in the *Tour Eiffel* link.
In the Behaviors panel, click the Add Behavior icon **+**.
Choose Swap Image from the pop-up menu.

As long as the cursor is still inserted anywhere in the link, the behavior will be applied to the entire link markup.

3 In the Swap Image dialog, select the item `image "ecotour"`.
Browse to and select **tower.jpg** from the site images folder.
Click OK/Open.

4 In the Swap Image dialog, select the Preload Images option and Restore Images onMouseOut option, if necessary, and click OK.

The Swap Image event appears in the Behaviors panel along with a Swap Image Restore event. Since the behavior was applied all at once, Dreamweaver provides the restore functionality as a productivity enhancement.

5 Select and apply a link placeholder (#) to the *Paris Underground* text.
Apply the Swap Image behavior to the link.
Use the **underground.jpg** image from the site images folder.

6 Repeat step 5 for the *Seine River Dinner Cruise* text. Select the image **cruise.jpg**.

7 Repeat step 5 for the *Champs Élysées* text. Select the image **champs.jpg**.

The Swap Image behaviors are now complete, but the text and link appearances don't match the site's color scheme. Let's create custom CSS rules to format them accordingly. You will create two rules: one for the heading element and another for the link itself.

8 Insert the cursor in any of the rollover links.

9 In the CSS Designer, select **mygreen_styles.css** > GLOBAL > `.content section h2`.
Create the new selector `.content section h3`

10 Create the following properties in the new rule:

```
margin-top: 0px
margin-bottom: 5px
```

11 Select **mygreen_styles.css** > GLOBAL > `.content section h3`.
Create a new selector `.content section h3 a:link,`
`.content section h3 a:visited`

12 Create the following properties in the new rule:

```
font-size: 120%
color: #090
```

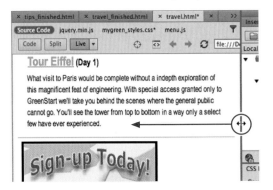

The headings are now more prominent and styled to match the site theme. Note how the link underline disappears when the mouse moves over the link based on the styling inherited from the existing `a:hover` styling.

13 Save all files, and test the behaviors in Live view.

The Swap Image behavior should work successfully on all links. If one or more of the links do not function, check to make sure the behavior was assigned to the link successfully.

Making it responsive

Once you're satisfied that all the rollover effects are functioning properly, you should check to make sure that the new components adapt properly to the responsive page design, too. You can check the functionality in Dreamweaver or in any modern browser installed on your computer.

1 Drag the right edge of the screen to the left to test how the new table responds to the existing set of media queries.

The table adapts to the changing screen in a fashion similar to the tables created and styled in Lesson 8. Everything seems to display fine, although the Ecotour ad does not scale or resize in any way.

At a width of 810 pixels, the cells of the table begin to stack one atop the other, and the cell containing the ad follows suit. The image no longer appears beside the text describing the tours. At this point, the purpose of the rollover effect will be lost completely. The simplest plan would be just to hide the ad on smaller screens and allow the text to speak for itself.

At this moment, there's a custom id applied to the ad image but nothing applied to the cell containing it. CSS can hide the image, but it will leave a blank cell behind. Let's create a custom class to hide the cell containing the ad.

2   If necessary, choose Window > CSS Designer.
    Select **mygreen_styles.css** > screen and (max-width 810px) >
    .content section table.
    Create a new selector table .ad_hide.

    This rule limits the styling to elements within a table.

3   Create the following property in the new rule display: none.

    Once it's created, you can apply the class to the appropriate cell. You can do this in Live or Design view.

4   Select the Ecotour ad image.

5   Select the td tag selector for the cell containing the ad.

6   In Live view, click the Add Class/Id icon ⊞ in the Element View interface.
    Type .ad_hide and press Enter/Return.

    Or

    In Design view, choose .ad_hide from the Class menu in the Property inspector.

The table cell and ad will display in the document window whenever it is wider than 810 pixels.

7   Choose **mygreen_styles.css** > GLOBAL to reset document display.
    Drag the right edge of the document window to the left until it is narrower than 810 pixels. Observe the changes to the table and its content.

    The Ecotour ad hides once the screen is narrower than 810 pixels. It reappears as soon as the screen gets wider than 810 pixels.

8 Save all files.

9 Close **travel.html**.

In addition to eye-catching effects such as the dynamic behaviors you've just been learning about, Dreamweaver also provides structural components—such as jQuery widgets—that conserve space and add more interactive flair to your website.

Working with jQuery Accordion widgets

The jQuery Accordion widget allows you to organize a lot of content into a compact space. In the Accordion widget, the tabs are stacked, and when opened, they expand vertically rather than side by side. Let's preview the completed layout.

1 In the Files panel, select **tips_finished.html** from the lesson11 folder, and preview it in your primary browser.

The page content is divided among three panels using the jQuery Accordion widget.

2 Click each panel in turn to open and close each.

When you click a tab, the panel slides open with a smooth action. The panels are set to a specific height; if the content is taller or wider than the panel itself, scroll bars appear automatically. When the panels open and close, the bulleted lists of green tips are revealed. The accordion allows you to display more content in a smaller, more efficient footprint.

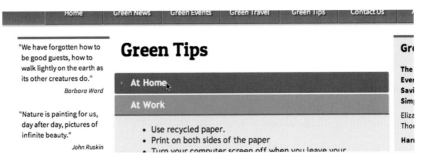

3 Close your browser, and return to Dreamweaver.
Close **tips_finished.html**.

Inserting a jQuery Accordion widget

In this exercise, you'll incorporate a jQuery Accordion widget into one of your existing layouts.

1   Open **tips.html** in Design view.

The page consists of three bulleted lists separated by <h2> headings. Let's start by inserting a jQuery Accordion before the first <h2>.

2   Insert the cursor in the *At Home* heading, and select the <h2> tag selector. Press the left arrow key once to move the cursor before the opening <h2> tag.

3   In the Insert panel jQuery UI category, select Accordion.

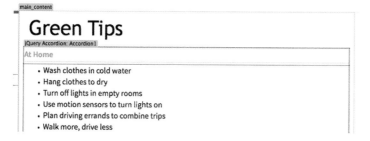

Dreamweaver inserts the jQuery Accordion widget element above the heading. The initial element is a three-panel Accordion widget that appears with the top panel (panel 1) open. A blue tab appears above the new object, with the title *jQuery Accordion: Accordion1*.

4   Scroll down, and insert the cursor in the first bullet, *Wash clothes in cold water.* Select the <ul> tag selector. Press Ctrl+X/Cmd+X to cut the whole list.

5   Insert the cursor in the *Content 1* text in the top Accordion widget panel. Select the <p> tag selector, and paste the bulleted list.

6   Insert the cursor in the <h2> heading *At Home.* Select the <h2> tag selector, and press Delete.

The <h2> element and the original heading are now gone.

7   Select the placeholder text *Section 1*, and type **At Home** to replace it.

> ### Green Tips
>
> jQuery Accordion: Accordion1
>
> At Home
>
> - Wash clothes in cold water
> - Hang clothes to dry
> - Turn off lights in empty rooms
> - Use motion sensors to turn lights on
> - Plan driving errands to combine trips
> - Walk more, drive less

In Design view, the bulleted list appears in the first content panel.

8 Select and cut the subsequent `<ul>` element containing the "Work" tips. Select and delete the empty `<section>` containing the *At Work* heading.

9 Position the cursor over the bar displaying the *Section 2* text. Click the eye icon 👁 to open panel 2, if necessary.

Panel 2 opens; panel 1 closes automatically.

10 Select the text *Section 2*, and type **At Work** to replace it.

▶ **Tip:** Remember to use the tag selectors to select and replace the entire element.

11 Select the `<p>` element containing the text *Content 2*, and paste the `<ul>` element.

The list of tips At Work replaces the placeholder for Content 2.

12 Repeat steps 7–10 to create the content section for *In the Community*.

When you're finished, all three lists are now contained within Accordion 1, and all the empty `<section>` elements have been deleted.

You inserted a jQuery Accordion and added content to it. Although the content added in this exercise was already on the page, it should be clear that you can enter and edit content directly in the content panels, too. You can also copy material from other sources, such as Microsoft Word and text editors, among others.

13 Save all files.

14 Click OK.

A dialog appears reporting that several jQuery asset files will be copied to the site folder to support Accordion 1's functionality. In the next exercise, you'll learn how to apply the site color scheme to the Accordion widget.

Customizing a jQuery Accordion

Like other widgets that can be created by Dreamweaver, the jQuery Accordion is formatted by its own separate CSS and JavaScript files. If you look at the related file display at the top of the document window, you'll see three new style sheets and two new .js files linked to this page that are formatting and controlling the behavior of the widget.

The jQuery style sheets are very complex and should be avoided unless you know what you are doing. Instead, in this exercise, you'll learn how to apply the site design theme to Accordion 1 by using the existing site style sheet and the skills you have already learned.

1 Insert the cursor into the *At Home* tab.
   Examine the names and order of the tag selectors.

   The tabs are comprised of three main elements: `<div#Accordion1>`, `<h3>`, and `<a>`. But that's only on the surface. Behind the scenes, the jQuery functions are manipulating the HTML and CSS to produce the various behaviors controlling the Accordion. As you move your mouse over the tabs and click them, class attributes are being changed on the fly to produce the hover effects and animated panels.

   As you learned earlier, hyperlinks exhibit four basic behaviors: link, visited, hover, and active. jQuery is taking advantage of these default states to apply the various effects you see when interacting with Accordion 1. Your job will be to create several new rules that will override the jQuery styling and apply the GreenStart theme instead. The first step is to format the default state of the tabs.

2 Switch to Design view. Insert the cursor into one of the heading tabs above a closed accordion section.

   The tabs above the closed panels are considered the default state, since only one tab can be open at a time.

3 Select the h3 tag selector for the closed tab.
   Select **mygreen_styles.css** > GLOBAL > `.content section h3`. Click the Add Selector icon ➕.

The selector name field opens, filled automatically by a descendant selector based on the selection in the document window. This selector needs to be more specific in order to override the original jQuery styling. While the selector name is still open, you can make it more or less specific by pressing the up or down arrow key. You may also have to edit the selector names manually.

Tip: Pressing the down arrow should create the desired selector. But it's hard to view the entire selector since the field window is so small. You can press the right or left arrow to scroll through the entire name.

4   Press the down arrow once to create the following new selector
    `.content section #Accordion1 .ui-helper-reset.ui-state-default`

5   Select Show Set and create the following properties for the new rule:

    ```
    font-size: 90%
    border-bottom: solid 3px #060
    margin-bottom: 0px
    background-color: #090
    background-image: none
    ```

This styling will apply to the default state of the accordion tabs and then automatically to all others by inheritance. By starting with this state, you have to style only the behaviors you want to change through user interaction.

The accordion tabs are enabled in very much the same way we built the rollover effect earlier using a dummy hyperlink. So, that means that the text color is controlled by the <a> element.

6   Select the a tag selector for the closed tab.

7   Select **mygreen_styles.css** > GLOBAL > `.content section h2`

8   Click the Add Selector icon ➕.

A new selector name appears, targeting the <a> element in Accordion 1. Typically, hyperlinks change color when you click the link and visit the targeted destination. Since this is more like a navigation menu than a simple link, it would not look good to have the tab heading show two different colors in the layout. The new rule should format both the default (`a:link`) and visited state of the hyperlink. That means, you'll need to modify the selector name created by the CSS Designer.

9 Press the down arrow to make the default selector name more specific.

The tag name `section` is added to the selector name.

10 Press the down arrow again.

The class `.content` is added to the selector. The new selector now targets the basic hyperlink (`a`) in the current accordion element, but there is one problem: The selectors in the jQuery style sheet uses `a:link` to format this element. The pseudo-class `a:link` is more specific than the `a` tag by itself and may override your new rule, which defeats the purpose of making it in the first place. When resetting properties from other style sheets, it's important to match the specificity of any conflicting rule, or exceed it.

11 If the selector field is still open and editable, press the right arrow to move the cursor to the end of the selector name, or press the End key. Otherwise, double-click the selector to edit the name and move the cursor to the end of the name.

When cursor arrives at the end of the selector you will see the `a` tag at the end of the name.

12 Type `:link` to complete the first part of the selector name. Make sure there is no space between the tag and the pseudo-class.

You could create a second selector for the visited state, but it's easier to simply add it to this one.

13 Press Ctrl-A/Cmd-A to select the entire selector name.
Press Ctrl-C/Cmd-C to copy the selector.

14 Insert the cursor at the end of the current selector name. Type , (comma), and press the spacebar. Press Ctrl-V/Cmd-V to paste the selector name.

An exact duplicate of the selector name appears following the comma.

15 Change `a:link` at the end of the selector name to `a:visited` and press Enter/Return to complete the selector name.

The selector name is complete. This rule will target the tab heading for the default and visited state.

16 Create the following property in the new rule: `color: #FFC`

The text in the tab appears pale yellow. The base design of Accordion 1 is complete. Now, let's add a little flair by creating a custom `a:hover` state for the tabs.

▶ **Tip:** Use copy and paste to make complex selector names like this one. Don't forget to insert the comma between the two parts.

◐ **Note:** As you learned in Lesson 5, the pseudo-classes must be declared in a specific order. The `a:link` pseudo-class must precede `a:visited`, even in a selector name.

17 Select **mygreen_styles.css** > GLOBAL > `.content section #Accordion1 .ui-helper-reset.ui-state-default` rule.

18 Right-click the rule, and duplicate it.

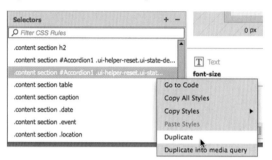

19 Edit the new selector to add the `:hover` state to it, such as: `.content section #Accordion1 .ui-helper-reset.ui-state-default:hover`

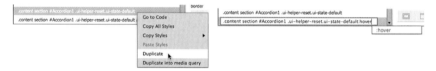

The new `:hover` rule is identical to the original. Since it inherits the styling from the default state, there's no need to keep all the properties.

20 Delete the following specifications from the new `:hover` state rule:

~~font-size: 90%~~
~~border-bottom-color: #060~~
~~border-bottom-width: 3px~~
~~border-bottom-style: solid~~
~~margin-bottom: 0px~~

21 Edit the remaining specifications as follows:

`background-color: #060`

These changes will provide a visual interactivity for the hover state. Let's also modify the text color.

22 In **mygreen_styles.css** > GLOBAL, duplicate the following rule:

`.content section #Accordion1 .ui-helper-reset.ui-state-default a:link, .content section #Accordion1 .ui-helper-reset.ui-state-default a:visited`

23 Delete the complete `a:visited` selector and change the remaining selector as shown:

`.content section #Accordion1 .ui-helper-reset.ui-state-default a:hover`

24 Edit the following specification:

`color: #FFF`

25 Save all files.

26 Switch to Live view.
Test and examine the accordion behavior.

The tabs display a hover behavior, changing color as you position the pointer over them, and a drop shadow behind the text.

There are two detractions from the overall effect: The content windows display at the same height regardless of the amount of content, and the background fill doesn't seem to fit properly. One fix is simple; the other not so much.

27 Switch to Design view, and insert the cursor in Accordion 1.

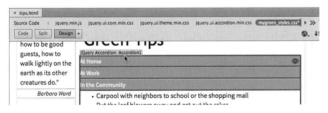

A blue tab appears above the widget, identifying it as a jQuery Accordion.

28 Select the blue tab (jQuery Accordion: Accordion1) that appears above the widget.

The Property inspector displays various specifications for the jQuery Accordion. In this interface, you can easily add new content windows and remove existing ones and control other important properties without having to access the HTML or CSS code. The height style is currently set for auto, which makes each panel the same size.

29 From the Height Style pop-up menu, choose `content`.

30 Save all files, and preview the document in Live view.
Test and examine the accordion behavior.

The panels now scale individually to the height of their actual content. The gradient background is still not conforming to the entire content window. The fix for this will be a little more convoluted. The first step is to figure out what rules are formatting this element.

31 Insert the cursor in the open content window of the accordion.
Observe the tag selectors, and try to identify the element holding the list.

The only element that seems to contain the content is a <div>.

32 Observe the CSS Designer Selectors window.
Try to identify the source of the styling of this <div>.

The display in the Properties window shows a background color but no gradient. It shows no classes or ids, either. If you relied solely on Design view, you would remain stumped and would be unable to discover the source of the formatting. Luckily, Live view has additional capabilities as well as a more accurate display.

Editing dynamic jQuery styling

Widgets, like the jQuery Accordion, are often formatted dynamically. Some or all of their styling is not intrinsic to the element; they are actually applied, swapped, and even removed programmatically. Dynamic styling can give you huge advantages over static formatting.

For example, by using scripts you can have the component poll, or query, the browser to find out its dimensions, orientation, and even operating system. Once this information is known, the script can then apply custom styling optimized for that environment and even remove styles known not to work properly.

In most cases, you can use Design view to identify the styling applied to any individual component or element. However, when the answers are not apparent, as in this case, you've reached the limit of Design view's functionality. The next step is to turn to Live view.

1 If necessary, open **tips.html** in Design view, or switch to it if the file is still open.

2 Insert the cursor in the open accordion content section.
   Observe the tag selector interface.

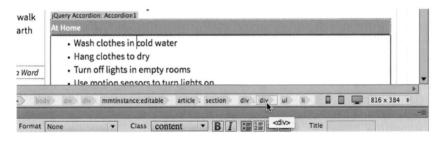

There is nothing different in the tag selectors. There are no additional tags, classes, or ids. By all appearances, it looks like an unstyled, generic `<div>`.

3 Switch to Live view.
   Using the tag selector, select the first `<div>` containing the `<ul>` element.
   Observe the Element Display interface.

In Design view, the `<div>` itself displayed no classes or ids at all. But in the Live view Element Display, the `<div>` now shows five classes and one id assigned to it. Where did they come from?

Live view processes all the HTML, CSS, and JavaScript, and then renders the page as it would appear in a modern browser. The fact that nothing appears in the tag selectors or in the underlying HTML code itself suggests that jQuery or JavaScript is applying these classes and id on the fly. Fortunately, Dreamweaver provides a method that enables us to prove this theory.

4   Click the Inspect mode icon ⊕ to turn Inspect mode on.
Position the cursor over the unordered list, but do not click it.

Inspect mode displays the element name directly under the cursor, and displays the element's width and height and any classes or ids associated with it. Combining Inspect mode with Live Code mode enables you to see exactly what things are being done behind the scenes.

5   Select Split view.

The document window splits in half. Depending on your own defaults, it may appear split vertically or horizontally. You can change this display preference from the View menu.

6   If necessary, choose View > Split Vertically to display the Live and Code views side by side. Observe the `<div>` containing the `<ul>` in Accordion 1.

With only Live view turned on, the Code view window shows the raw, static HTML. The code highlights as you move your cursor, but it does not show any dynamic functionality. Note how the `<div>` element has no classes or ids assigned to it in the Code view window, yet in Inspect mode the Element View interface tells a different story. To see what's really happening, you need to turn on Live Code.

7   Click the Live Code icon `<>` to turn Live Code on.
Position the cursor over various elements on the screen.
Observe the code display.

With Live Code on, Code view shows what's really going on in the browser. Not only do the elements show classes and ids that did not appear before, they also change attributes dynamically as you move your cursor. The `<div>` holding the list element now shows the classes assigned to it via the jQuery commands.

Using Live view with Live Code and Inspect mode makes the job of troubleshooting and styling dynamic elements much faster and easier, and takes away a lot of the guesswork that was a major factor in web design in the past. As you move the cursor around the layout, Inspect mode takes over control of the CSS Designer display. The Source, @Media, Selectors, and Properties windows change as you hover over each element, showing you the source of any CSS styling. Often this interaction will be sufficient to identify the pertinent styling information you're looking for, but not in every instance.

Note: Clicking the element turns off Inspect mode.

8 Position the cursor over the open list in Accordion 1 in the Live view window, and try to identify the parent `<div>` of the list.

It takes some practice to learn where to position the cursor to select various elements on the page. Be careful not to click in the Live view window. Clicking an element turns Inspect mode off. If you can't find a specific element by moving the cursor around, you can use the tag selector interface to get the information you want.

9 Click the tag selector for the open content `<div>` in Accordion 1.

When you select the `<div>`, two things happen at once. First, Inspect mode is turned off. Then, the CSS Designer displays the various rules and styling assigned to the `<div>`. However, just seeing the raw display of styling isn't very helpful all the time. Since elements can inherit and combine styling from multiple rules, tracking down the exact rule you need to override can be daunting. In these situations the Code Navigator excels.

10 Right-click the tag selector for the `<div>` element, or press Ctrl+Alt+N/ Cmd+Opt+N.

Code Navigator appears, displaying the full list of CSS rules applied to this element. This display works in all modes, but shows only dynamic styling when you are in Live view. If you don't see the list of dynamically applied rules, you may need to move your insertion point from the Code window to the Live view window.

Finding the rule or rules that are responsible for the background effects in the Accordion content element will take a bit of detective work. As you look for the specific styling reference, make note of the class or id names applying the styles. Often, the name itself will give you a clue to what styling it's responsible for.

11 Hover the cursor over each rule in the Code Navigator display, and note the specification(s) applied by each.

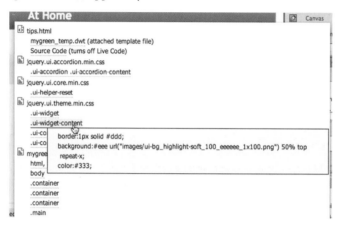

The rule that seems to be applying the background is ui-widget-content. To change or override this rule, you need to create a more specific selector and either turn off the background effect or make one of your own.

12 In the CSS Designer, select **mygreen_styles.css** > Global > .content section h2.

Create a new selector .content section .ui-widget-content

13 Create the following properties:

```
background-color: #CFC
background-image: none
```

The background for the Accordion content window now displays as a light green over the entire height of the area.

14 Save all files, and preview the page in a browser.
Test the Accordion in various screen sizes.

The Accordion works fine at all screen sizes and is naturally responsive when the media queries kick in. The only issue seems to be that the content of the Accordion is indented awkwardly on smaller screens. Before you can make a new rule to reset this spacing, you'll need to once more identify the rule that's setting it in the first place.

15 Insert the cursor in a list in an open Accordion content window.
Select the various elements containing the list to identify the current styling. Use the tag selector interface with the CSS Designer and/or Code Navigator to pinpoint specifications providing margin or padding to the elements.

You'll find that the rule `.content ul, .content ol` applies left padding of 40 pixels and right padding of 15 pixels. You need to reset this styling only for screens under 665 pixels.

16 Select **mygreen_styles.css** > `screen and (max-width 665px)` > `.content section`.
Create a new selector `.content section div div ul,` `.content section div div ol`

This selector will target only ordered and unordered lists contained within the Accordion or similar elements. Note how we did not use the `#Accordion1` id in the selector. Using it would limit the styling only to Accordion 1. By using a more generic name it broadens the usefulness of the rule and limits the amount of code you have to create overall.

17 Create the following property: `padding: 0px 0px 25px 0px`

18 Save all files, and preview the changes in Live view or a browser.

The padding on the list has been reduced but not removed. This means that the spacing is probably being applied by another rule.

19 Switch to Live view, and insert the cursor in a list in an open content window.

20 Select the tag selector for the parent `<div>`.
Examine the list of rules pertinent to this element.
Check each one for any spacing that indents the list.

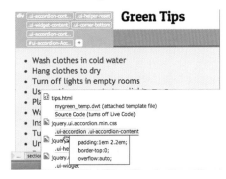

By checking each one, you should find that the `.ui-accordion` `.ui-accordion-content` rule applies left and right padding of 2.2 ems. The indent looks fine in wider screens, but makes the text too hard to read on narrower ones.

21 Choose **mygreen_styles.css** > `screen` and `(max-width 665px)` > `.content section`.

Create a new selector `.content section div div`

22 Create the following property: `padding: 0px`

23 Save all files, and preview the changes in Live view or a browser.

That did it. When the document window becomes narrower than 665 pixels, the padding is removed from the element. The text stretches across the entire screen, using the space more effectively.

You've learned how to identify the styling applied to a dynamic jQuery accordion and successfully reformatted it to to the Accordion widget so it match the website color scheme and adjusted the component height to allow the content to display more efficiently.

The Accordion is just one of the 33 jQuery widgets and components offered by Dreamweaver that allow you to incorporate advanced functionality into your website, requiring little or no programming skill. All of these components can be accessed via either the Insert menu or panel.

Adding interactivity to your webpages opens up new possibilities of interest and excitement for your visitors, engaging them in new ways. It can easily be overdone, but a wise use of interactivity can help bring in new visitors and keep your frequent visitors coming back for more.

Review questions

1 What is a benefit of using Dreamweaver behaviors?

2 What three steps must be used to create a Dreamweaver behavior?

3 What's the purpose of assigning an id to an image before applying a behavior?

4 What does a jQuery Accordion widget do?

5 Where can you add or remove panels from a jQuery Accordion widget?

6 What Dreamweaver tools are helpful in troubleshooting CSS styling on dynamic elements?

Review answers

1 Dreamweaver behaviors add interactive functionality to a webpage quickly and easily.

2 To create a Dreamweaver behavior, you need to create or select a trigger element, select a desired behavior, and specify the parameters.

3 The id is essential for selecting the specific image during the process of applying a behavior.

4 A jQuery Accordion widget includes multiple collapsible panels that hide and reveal content in a compact area of the page.

5 Select the widget in the document window using the blue tab, and use the Property inspector jQuery interface.

6 Inspect mode, Live Code, and Code Navigator make it faster and easier to identify CSS styling and to create new specifications.

12 WORKING WITH WEB ANIMATION AND VIDEO

Lesson overview

In this lesson, you'll learn how to incorporate web-compatible animation and video components into your webpage and do the following:

- Insert web-compatible animation

- Insert web-compatible video

 This lesson will take about 40 minutes to complete. Download the project files for this lesson from the Lesson & Update Files tab on your Account page at www.peachpit.com, store them on your computer in a convenient location, and define a new site based on the lesson12 folder, as described in the "Getting Started" section of this book. Your Account page is also where you'll find any updates to the lessons or to the lesson files. Look on the Lesson & Update Files tab to access the most current content.

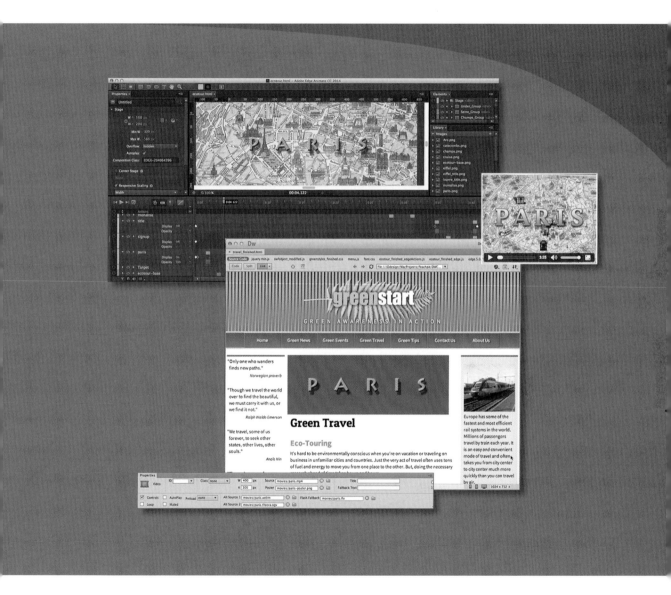

Dreamweaver allows you to integrate HTML5-compatible animation and video.

Understanding web animation and video

The web can provide a variety of experiences to the average user. One second, you are downloading and reading a best-selling novel. Next, you're listening to your favorite radio station or performing artist. Then, you're watching live television coverage or a feature-length movie. Before Adobe Flash, animation and video were hard to incorporate on websites. That's because HTML was invented at a time when even static images were difficult to use on the Internet; video was a dream far off in the future.

Video and animation content was eventually provided in a variety of formats using a hodgepodge of applications, plug-ins, and coder-decoders (codecs) that could transfer data across the Internet to your computer and browser. Often this was accomplished with enormous difficulties and incompatibilities. Frequently, a format that worked in one browser was incompatible with another. Applications that worked in Windows didn't work on the Mac. Most formats required their own proprietary players or plug-ins.

For a time, Adobe Flash brought order to this chaos. It provided a single platform for creating both animation and video. Flash started as an animation program and changed the web for everyone. A few years ago, it revolutionized the industry again by making it a simple task to add video to a site. By inserting a video into Flash and saving the file as a SWF or FLV file, web designers and developers were able to take advantage of the almost universal distribution of the Flash Player (installed on over 90 percent of all desktop computers). No more worries over formats and codecs—Flash Player took care of all that.

With the invention and rise in popularity of smartphones and tablet devices over the last decade, Flash has fallen on hard times. For most manufacturers, the power and capability of Flash were too difficult to support on these devices, and it was abandoned. Flash is not dead. It's still unmatched for its multimedia power and functionality. But today, all bets are off when it comes to animation and video. The techniques for creating web-based media are being reinvented. As you may have guessed, this trend away from Flash is ringing in a new era of chaos on the web media front. Half a dozen or more codecs are competing to become the "be-all end-all" format for video distribution and playback for the web.

The only ray of sunshine in this morass is that HTML5 was developed with built-in support for both animation and video. Great strides have already been made to replace much of the capability of Flash-based animation using native HTML5 and CSS3 functionality. The status of video is not as clear. So far, a single standard has not yet emerged, which means that to support all the popular desktop and mobile browsers, you'll have to produce several different video files. In this lesson, you'll learn how to incorporate different types of web animation and video into your site.

Previewing the completed file

To see what you'll work on in this lesson, preview the completed page in a browser. The finished page is based on the travel page you created in Lesson 11, "Adding Interactivity."

1 Launch Adobe Dreamweaver CC (2014.1 release) or later.

2 If necessary, define a site based on the lesson12 folder.
   Press F8 to open the Files panel, and choose lesson12 from the site list drop-down menu.

3 Open **travel_finished.html** from the site root folder.
   Preview the page in your default browser.

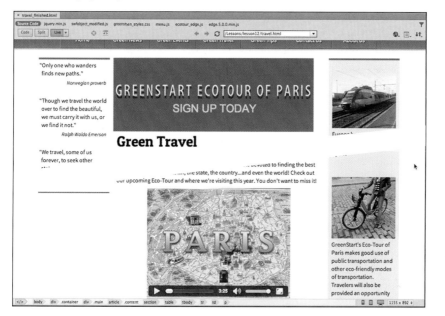

The page includes two media elements: the banner animation at the top of the `main_content` region and the video inserted below. Depending on the browser used to view the page, the video may be generated from one of four different formats: MP4, WebM, Ogg, or Flash Video.

4 Note that the banner ad plays when the page loads and stops with a call to sign up for the Eco-Tour.

5 To view the video, click the Play button. If you do not see a Play button, your browser may be showing a Flash fallback version of the video. Move the cursor over the video to display the control skin, and click the Play button.

Note: Internet Explorer may block dynamic content from playing when it's on your local hard drive.

Note: The video may not play properly until you upload the page and its resources to an actual web server.

Different browsers support different types of video. Depending on the video format your browser supports, you may notice that the controls fade if you move the cursor away from the video, but that they return once you position the cursor over the video again.

6   When you're finished previewing the media, close your browser. Return to Dreamweaver, and close **travel_finished.html**.

Video and animation provide powerful venues for rich web content, and Dreamweaver makes it a simple matter to insert this type of content.

Introducing Adobe Edge Animate

The animation used in this lesson was built in Edge Animate, a new program developed by Adobe—not to replace Flash, but to create web animation and interactive content natively, using HTML5, CSS3, and JavaScript. A new Creative Cloud version of the program is now available to all Creative Cloud subscribers. At the time of this writing, there were plans to offer Edge Animate as an individual product on Creative Cloud. For subsequent versions and upgrades, this model may change. The name "Edge" was coined by Adobe to brand a set of new HTML applications under development to support designers and developers creating webpages and content for the modern web. You can check out all the new offerings at html.adobe.com.

Adding web animation to a page

Dreamweaver has a built-in and simplified workflow for inserting Edge Animate compositions, making the process a point-and-click operation. Dreamweaver takes advantage of a feature in Edge Animate designed to assist in deploying compositions to other programs and workflows, such as Adobe InDesign, Adobe Dreamweaver, and Apple's iBooks Author. The File > Publish Settings command (shown in the figure) enables you to export your Edge Animate compositions into a single file or folder.

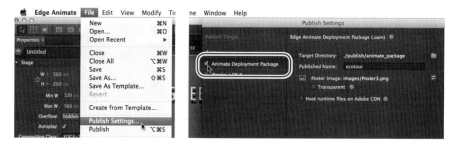

By defining your Publish Settings appropriately, you can create a complete set of files that are compatible with these applications. For the purposes of this exercise, we published an OAM file for you, which is an archive file format that contains all the constituent elements needed to support the animation in Dreamweaver.

1 Open **travel.html** from the site root folder in Design view.

   The banner should be inserted outside any text elements.

2 Insert the cursor in the *Green Travel* heading text, and select the h1 tag selector. Press the left arrow key to move the cursor outside the <h1> element.

3 Choose Insert > Media > Edge Animate Composition. You may also use the Edge Animate Composition option in the Insert panel's Media category.

4 Navigate to the resources folder in lesson12.
   Select **ecotour.oam**.

5 Click OK/Open to insert the composition.

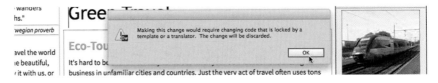

Normally, this command will be all you need to insert an Edge Animate composition. The banner animation should appear in the layout. In files based on a template, however, you may receive an error message that says Dreamweaver cannot insert the animation because it would require changing code that is locked in the template. If you see this message, you'll have to insert the composition and its support code by hand.

6 If you see the insertion error message associated with the template, click OK to dismiss the warning, and complete the following steps; otherwise, skip to step 24.

7 Choose File > New.

First, we'll create a new webpage that isn't based on the site template, and then you will insert the composition into that file and then transfer the various markup and code elements into **travel.html** by hand.

8 Create a blank HTML file using the <none> option.

A blank HTML file appears in a new document window.

9 Save the file as **animation_transfer.html**, and switch to Code view.

10 Examine the HTML code.

```
× travel.html*   × animation_transfer.html
Code  Split  Design ▼
     1  Show Code and Design views (Press Command key for all open documents)
     2  <html>
     3  <head>
     4  <meta charset="UTF-8">
     5  <title>Untitled Document</title>
     6  </head>
     7
     8  <body>
     9  </body>
    10  </html>
```

The file contains the structure of a basic webpage, including <head> and <body> sections, but no other content.

11 Insert the cursor at the end of the opening <body> tag.
Press Enter/Return to insert a new line in the code.

12 Choose Insert > Media > Edge Animate Composition.

13 Select **ecotour.oam** in the resources folder in lesson12.
Click OK/Open to insert the composition.

The code for the Edge Animate stage appears at the cursor location, while some support code is simultaneously inserted in the <head> section. Dreamweaver can preview the content of the animation in Live view.

14 Switch to Split view so that the Live view window displays on the right side.

The Live view window renders the animation as it would appear in a browser. You can use copy and paste to transfer the necessary code into the travel page.

15 In the Code view window, select and copy all the markup contained between the <!--Adobe Edge Runtime--> and <!--Adobe Edge Runtime End--> comments.

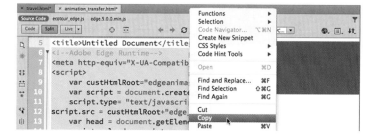

16 Click the document tab for **travel.html**, and switch to Code view.

17 In the Code view window, scroll to the <head> section.

Insert the cursor at the end of the notation `<!-- InstanceBeginEditable name="head" -->`, and press Enter/Return to create a new line.

18 Right-click the open line in Code view.

Choose Paste from the context menu, or press Ctrl+V/Cmd+V to paste the runtime markup copied in step 16.

The next step is to transfer the composition stage.

19 Switch to **animation_transfer.html**.

20 In Code view, select the markup `<div id="Stage" class="EDGE-204064396"></div>`, and copy it.

21 Switch to **travel.html**.

22 In the Code view window, scroll to the <body> section.

Insert the cursor at the end of the notation `<article class="content">` (around line 108), and insert a new line.

23 Press Ctrl+V/Cmd+V to paste the stage.

24 Switch to Live view.

The banner animation plays automatically in Live view once the code is processed, but what you cannot see is that Dreamweaver just created a new folder in the site root directory.

25 Open the Files panel, and examine the list of folders in the site root.

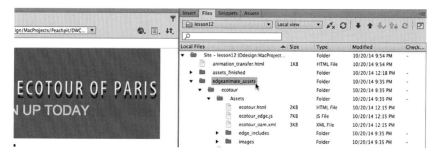

◆ **Warning:** Dreamweaver will not automatically upload all the support files needed for the Edge Animate composition. Be sure to upload the entire contents of the edgeanimate_assets folder when publishing the site to the web.

The folder named edgeanimate_assets now appears in the root directory. The folder was generated automatically and contains all the files needed to support the composition. The entire folder must be uploaded to the web host when **travel.html** is posted.

26 Save all files.

Congratulations, you've successfully incorporated an HTML5- and CSS3-based animation in your page.

Poster child

The widespread popularity and support of HTML5 should mean that your animation will run in most browsers and mobile devices. But there's a very small possibility the animation may be incompatible with older computers and software. Edge Animate can include either a down-level stage or a static poster, image that will be viewed in these circumstances.

To add or create a down-level stage or poster within Edge Animate, select the project stage, and then add the appropriate content using the Properties panel.

Adding web video to a page

Implementing HTML5-compatible video in your site is a bit more involved than it was when you had to insert only a single Flash-based file. Unfortunately, no single video format is supported by all browsers in use today. To make sure your video content plays everywhere, you'll have to supply several different formats. Dreamweaver CC now provides a built-in technique to add multiple video files so you won't have to do all the coding yourself. In this exercise, you will learn how to insert HTML5-compatible video on a page in your site.

1   If necessary, open **travel.html** in Design view.

    You will insert the video in the `main_content` section of the page.

2   Insert the cursor in the paragraph *Click here to sign up*.
    Click the p tag selector, and press the left arrow key once.

    The cursor should appear before the opening <p> tag.

3   Choose Insert > HTML5 Video.

    This command creates the HTML5-compatible video element. A video placeholder appears on the page, and the Property inspector displays new options for targeting the video source files. Note that the interface enables you to specify up to three video source files and one Flash fallback file. The first step is to select your primary video source.

4   In the Property inspector, click the Browse icon ![icon] in the Source field. Navigate to the movies folder, and select the **paris.mp4** file. Click OK/Open.

    The MP4 file format will be the primary video format loaded. MP4, also known as MPEG-4, is a video format based on Apple's QuickTime standard. It is supported natively by iOS devices and will load the MP4 file, which is compatible with iOS devices and Apple's Safari browser. Many experts advise loading MP4 files first, because otherwise iOS devices may ignore the video element altogether.

5 Enter the following specifications in the Property inspector:

W: **400**

H: **300**

If you did not create the video yourself, you can often obtain the width and height of an MP4 in the File Manager in Windows by selecting properties, or choosing Get Info in the Finder in OS X.

The next format you will load is WebM, which is an open-source, royalty-free video format sponsored by Google. It is compatible with Firefox 4, Chrome 6, Opera 10.6, and Internet Explorer 9 and later.

6 If Dreamweaver has automatically inserted WebM as the file for Alt Source 1, go to step 7. Otherwise, click the Browse icon for the Alt Source 1 field. Navigate to the movies folder, select the file **paris.webm**, and click OK/Open.

To round out our HTML5 video selections, the next format you'll load is a lossy, open-source multimedia format: Ogg. It is designed for the distribution of multimedia content that is free of copyright and other media restrictions.

Note: Ogg is a container format. When the container contains a video, it uses the extension ogv.

7 Click the Browse icon for the Alt Source 2 field.

Select the file **paris.theora.ogv** from the movies folder, and click OK/Open.

These three formats support all the modern desktop and mobile browsers. But to support older software and devices, using a stalwart old friend—Flash video—may be necessary. By adding it last, you ensure that only browsers that don't support the other three formats will load the Flash content. Although many are abandoning Flash, Dreamweaver still provides support for inserting both FLV and SWF files.

8 Click Browse in the Flash Fallback field.

Select the **paris.flv** file from the movies folder, and click OK/Open.

9 Save the file.

10 If necessary, switch to Live view.

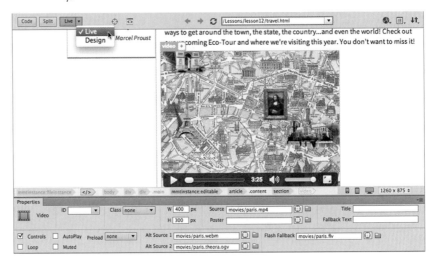

In some browsers, the `<video>` element won't generate a preview of the video content. You can add an image placeholder by using the Poster field in the Property inspector.

11 If necessary, select the `<video>` tag selector.
In the Property inspector, click Browse in the Poster field.
In the movies folder, select **paris-poster.png**, and click OK/Open.

A preview image has been applied to the `<video>` element. It won't be visible in Design view, but you can see the poster in Live view and, more importantly, in the browser. The advantage of using a poster is that something will always appear on the page, even in the browsers that do not support HTML5 or Flash video formats.

12 Save all files. Preview the page in Live view.

The poster appears within the layout; video controls appear below the poster depending on what video format is displayed. Flash video controls will appear within the video itself. In the next exercise, you will learn how to configure these controls and how the video will respond to the user.

Buggy video

At this point, you normally would be finished and ready to test your video configuration in multiple browsers. Unfortunately, the Flash fallback using an FLV source file is missing some essential support files and will not play the FLV correctly as is. Dreamweaver has a bug affecting the proper support of both FLV and SWF video using the new HTML5 video workflow described in this section.

The Dreamweaver engineers promised to fix this issue in a subsequent cloud update, but until then you can correct the issue yourself by simply replacing the new code element using the legacy Flash video workflow, like this:

1   Select the `<video>` tag selector.

2   Switch to Code view.
    If necessary, select Source Code in the Related Files interface.

3   Select the entire `<embed>` element containing the reference to **paris.flv**, and delete it.

4   Choose Insert > Media > Flash Video.

5   In the Insert FLV dialog, click the Browse icon. Select **paris.flv** from the movies folder, and click OK/Open.

    The filename **paris.flv** appears in the URL field of the dialog. Flash video supplies its own controls via a SWF skin interface. You can choose your own skin design in this dialog.

6   Choose **Corona Skin 2** from the Skin pop-up menu.

    Before you can insert the file, you have to specify the dimensions of the video.

7   Click the Detect Size button.

    Dreamweaver inserts the dimension 400 by 300 into the Width and Height fields. You can use the options below these fields to specify whether you want the video to autoplay and autorewind.

8   Click OK to insert the FLV video.

The `<embed>` element is now replaced by an `<object>` tag, along with all the code necessary to run the Flash video and even detect the presence and version of the needed Flash Player. This is the simplest method to insert FLV-compatible video so it will play properly in all browsers that don't support HTML5 video. But you should use this method only until the feature described within the exercise is fixed.

Choosing HTML5 video options

The final step for configuring the video is to decide what other HTML5-supported options to specify. The options are displayed within the Property inspector whenever the `<video>` element is chosen. The options are selectable in all views.

1   If necessary, open **travel.html** in Live view.
Select the `<video>` tag selector.
Observe the left side of the Property inspector.

*   **Controls** displays visible video controls.

*   **AutoPlay** starts the video automatically after the webpage loads.

*   **Loop** causes the video to replay from the beginning automatically once it finishes.

*   **Muted** silences the audio.

*   **Preload** specifies the method in which the video loads.

2   If necessary, select the Controls option, and deselect the AutoPlay, Loop, and Muted options. Set Preload to **none**.

Video is very memory- and bandwidth-intensive. This is especially true for phones and tablets. Setting the Preload to none prevents any video resources from downloading until the user actually clicks the video. It may take the video a few more seconds to download when launched, but your visitors will appreciate that you are respectful of their minutes and data plan. The `<video>` element is now complete. The placeholder appears in the layout flush to the left side of `<div.content>`. Let's center it.

3 Select the `video` tag selector.

By default, the `<video>` tag is an inline element. By assigning it the `block` property, you can control how the video aligns on the page and relates to other elements.

4 In the CSS Designer, select **mygreen_styles.css** > GLOBAL > `.content`. Create a new rule `.content section video,` `.content section video object`.

5 Create the following properties:

```
display: block
margin: 10px auto
```

6 Preview the page in Live view or in a browser. If the video controls are not visible, move your cursor over the still image to display them. Click the Play button to view the movie.

| Dreamweaver | Chrome | Internet Explorer |

Depending on where you preview the page, you will see one of the four video formats. For example, in Live view you will see the MP4-based video. The controls will appear differently depending on what format is displayed. This movie has no sound, but the controls will often include a speaker button to adjust the volume or mute the audio.

7 When you're finished, switch back to Design view.

● **Note:** This rule will center all `<video>` elements inserted in `.content`. If you need to target a specific video, an alternate method is to create a custom CSS class and apply it as needed.

● **Note:** In Microsoft Internet Explorer, a notice may appear notifying you that the active content was blocked. Click the button Allow Blocked Content to play the video.

● **Note:** In Live view, you may not see a "play" control, but if you click to the left of the progress bar, the video will play.

You've embedded three HTML5-compatible videos and an FLV fallback, which gives you support for most browsers and devices that can access the Internet. But you've learned only one possible technique for supporting this evolving standard. To learn more about HTML5 video and how to implement it, check out the following links:

- http://tinyurl.com/video-HTML5-1
- http://tinyurl.com/video-HTML5-2
- http://tinyurl.com/video-HTML5-3

To learn more about implementing video for mobile devices, check out these links:

- http://tinyurl.com/fluid-video
- http://tinyurl.com/fluid-video-1

Review questions

1 What advantage does HTML5 have over HTML 4 regarding web-based media?

2 What programming language(s) created the HTML5-compatible animation used in this lesson?

3 True or false: To support all web browsers, you can select a single video format.

4 In browsers or devices that do not support video, what can you do to provide some form of content to these users?

5 What video format is recommended to support older browsers?

Review answers

1 HTML5 has built-in support for web animation and video.

2 The animation used in this lesson was created by Adobe Edge Animate natively using HTML5, CSS3, and JavaScript.

3 False. A single format supported by every browser has not emerged. Developers recommend incorporating four video formats to support the majority of browsers: MP4, WebM, Ogg, and FLV.

4 You can add a static poster image (GIF, JPG, or PNG) via an option in the Property inspector to provide a preview of the video content in incompatible browsers and devices.

5 FLV (Flash video) is recommended as the fallback format for older browsers because of the widespread installation of the Flash Player.

13 PUBLISHING TO THE WEB

Lesson overview

In this lesson, you'll publish your website to the Internet and do the following:

- Define a remote site
- Define a testing server
- Put files on the web
- Cloak files and folders
- Update out-of-date links site-wide

 This lesson will take about one hour to complete. If you have not already done so, download the project files for this lesson from the Lesson & Update Files tab on your Account page at www.peachpit.com, store them on your computer in a convenient location, and define a new site based on the lesson13 folder, as described in the "Getting Started" section of this book. Your Account page is also where you'll find any updates to the lessons or to the lesson files. Look on the Lesson & Update Files tab to access the most current content.

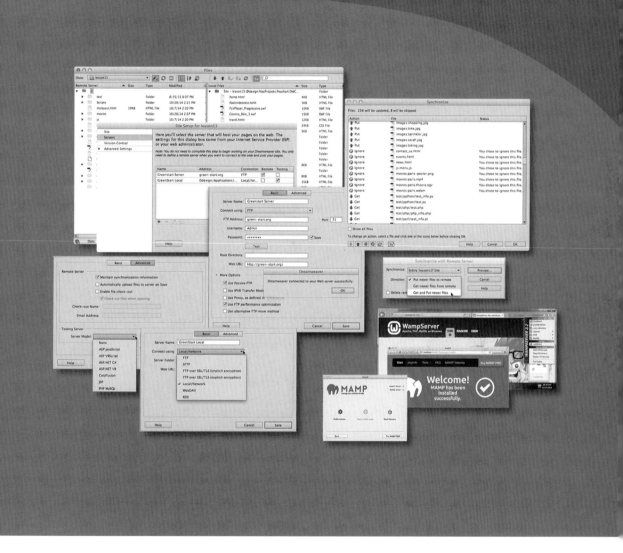

The goal of all the preceding lessons is to design, develop, and build pages for a remote website. But Dreamweaver doesn't abandon you there. It also provides powerful tools to upload and maintain any size website over time.

Defining a remote site

● **Note:** If you have not already downloaded the project files for this lesson to your computer from your Account page and defined a site based on this folder, make sure to do so now. See "Getting Started" at the beginning of the book.

Dreamweaver's workflow is based on a two-site system. One site is in a folder on your computer's hard drive and is known as the *local site*. All work in the previous lessons has been performed on your local site. The second site, called the *remote site*, is established in a folder on a web server, typically running on another computer, and is connected to the Internet and publicly available. In large companies, the remote site is often available only to employees via a network-based intranet. Such sites provide information and applications to support corporate programs and products.

Dreamweaver supports several methods for connecting to a remote site:

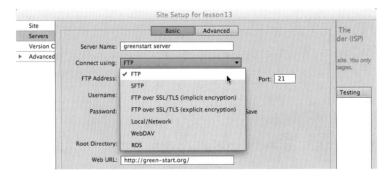

- **FTP** (File Transfer Protocol)—The standard method for connecting to hosted websites.

- **SFTP** (Secure File Transfer Protocol)—A protocol that provides a method to connect to hosted websites in a more secure manner to preclude unauthorized access or interception of online content.

- **FTP over SSL/TLS** (implicit encryption)—A secure FTP (FTPS) method that requires all clients of the FTPS server be aware that SSL is to be used on the session. It is incompatible with non-FTPS-aware clients.

- **FTP over SSL/TLS** (explicit encryption)—A legacy-compatible, secure FTP method where FTPS-aware clients can invoke security with an FTPS-aware server without breaking overall FTP functionality with non-FTPS-aware clients.

- **Local/network**—A local or network connection is most frequently used with an intermediate web server, called a *staging server*. Staging servers are typically used to test sites before they go live. Files from the staging server are eventually published to an Internet-connected web server.

- **WebDav** (Web Distributed Authoring and Versioning)—A web-based system also known to Windows users as Web Folders and to Mac users as iDisk.

- **RDS** (Remote Development Services)—Developed by Adobe for ColdFusion and primarily used when working with ColdFusion-based sites.

Dreamweaver now can upload larger files faster and more efficiently and as a background activity, allowing you to return to work more quickly. In the following exercises, you'll set up a remote site using the two most common methods: FTP and Local/Network.

Setting up a remote FTP site

The vast majority of web developers rely on FTP to publish and maintain their sites. FTP is a well-established protocol, and many variations of the protocol are used on the web—most of which are supported by Dreamweaver.

◆ **Warning:**
To complete the following exercise, you must have a remote server already established. Remote servers can be hosted by your own company or contracted from a third-party web-hosting service.

1 Launch Adobe Dreamweaver CC (2014.1 release) or later.

2 Choose Site > Manage Sites, or choose Manage Sites from the site list drop-down menu in the Files panel.

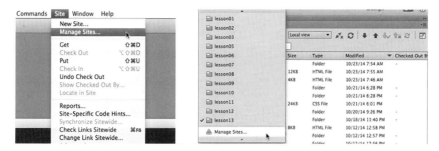

3 In the Manage Sites dialog is a list of all the sites you may have defined. Make sure that the current site, lesson13, is chosen. Click the Edit icon ✏.

4 In the Site Setup for lesson13 dialog, click the Servers category.

The Site Setup dialog allows you to set up multiple servers, so you can test several types of installations, if desired.

5 Click the Add New Server icon ✚.

Enter **GreenStart Server** in the Server Name field.

6 From the Connect Using pop-up menu, choose FTP.

7 In the FTP Address field, type the URL or IP (Internet protocol) address of your FTP server.

If you contract a third-party service as a web host, you will be assigned an FTP address. This address may come in the form of an IP address, such as 192.168.1.100. Enter this number into the field exactly as it was sent to you. Frequently, the FTP address will be the name of your site, such as **ftp.green-start.org**. Dreamweaver doesn't require you to enter the characters *ftp* into the field.

8 In the Username field, enter your FTP user name.
In the Password field, enter your FTP password.

Usernames may be case sensitive, but password fields almost always are; be sure you enter them correctly. Often, the easiest way to enter them is to copy them from the confirmation email from your hosting company and paste them into the appropriate fields.

▶ **Tip:** Check with your web-hosting service or IS/IT manager to obtain the root directory name, if any.

9 In the Root Directory field, type the name of the folder that contains documents publicly accessible to the web, if any.

Some web hosts provide FTP access to a root-level folder that might contain nonpublic folders—such as cgi-bin, which is used to store common gateway interface (CGI) or binary scripts—as well as a public folder. In these cases, type the public folder name—such as public, public_html, www, or wwwroot—in the Root Directory field. In many web host configurations, the FTP address is the same as the public folder, and the Root Directory field should be left blank.

10 Select the Save option if you don't want to re-enter your user name and password every time Dreamweaver connects to your site.

11 Click Test to verify that your FTP connection works properly.

▶ **Tip:** If Dreamweaver does not connect to your host, first check the username and password, as well as the FTP address and root directory for any errors.

FTP Address: green-start.org   Port: 21

Username: admin

Passw   **Dreamweaver**

Dreamweaver connected to your Web server successfully.

OK

Root Direct

Web URL: http://green-start.org/

Dreamweaver displays an alert to notify you that the connection was successful or unsuccessful.

12 Click OK to dismiss the alert.

If Dreamweaver connects properly to the webhost, skip to step 14. If you received an error message, your web server may require additional configuration options.

13 Click the More Options triangle to reveal additional server options.

Web URL: http://green-start.org/

▼ More Options

☑ Use Passive FTP

☐ Use IPV6 Transfer Mode

☐ Use Proxy, as defined in *Preferences*

☑ Use FTP performance optimization

☐ Use alternative FTP move method

Help   Cancel   Save

Consult the instructions from your hosting company to select the appropriate options for your specific FTP server:

- **Use Passive FTP**—Allows your computer to connect to the host computer and bypass a firewall restraint. Many web hosts require this setting.

- **Use IPV6 Transfer Mode**—Enables connection to IPV6-based servers, which use the most recent version of the Internet transfer protocol.

- **Use Proxy**—Identifies a secondary proxy host connection as defined in your Dreamweaver preferences.

- **Use FTP Performance Optimization**—Optimizes the FTP connection. Deselect if Dreamweaver can't connect to your server.

- **Use Alternative FTP Move Method**—Provides an additional method to resolve FTP conflicts, especially when rollbacks are enabled or when moving files.

Troubleshooting your FTP connection

Connecting to your remote site can be frustrating the first time you attempt it. You can experience numerous pitfalls, many of which are out of your control. Here are a few steps to take if you have issues connecting:

- If you can't connect to your FTP server, double-check your username and password and re-enter them carefully. Remember that usernames may be case sensitive, while most passwords frequently are. (This is the most common error.)

- Select Use Passive FTP, and test the connection again.

- If you still can't connect to your FTP server, deselect the Use FTP Performance Optimization option, click OK, and click Test again.

- If none of these steps enable you to connect to your remote site, check with your IS/IT manager or your remote site administrator or webhosting service.

Once you establish a working connection, you may need to configure some advanced options.

14 Click the Advanced tab. Select among the following options for working with your remote site:

- **Maintain Synchronization Information**—Automatically notes the files that have been changed on the local and remote sites so that they can be easily synchronized. This feature helps you keep track of your changes and can be helpful if you change multiple pages before you upload. You may want to use cloaking with this feature. You'll learn about cloaking in an upcoming exercise. This feature is usually selected by default.

- **Automatically Upload Files To Server On Save**—Transfers files from the local to the remote site when they are saved. This option can become annoying if you save often and aren't yet ready for a page to go public.

- **Enable File Check-Out**—Starts the check-in/check-out system for collaborative website building in a workgroup environment. If you choose this option, you'll need to enter a check-out name and, optionally, an email address. If you're working by yourself, you do not need to select this option.

It is acceptable to leave any or all these options unselected, but for the purposes of this lesson, select the Maintain Synchronization Information option.

15 Click Save to finalize the settings in the open dialogs.

A dialog appears, informing you that the cache will be re-created because you changed the site settings.

16 Click OK to build the cache. When Dreamweaver finishes updating the cache, click Done to close the Manage Sites dialog.

You have established a connection to your remote server. If you don't currently have a remote server, you can substitute a local testing server instead as your remote server.

Installing a testing server

When you produce sites with dynamic content, you need to test functionality before the pages go live on the Internet. A testing server can fit that need nicely. Depending on the applications you need to test, the testing server can simply be a subfolder on your actual web server, or you can use a local web server such as Apache or Internet Information Services (IIS) from Microsoft.

For detailed information about installing and configuring a local web server, check out the following links:

- Apache/ColdFusion—http://tinyurl.com/setup-coldfusion
- Apache/PHP—http://tinyurl.com/setup-apachephp
- IIS/ASP—http://tinyurl.com/setup-asp

Once you set up the local web server, you can use it to upload the completed files and test your remote site. In most cases, your local web server will not be accessible from the Internet or be able to host the actual website for the public.

Establishing a remote site on a local or network web server

◆ **Warning:**
To complete the following exercise, you must have already installed and configured a local or network web server.

If your company or organization uses a staging server as a "middleman" between web designers and the live website, it's likely you'll need to connect to your remote site through a local or network web server. Local/network servers are often used as testing servers to check dynamic functions before pages are uploaded to the Internet.

1 Launch Adobe Dreamweaver CC (2014.1 release) or later.

2 Choose Site > Manage Sites.

3 In the Manage Sites dialog, make sure that lesson13, is chosen. Click the Edit icon ✎ .

4 In the Site Setup for lesson13 dialog, select the Servers category.

5 If you have a testing server already set up in the dialog, select the Remote option.

6 Click the Add New Server icon ➕ .
In the Server Name field, enter **GreenStart Local**.

7 From the Connect Using pop-up menu, choose Local/Network.

8 In the Server Folder field, click the Browse icon 📁 .
Select the local web server's HTML folder, such as C:\wamp\www\lesson13.

● **Note:** The paths you enter here are contingent on how you installed your local web server and may not be the same as the ones displayed.

9 In the Web URL field, enter the appropriate URL for your local web server. If you are using WAMP or MAMP local servers, your web URL will be something like http://localhost:8888/lesson13 or http://localhost/lesson13.

You must enter the correct URL, or Dreamweaver's FTP and testing features may not function properly.

Windows

OS X

10 Click the Advanced tab, and as with the actual web server, select the appropriate options for working with your remote site: Maintain Synchronization Information, Automatically Upload Files To Server On Save, and/or Enable File Check-Out.

Although leaving these three options unselected is acceptable, for the purposes of this lesson, select the Maintain Synchronization Information option.

11 If you'd like to use the local web server as the testing server too, select the server model in the Advanced section of the dialog. If you are creating a dynamic site using a specific programming language, like ASP, ColdFusion, or PHP, select the matching Server Model so you'll be able to test the pages of your site properly.

12 Click Save to complete the remote server setup.

13 In the Site Setup for lesson13 dialog, select Remote. If you want to use the local server as a testing server too, select Testing. Click Save.

14 In the Manage Sites dialog, click Done. If necessary, click OK to rebuild the cache.

Only one remote and one testing server can be active at one time, but you may have multiple servers defined. One server can be used for both roles, if desired. Before you upload files for the remote site, you may need to cloak certain folders and files in the local site.

Cloaking folders and files

Not all the files in your site root folder may need to be transferred to the remote server. For example, there's no point in filling the remote site with files that won't be accessed or that will remain inaccessible to website users. Minimizing files stored on the remote server may also pay financial dividends, since many hosting services base part of their fee on how much disk space your site occupies. If you selected Maintain Synchronization Information for a remote site using FTP or a network server, you may want to cloak some of your local materials to prevent them from being uploaded. Cloaking is a Dreamweaver feature that allows you to designate certain folders and files that will not be uploaded to or synchronized with the remote site.

Folders you don't want to upload include the Templates and resource folders. Some other non-web-compatible file types used to create your site, like Photoshop (.psd), Flash (.fla), or Microsoft Word (.doc) files, also don't need to be on the remote server. Although cloaked files will not upload or synchronize automatically, you may still upload them manually, if desired. Some people like to upload these items to keep a backup copy of them off-site.

The cloaking process begins in the Site Setup dialog.

1   Choose Site > Manage Sites.

2   Select lesson13 in the site list, and click the Edit icon ✐.

3   Expand the Advanced Settings category.
    Select the Enable Cloaking and Cloak Files Ending With options.

The field below the checkboxes displays the extensions .fla and .psd.

4   Insert the cursor after .*psd,* and insert a space. Type **.doc .txt .rtf**

Be sure to insert a space between each extension. By specifying the extensions of file types that don't contain desired web content, you prevent Dreamweaver from uploading and synchronizing these file types automatically no matter where they appear in the site.

5   Click Save. If Dreamweaver prompts you to update the cache, click OK. Then, click Done to close the Manage Sites dialog.

    Although you have cloaked several file types automatically, you can also cloak specific files or folders manually from the File panel.

6   Open the Files panel, and click the Expand icon ⬚ to fill the workspace.

    The Files panel displays as a separate standalone window.

7 Right-click the resources folder.

From the context menu, choose Cloaking > Cloak.

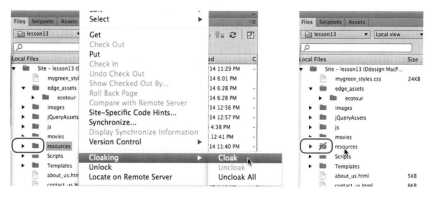

The Templates folder is not needed on the remote site because your webpages do not reference these assets in any way. But if you work in a team environment, it may be handy to upload and synchronize these folders so that each team member has up-to-date versions of each on their own computers. For this exercise, let's assume you work alone.

8 Apply cloaking to the Templates folder.

9 In the warning dialog that appears, click OK.

Using the Site Setup dialog and the Cloaking context menu, you cloaked file types, folders, and files. The synchronization process will ignore cloaked items and not upload or download them automatically.

Wrapping things up

Over the last 12 lessons, you have built an entire website, beginning with a starter layout and including text, images, movies, and interactive content, but a few loose strings remain for you to tie up. Before you publish your site, you'll need to create one important webpage and make some crucial updates to your site navigation.

The file you need to create is one that is essential to every site: a home page. The home page is usually the first page most users see on your site. It is the page that loads automatically when a user enters your site's domain name into the browser window. Since the page loads automatically, there are a few restrictions on the name and extension you can use.

Basically, the name and extension depend on the hosting server and the type of applications running on the home page, if any. Today, the majority of home pages will simply be named *index*. But *default*, *start*, and *iisstart* are also used.

Extensions identify the specific types of programming languages used within a page. A normal HTML home page will use an extension of .htm or .html. Extensions like .asp, .cfm, and .php, among others, are required if the home page contains any dynamic applications specific to that server model. You may still use one of these extensions—if they are compatible with your server model—even if the page contains no dynamic applications or content. But be careful—in some instances, using the wrong extension may prevent the page from loading altogether. Whenever you're in doubt, use .html, because it's supported in all environments.

The specific home page name or names honored by the server are normally configured by the server administrator and can be changed, if desired. Most servers are configured to honor several names and a variety of extensions. Check with your IS/IT manager or web server support team to ascertain the recommended name and extension for your home page.

1   Create a new page from the site template.
    Save the file as **index.html**, or use a filename and extension compatible with your server model.

2   Open **home.html** from the lesson13 site root folder in Design view.

3   Insert the cursor in the heading, *Welcome to Meridien GreenStart*.
    Select the `article` tag selector, and copy all the content.

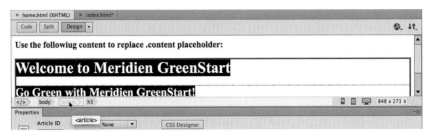

● **Note:** Pasting to replace an element works only in Design and Code views.

4   Switch to **index.html**, and select Design view.
    Insert the cursor anywhere in the text *Add main heading here*.
    Select the `article` tag selector, and paste the content.

The new content replaces the placeholder text in the center of the page, but it needs to be formatted.

5 Select the `article` tag selector.

Select `.content` using the class drop-down menu in the Property inspector.

6 Replace Sidebar 1 with the first aside element in **home.html**.

Apply `.sidebar1` to this element from the class menu.

7 Replace Sidebar 2 with the second aside element in **home.html**.

Apply `.sidebar2` to this element from the class menu.

Note the hyperlink placeholders in the main_content region.

8 Insert the cursor in the *News* link.

In the Property inspector, browse and connect the link to **news.html**.

9 Repeat step 8 with each link.

Connect the links to the appropriate pages in your site root folder.

10 Save and close all files.

The home page is complete. Let's assume you want to upload the site at its current state of completion even though some pages have yet to be created. This happens in the course of any site development. Pages are added and deleted over time; missing pages will be completed and uploaded at a later date. Before you can upload the site to a live server, you should always update any out-of-date links and remove dead ones.

Putting your site online

◆ Warning: Dreamweaver does a good job trying to identify all the dependent files in a particular workflow. In some cases, it may miss files crucial to a dynamic or extended process. It is imperative that you do your homework to identify these files and make sure they are uploaded.

For the most part, the local site and the remote site are mirror images, containing the same HTML files, images, and assets in identical folder structures. When you transfer a webpage from your local site to your remote site, you are publishing, or *putting*, that page. If you *put* a file stored in a folder on your local site, Dreamweaver transfers the file to the equivalent folder on the remote site. It will even automatically create the remote folder or folders, if necessary if it does not already exist. The same is true when you download files.

Using Dreamweaver, you can publish anything—from one file to a complete site—in a single operation. When you publish a webpage, by default Dreamweaver asks if you would also like to put the dependent files, too. Dependent files are the images, CSS, HTML5 movies, JavaScript files, server-side includes (SSI), and all other files necessary to complete the page.

You can upload one file at a time or the entire site at once. In this exercise, we will upload one webpage and its dependent files.

1 Open the Files panel, and click the Expand icon 🗗, if necessary.

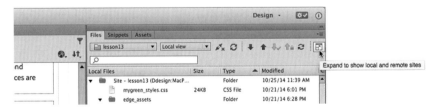

2 Click the Connect To Remote Server icon ![icon] to connect to the remote site.

If your remote site is properly configured, the Files panel will connect to the site and display its contents on the left half of the panel. When you first upload files, the remote site may be empty or mostly empty. If you are connecting to your Internet host, specific files and folders created by the hosting company may appear. Do not delete these items unless you check to see whether they are essential to the operation of the server or your own applications.

3 In the local file list, select **index.html**.
In the Document toolbar, click the Put icon ![icon].

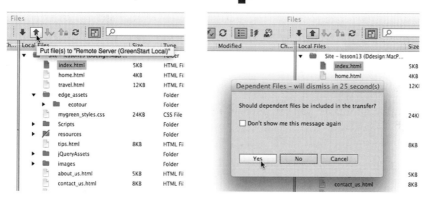

Note:
If Dreamweaver doesn't prompt you to upload dependent files, this option may be turned off. To turn this feature on, access the option in the Site category of the Dreamweaver Preferences panel.

By default, Dreamweaver will prompt you to upload dependent files. If a dependent file already exists on the server and your changes did not affect it, you can click No. Otherwise, for new files or files that have had any changes, click Yes. Dreamweaver will then upload images, CSS, JavaScript, server-side includes, and other dependent files needed to properly render the selected HTML file.

The file panel enables you to upload multiple files as well as the entire site at once.

Note: Dependent files include but are not limited to images, style sheets, and JavaScript used within a specific page and are essential to the proper display and function of the page.

▶ Tip: If you are
using a third-party
webhosting service, be
aware that they often
create placeholder
pages on your domain.
If your home page
does not automatically
appear when you
access your site, check
to make sure that
there is no conflict
with the webhost's
placeholder pages.

4   Select the site root folder for the local site, and then click the Put icon ⬆ in the
    Files panel.

A dialog appears, asking you to confirm that you want to upload the entire site.

5   Click OK.

Dreamweaver begins to upload the site. It will re-create your local site structure
on the remote server. When it's complete, note that none of the cloaked lesson
folders were uploaded. Dreamweaver will automatically ignore all cloaked items
when putting a folder or an entire site. If desired, you can manually select and
upload individually cloaked items.

● **Note:** A file
that is uploaded or
downloaded will
automatically overwrite
any version of the file at
the destination.

6   Right-click the Templates folder, and choose Put from the context menu.

Dreamweaver prompts you to upload dependent files for the Templates folder.

● **Note:** When
accessing Put and Get, it
doesn't matter whether
you use the Local or
Remote pane of the
Files panel. Put always
uploads to Remote;
Get always downloads
to Local.

7   Click Yes to upload dependent files.

The Templates folder is uploaded to the remote server. Note that the remote
Templates folder displays a red slash, indicating that it, too, is cloaked. At
times, you will want to cloak local and remote files and folders to prevent these
items from being replaced or accidentally overwritten. A cloaked file will not
be uploaded or downloaded automatically. But you can manually select any
specific files and perform the same action.

The opposite of the Put command is Get, which downloads any selected file or
folder to the local site. You can get any file from the remote site by selecting it in
the Remote or Local pane and clicking the Get icon ⬇. Alternatively, you can
drag the file from the Remote pane to the Local pane.

8 Use a browser to connect to the remote site on your network server or the Internet. Type the appropriate address in the URL field—depending on whether you are connecting to the local web server or the actual Internet site—such as http://localhost/*domain_name* or http://www. *domain_name*.com.

The GreenStart site appears in the browser. Click to test the hyperlinks to view each of the completed pages for the site. Once the site is uploaded, keeping it up to date is an easy task. As files change, you can upload them one at a time or synchronize the whole site with the remote server. Synchronization is especially important in workgroup environments where files are changed and uploaded by several individuals. You can easily download or upload files that are older, overwriting files that are newer in the process. Synchronization can ensure that you are working with only the latest versions of each file.

Synchronizing local and remote sites

Synchronization in Dreamweaver keeps the files on your server and your local computer up to date. It's an essential tool when you work from multiple locations or with one or more coworkers. Used properly, it can prevent you from accidentally uploading or working on out-of-date files.

At the moment, your local and remote sites are identical. To better illustrate the capabilities of synchronization, let's make a change to one of the site pages.

1 Open **about_us.html** in Design view.

2 In the CSS Designer, select **mygreen_styles.css** > GLOBAL. Create a new `.green` selector.

3 Add the following property to the new rule:
`color: #090`

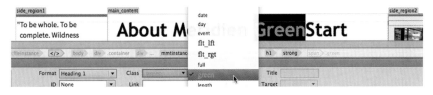

4 In the main heading, select the characters *Green* in the name *GreenStart*.

5 Apply the CSS `.green` class to this text.

6 Apply the CSS `.green` class to each occurrence of the word *green* anywhere on the page where the text is not already green in color.

7 Save all files and close the page.

8 Open and expand the Files panel.
In the Document toolbar, click the Synchronize icon .

The Synchronize Files dialog appears.

9 From the Synchronize pop-up menu, choose the option Entire 'lesson13' Site. From the Direction menu, choose the Get And Put Newer Files option.

Choose specific options in this dialog that meet your needs and workflow.

Note: Synchronize does not compare cloaked files or folders.

10 Click Preview.

The Synchronize dialog appears, reporting what files have changed and whether you need to get or put them. Since you just uploaded the entire site, only the file **about_us.html** appears in the list, which indicates that Dreamweaver wants to put it to the remote site.

Synchronization options

During synchronization, you can choose to accept the suggested action or override it by selecting one of the other options in the dialog. Options can be applied to one or more files at a time.

Get—Downloads the selected file(s) from the remote site

Put—Uploads the selected file(s) to the remote site

Delete—Marks the selected file(s) for deletion

Ignore—Ignores the selected file(s) during synchronization

Synchronized—Identifies the selected file(s) as already synchronized

Compare—Uses a third-party utility to compare the local and remote versions of a selected file

11 Click OK to put the file.

If other people access and update files on your site, remember to run synchronization *before* you work on any files to be certain you are working on the most current versions of each file in your site. Another technique is to set up the Check-out/ Check-in functionality in the advanced options of the server's setup dialog.

In this lesson, you set up your site to connect to a remote server and uploaded files to that remote site. You also cloaked files and folders and then synchronized the local and remote sites.

Congratulations! You've designed, developed, and built an entire website and uploaded it to your remote server. By finishing all the exercises in this book, you have gained experience in all aspects of the design and development of a standard website compatible with desktop computers. Now you are ready to build and publish a site of your own. Good luck!

Review questions

1   What is a remote site?

2   Name two types of file transfer protocols supported in Dreamweaver.

3   How can you configure Dreamweaver so that it does not synchronize certain files in your local site with the remote site?

4   True or false: You have to manually publish every file and associated image, JavaScript file, and server-side include that are linked to pages in your site.

5   What service does synchronization perform?

Review answers

1   A remote site is typically the live version of the local site stored on a web server connected to the Internet.

2   FTP (file transfer protocol) and local/network are the two most commonly used file transfer methods. Other file transfer methods supported in Dreamweaver include Secure FTP, WebDav, and RDS.

3   Cloaking the files or folders prevents them from synchronizing.

4   False. Dreamweaver can automatically transfer dependent files, if desired, including embedded or referenced images, CSS style sheets, and other linked content, although some files may be missed.

5   Synchronization automatically scans local and remote sites, comparing files on both to identify the most current version of each. It creates a report window to suggest which files to get or put to bring both sites up to date, and then it will perform the update.

APPENDIX
Tiny URLs

This book uses some Tiny URLs that resolve to full website addresses. Occasionally, tiny URLs expire, so in this appendix we have supplied the tiny URL followed by the full address.

LESSON 6

page 204   http://tinyurl.com/adobe-media-queries
www.adobe.com/devnet/dreamweaver/articles/introducing-media-queries.html?PID=6154686

http://tinyurl.com/w3c-media-queries
www.w3.org/TR/css3-mediaqueries/

http://tinyurl.com/media-queries-smashing
www.smashingmagazine.com/2010/07/19/
how-to-use-css3-media-queries-to-create-a-mobile-version-of-your-website/

LESSON 12

page 378   http://tinyurl.com/video-HTML5-1
www.w3schools.com/html/html5_video.asp

http://tinyurl.com/video-HTML5-2
www.808.dk/?code-html-5-video

http://tinyurl.com/video-HTML5-3
www.htmlgoodies.com/html5/client/how-to-embed-video-using-html5.html#fbid=YQb48VBD_FG

http://tinyurl.com/fluid-video
ulrich.pogson.ch/complete-responsive-videos-breakdown

http://tinyurl.com/fluid-video-1
css-tricks.com/NetMag/FluidWidthVideo/Article-FluidWidthVideo.php

LESSON 13

page 387   http://tinyurl.com/setup-coldfusion
www.adobe.com/devnet/dreamweaver/articles/setup_cf.html?PID=4166869

http://tinyurl.com/setup-apachephp
www.adobe.com/devnet/dreamweaver/articles/setup_php.html?PID=4166869

http://tinyurl.com/setup-asp
www.adobe.com/devnet/dreamweaver/articles/setup_asp.html?PID=4166869

INDEX

NUMBERS

4-bit color space, 280
8-bit palette, 280
100% font size, using, 145–146
256 colors, 280
256 shades of gray, 280

SYMBOLS

* (asterisk), appearance in document
    tab, 226
<!-- --> comment, 52, 140
< > (opening and closing tags), using in
    HTL, 41

A

<a> tag, described, 52, 167
absolute hyperlinks. *See also* hyperlinks
    creating in Live view, 318–320
    explained, 308–309
Adobe Add-ons link, checking, 13
Adobe Authorized Training Centers,
    contacting, 13
Adobe Creative Cloud Learn & Support
    site, 12. *See also* Creative Cloud
Adobe Dreamweaver CC product home
    page, 13. *See also* Dreamweaver
Adobe Dreamweaver Learn and Support
    site, 12
Adobe Edge Inspect. *See* Edge Inspect
Adobe Generator
    exporting assets from Photoshop,
        125–126
    features of, 123
    using, 124–125
    using to create assets, 127–128
Adobe Muse program, features of, 41

Adobe website, 204
all media type property, intended
    use, 184
alpha transparency, 281
Alt key. *See* keyboard shortcuts
Alt text, using, 285
animation
    adding to pages, 367–371
    defining Publish Settings, 367
    overview of, 364
Apache/ColdFusion web server, 387
Apache/PHP web server, 387
<article> tag, described, 56, 58
<aside> tag, described, 56
Asset panel, identifying, 16
assets
    creating using Adobe Generator,
        123–128
    exporting from Photoshop, 125–126
Assets panel, docking, 232
asterisk (*), appearance in document
    tab, 226
<audio> tag, described, 56
aural media type property, intended
    use, 184

B

background effects, adding, 158–162
background HTML default,
    described, 66
backgrounds, creating using CSS,
    98–101. *See also* CSS backgrounds
behaviors
    adding to hyperlinks, 342–344
    availability of, 335
    creating page for, 337
    explained, 334

J

JPEG (Joint Photographic Experts Group), 282
jQuery Accordion widgets. *See also* dynamic jQuery styling
    creating selectors, 350–351
    customizing, 349–355
    declaring pseudo-classes, 351
    inserting, 347–348
    previewing layout, 346
    replacing elements, 348
    style sheets, 349

K

keyboard shortcuts
    copying text, 222
    customizing, 28–29
    Cut action, 211
    Duplicate Set icon, 28
    New Document dialog, 220
    nonbreaking space, 43
    pasting text from clipboard, 241
    Quick Tag Editor, 239
    refreshing page view, 43
    select all, 222, 295

L

layout_finished.html file, opening, 133
layouts, determining basic settings for, 145–146. *See also* page layouts; predefined layouts; templates
leading, setting for type, 146
lesson order, recommendation for, 16
`<li>` tag, described, 52
line breaks, using with CSS rules, 74
line height, setting for type, 146
line numbers, displaying in Code view, 140
`<link />` tag, described, 52
link destination, creating using id, 327–328
linking to pages, 314
links. *See* hyperlinks

lists
    creating, 239–242
    reformatting, 242
    selecting, 242
Live Code, explained, 20
Live view
    absolute hyperlinks, 318–320
    explained, 19
    selecting elements in, 234
local site, defining, 8–9
local sites, synchronizing with remote sites, 397–399
local/network connections, 382
Locked icon, appearance of, 208

M

margins, setting in CSS, 106–107
`margins` HTML default, described, 66
media queries. *See also* mobile devices
    adding, 263
    adding rules to, 201–203
    identifying, 190–191
    order of CSS rules, 196
    resources, 186, 204
    in responsive design, 185
    syntax, 185–186
    targeting, 191–192
    targeting selectors, 192–195
    troubleshooting styles, 195–198
    writing, 264
media type properties
    `all`, 184
    `aural`, 184
    `braille`, 184
    `handheld`, 184
    `print`, 184
    `projection`, 184
    `screen`, 184
    `tty`, 184
    `tv`, 184
menu bar, identifying, 16
Meridien GreenStart scenario, described, 119
`<meta />` tag, described, 52

S

Safari browser, HTML default for, 67

Save All command, using, 226

saving, web pages, 290

screen, resizing manually, 247

`screen` media type property, intended use, 184

`<script>` tag, described, 52

searching and replacing text, 270–272

`<section>` tag, described, 56, 58

semantic content, building, 172–175

semantic structures, creating, 234–235

semantic web design, overview of, 57–58

SFTP (Secure File Transfer Protocol), 382

Sharpen tool, described, 304

Shift key. *See* keyboard shortcuts

Show Set option, enabling in Properties window, 266

site root folder, explained, 9

sites. *See* websites

Smart Objects, using with images, 292–294

Smashing Magazine, 204

Source Code option, choosing, 31

`<source>` tag, described, 56

spam, limiting, 324. *See also* email links

`<span>` tag, described, 52

specifications, creating manually, 246

specificity theory, impact on CSS formatting, 83–84

spellchecking webpages, 268–269

Split view

explained, 17–18

icon, 48

using, 48, 63

stories, moving individually, 233

`<strong>` tag, described, 45, 52

`<style>` tag, described, 52

styles, identifying with CSS Designer, 33

SVG (scalable vector graphic) format, 278

Swap Image behaviors, applying, 339–341

Synchronized option, explained, 398

synchronizing websites, 397–399

T

`table cell text` HTML default, described, 66

table cells

navigating, 250

selecting in Live view, 256

styling, 254–256

Table dialog, displaying, 249

table display, controlling, 256–258

`table header` HTML default, described, 66

`<table>` tag, described, 52

tables

adding rows to, 251

copying and pasting, 252

creating from scratch, 249–251

inserting, 258–260

making responsive, 262–268

navigating, 250

styling with CSS, 252–254

Tablet Size icon, clicking, 187

tag selectors

identifying, 16

using, 32, 249

tags, using for text formatting, 44

Target attribute, accessing in Property inspector, 320

`<td>` tag, described, 52

templates. *See also* embedded CSS; layouts

appearance of Locked icon, 208

creating, 240

creating from existing layouts, 213–214

editable regions, 208, 215–217

editing, 240

metadata, 217–219

opening in text editors, 219

updating, 224–226

workflow, 215

testing server, installing, 387

text

finding and replacing, 270–272

formatting in CSS, 71

formatting with HTML, 44

importing, 232–234

Production Notes

The Adobe Dreamweaver CC 2014 Classroom in a Book was created electronically using Adobe InDesign CS6. Art was produced using Adobe Illustrator and Adobe Photoshop. The Myriad Pro and Warnock Pro OpenType families of typefaces were used throughout this book.

References to company names in the lessons are for demonstration purposes only and are not intended to refer to any actual organization or person.

Images

Photographic images and illustrations are intended for use with the tutorials.

Typefaces used

Adobe Myriad Pro and Adobe Warnock Pro are used throughout the lessons. For more information about OpenType and Adobe fonts, visit www.adobe.com/type/opentype/.

Team credits

The following individuals contributed to the development of this edition of the Adobe Dreamweaver CC 2014 Classroom in a Book:

Writer: James J. Maivald
Project Editor: Nancy Peterson
Development Editor: Robyn Thomas
Technical Reviewers: Candyce Mairs, Clint Funk, Eva Brezenoff
Copyeditor: Wendy Katz
Indexer: Valerie Haynes Perry
Proofreader: Darren Meiss
Cover Designer: Eddie Yuen
Interior Designer: Mimi Heft